SANDSTEIN VERLAG · DRESDEN

A PLACE TO LEARN

FROM THE LANDESSCHULE DRESDEN TO THE ACADEMY

LERNRÄUME

VON DER LANDESSCHULE DRESDEN ZUR AKADEMIE

1927

Inhalt

2008

Contents

Liebe Leserinnen und Leser,

Lernen ist der individuelle oder kollektive Erwerb von geistigen, körperlichen und sozialen Kenntnissen und Fertigkeiten. Lernen bedeutet Veränderung des Verhaltens, Denkens oder Fühlens aufgrund von Erfahrung, Einsicht und Verständnis. Lernen wird durch die Umgebung, den Lernort oder die Lernräume, noch wesentlicher aber durch das Lernziel geprägt.

Dieses Buch beschreibt einen Ort des Lernens, mit dessen Geschichte diese Einflüsse deutlich belegt werden, und der für die Deutsche Gesetzliche Unfallversicherung besondere Bedeutung hat: ihre Akademie für Sicherheit und Gesundheit bei der Arbeit in Dresden.

Lernen hat hier eine lange Tradition, die dieses Buch, das Chronik und Bildband vereint, eingehend beleuchtet. In den 1920er Jahren wurde Klotzsche Standort der Sächsischen Landesschule Dresden. Die Architekten Heinrich Tessenow und Oskar Kramer setzten mit dem Gebäudekomplex einen Akzent in der Schularchitektur, der weit über die Landesgrenzen hinaus Beachtung fand. In den 1930er Jahren wandelten die Nationalsozialisten die Landesschule in eine Nationalpolitische Erziehungsanstalt um. Gleich einer antiken Tragödie folgte auf den Missbrauch als Kaderschmiede für eine menschenverachtende Ideologie der Niedergang des Ortes während der Stationierung der sowjetischen Streitkräfte. Für fast fünf Jahrzehnte verschwand er förmlich aus dem öffentlichen Bewusstsein.

Dear Readers,

Learning is the individual or collective acquisition of mental, physical and social knowledge and skills. Learning leads to the modification of behaviour, thought or perception on the basis of experience, insight and understanding. Learning is moulded by the environment, location or space in which it occurs and, to an even greater extent, the learning objective.

This book describes a seat of learning with a history clearly marked by such influences. The Dresden location in question has now taken on special importance within the framework of the statutory accident insurance network by becoming the location of its academy for occupational safety and health.

The long tradition of learning at the Klotzsche site, which became home to the Landesschule Dresden during the 1920s, is chronicled in detail by the text and images married together in this volume. Designed by architects Heinrich Tessenow and Oskar Kramer, the building complex set a tone in school architecture which echoed far beyond the limits of Saxony's borders. The 1930s saw the National Socialists transform the Landesschule into a National Political Educational Institution. The ensuing period played out in the manner of a classical tragedy, with the site initially abused as an establishment for the drilling of cadets in an inhuman ideology before being plunged into steep decline during its time as a Soviet military base. For nearly five decades it effectively vanished from the public consciousness.

von links nach rechts / from left to right
Marina Schröder, Dr. Hans-Joachim Wolff,
Lothar Szych, Hans-Gerd von Lennep

Vorstandsvorsitzende
der Deutschen Gesetzlichen Unfallversicherung
Chairpersons of the board at the DGUV
(German Social Accident Insurance)

Nach der Wiedervereinigung entschieden sich die Berufsgenossenschaften für die ehemalige Landesschule als Standort ihrer neuen Bildungseinrichtung. Ein Jahrzehnt nach dem Richtfest im Oktober 1999 ist der Campus in Klotzsche eine feste Größe für Qualifizierung, Beratung und Forschung in der Prävention. Die Deutsche Gesetzliche Unfallversicherung erforscht hier die Risiken und Veränderungen in der Arbeitswelt. Auf der Grundlage dieser Analysen passen die Sozialpartner die Prävention von Berufsgenossenschaften und Unfallkassen wiederum an neue Herausforderungen wie neue Arbeitsformen, psychische Belastungen und den demografischen Wandel an.

Die Einweihung der Akademie im Jahr 2001 markierte das Ende eines dunklen Kapitels in der Geschichte dieses Geländes. Heute lernen hier mehr als 20 000 Seminarteilnehmer jährlich, Gesundheit und Leben bei der Arbeit zu schützen.

Wir freuen uns über diesen Erfolg, denn er belegt: Das Engagement der Selbstverwaltung für diese Akademie war richtig. Mit Liebe und großem Einsatz haben wir hier einen Ort geschaffen, an dem Lernen und Forschen Freude bereiten und sich ergänzen. Einen Ort, an dem wir Zukunft machen.

Further to reunification, the former Landesschule was selected by the Berufsgenossenschaften (statutory accident insurance institutions) as the location for their new academy. One decade on from its topping-out ceremony in the October of 1999, the Klotzsche campus has become an established leader in preventative training, consultancy and research. It is here that the DGUV (German Social Accident Insurance) carries out studies into risks and changes in the working environment. The results of these analyses are used by social partners to adapt the preventative measures proposed by the statutory accident insurance institutions in order to overcome fresh challenges such as new forms of work, mental stress and demographic change.

The official opening of the academy in 2001 marked the end of a dark chapter in the history of the site. Over 20,000 seminar participants now arrive there each year to learn how to protect health and lives in occupational situations.

We are buoyed by this success, as it justifies the decision made by the social partners to go ahead with the academy project. Passion for the task and a great deal of effort have seen us create a place where learning and research are both gratifying and complementary. A place where the future is shaped today.

Dr. Hans-Joachim Wolff

Marina Schröder

Hans-Gerd von Lennep

Lothar Szych

Dank der Autoren und Herausgeber
The authors and publishers extend their thanks to

- Michail Alabugin, Odessa
- Brigitte Hoffmann, Dresden
- Michael Merchel, Sylvia Reinhardt, Gerd Schirok, Sächsisches Hauptsstaatsarchiv Dresden
- Gerhard Müller, Dresden
- Wolfgang Raquet, Dresden
- Sächsische Landesbibliothek – Staats- und Universitätsbibliothek Dresden, Deutsche Fotothek
- Dr. Karlheinz Ufert (†), Emmerich
- Dr. Johannes Zimmermann, Langebrück

Besonderer Dank der Herausgeber
Special thanks from the publishers

Ausgangspunkt dieses Buchprojektes war 2008 die Foto-Ausstellung »Tessenow re*F*ormt« der BGW Akademie für Arbeitssicherheit und Gesundheitsschutz in Dresden. Jörg Stojke und Sabine Terno von der Berufsgenossenschaft für Gesundheitsdienst und Wohlfahrtspflege sei an dieser Stelle für ihren Impuls besonders gedankt.
The starting point for this book project was the 2008 photo exhibition "Tessenow re*F*ormt" held by the BGW Academy for Occupational Safety and Health in Dresden. Jörg Stojke and Sabine Terno of the BG for Healthcare and Welfare are due special thanks here for their ideas.

Wenn die Bundesrepublik Deutschland in diesem Jahr 2009 mit besonderer Aufmerksamkeit auf die Ereignisse der Wende vor zwanzig Jahren zurückblickt und dabei auch allenthalben über die Leistung der deutschen Wiedervereinigung nachzudenken hat, wird in der positiven Bilanz ganz weit vorn die Rettung der baulichen Substanz des maladen Landes DDR rangieren. Seine Städte waren in einem sichtbar desolaten Zustand, seine Infrastruktur war verschlissen. Entsprechend intensiv drehten sich seit Anfang der 1990er Jahre die Kräne.

Auch die Akademie der Deutschen Gesetzlichen Unfallversicherung in Klotzsche entstand in diesem Bauboom der vergangenen zwei Jahrzehnte. Dass das Areal und seine Geschichte bisher in der Literatur kaum Beachtung fanden, hatte wohl mit seiner städtebaulichen »Zurückgezogenheit« zu tun. Man muss genau wissen, wohin man will, um dieses außergewöhnliche Gelände zu finden – um es dann allerdings, wer erstmals hierher kommt, staunend zu erkunden. Der großzügig in die Landschaft gelagerte Gebäude-Komplex ist von großer architektonischer Faszination, und es ist bedauerlich, dass dieses Beispiel gelungener Synthese von alter Substanz und Neubau so wenig im allgemeinen Bewusstsein angekommen ist. Vielleicht trägt ja dieses Buch zur verdienten Popularisierung bei. Es hat das Zeug dazu.

Nicht jedem Besucher wird sich auf den ersten Blick erschließen, was für eine verwickelte Geschichte mit dem Gebäudekomplex der Akademie verbunden ist – dazu ist der heutige Gesamteindruck vermutlich zu harmonisch. Das Haus selbst legt allerdings mit Dokumentarfotografie und Chronik in seinen weitläufigen Gängen und Korridoren genügend Spuren für die Historie seines Standortes.

The year is 2009, and twenty years have passed since the fall of the Wall. If the Federal Republic of Germany not only looks back on the events of that period with a particularly attentive eye, but also dedicates thorough thought to the achievements made possible by German reunification, the saving of the building fabric of the sickly GDR state will be at the forefront of the positive conclusions drawn. Though towns were in clearly desperate condition and infrastructure threadbare, cranes and earthmovers have worked overtime to rectify this since the start of the 1990s.

The academy operated by the DGUV (the German Social Accident Insurance body) in Klotzsche is just one product of the construction boom of the last two decades. The fact that the site and its history have previously been all but ignored in literature is likely to be a consequence of its locational "seclusion". Anyone wishing to find this remarkable site really has to know where they are going, yet once they have arrived they will only be able to marvel at it. Set against natural surroundings, its generously proportioned building complex is a work of great architectural fascination, and it is regrettable that the public is so unaware of this example of the successful synthesis of building fabric old and new. Perhaps this book will make a contribution to the popularisation of the site – it certainly has what it takes to do so.

The general impression made by the modern-day academy complex is probably too harmonious to enable all visitors to immediately fathom the intriguing story behind it. Documentary photographs and other chronicles on display along the academy's extensive walkways and corridors nevertheless leave many clues as to its past. What a chapter in German history! The pomp and misery of a totalitarian century are reflected in the varied and eventful usages of the property. Having been founded as the Landesschule Dresden at the beginning of the Weimar Republic era, the school's new premises were built in 1925/26 and included Heinrich Tessenow – one of the most feted exponents of New Realism architecture – amongst its architects.

Was für ein Kapitel deutscher Geschichte! In der wechselvollen Nutzungsgeschichte des Areals manifestieren sich Glanz und Elend eines totalitären Jahrhunderts. Gegründet wurde der Baukomplex als sächsische Landesschule Dresden zu Beginn der Weimarer Republik. Erbaut wurde sie 1925/26 u.a. von Heinrich Tessenow, einem der renommiertesten Vertreter einer neuen Sachlichkeit in der Architektur. Sofort mit der Eröffnung galt die Landesschule als einer der außergewöhnlichsten Neubauten der Stadt. Keine zehn Jahre später usurpierten 1934 die Nazis die Schule als Nationalpolitische Erziehungsanstalt im Sinne ihrer aggressiven Ideologie. Seit Kriegsende residierte hier als Besatzungsmacht die Sowjetarmee mit dem Stab der 11. Gardepanzerdivision. Übrig geblieben war nach 45 Jahren hermetischer Abgeschiedenheit dann ein völlig ruiniertes, auf etwa fünfzig Prozent dezimiertes Gebäudeensemble, dem keiner mehr ansehen konnte, wofür es einst erdacht war. Und in dieses Gelände hinein projektierte schließlich seit 1994 die spätere Akademie der Deutschen Gesetzlichen Unfallversicherung mit großem Wagemut ihr Zukunftsprojekt einer gemeinsamen Bildungsstätte für drei gewerbliche Berufsgenossenschaften und deren Spitzenverband. Seit 2001 steht sie so nunmehr gut 20000 Gästen im Jahr für ihre Weiterbildung zur selbstverständlichen Verfügung.

Soweit ein kleiner Abriss einer extremen Geschichte, wie sie Gebäude im 20. Jahrhundert gelegentlich erfuhren. Die Texte dieses Bandes gehen ihr auf Basis neuer, oft erstmaliger Forschungen nun bis in die Details nach. Dabei stellt sich heraus, wie ungenau unsere Kenntnis von dieser spezifischen Historie bisher war. So stand die Landesschule in direkter Nachfolge des Königlich-Sächsischen Kadettenkorps,

As soon as it opened, the Landesschule became one of the most exceptional new constructions in the city. Not even ten years had passed when, in 1934, the Nazis appropriated the school in order to create a State National Political Educational Institution which followed their aggressive ideology. From the end of the war onwards the site was occupied by the Soviet Army, which used it as the headquarters of its 11th Guards Tank Division. With the property having been hermetically sealed off from the outside world for 45 years, all that remained once the occupying Soviet forces had withdrawn was a completely dilapidated building complex which had been reduced by around fifty per cent in size. Its original usage was completely indiscernible. Almost unbelievably, this was the site for which a future DGUV-run academy was to draw up audacious plans for the creation of a shared training establishment for three statutory accident insurance institutions and their umbrella organisation. The planning process started in 1994, and the centre opened its doors for the first time in 2001. It now welcomes 20,000 guests a year to its facilities.

The above description is a brief summary of an extreme story as occasionally experienced by buildings during the 20th century. Contributions to this book have taken this story and investigated it in detail on the basis of new and often ground-breaking research. Their findings show just how vague our knowledge of the site and its specific history has been up to this point. It is now known, for example, that the Landesschule was the direct successor of the Königlich-Sächsisches Kadettenkorps, which had applied a strict disciplinary culture in its capacity as a military training facility for future officers from the late 17th century onwards. Under the Weimar Republic this tradition was to be replaced by a new concept which promoted gifted pupils and simultaneously followed a code of social responsibility which benefitted previously underprivileged social strata.

das seit dem späten 17. Jahrhundert als militärische Lehranstalt für Offiziere ein strenges Reglement von Disziplin praktizierte. Diese Tradition sollte in der Weimarer Republik mit einem neuen Konzept von Begabtenförderung bei gleichzeitiger sozialer Verantwortung für bislang unterprivilegierte Schichten abgelöst werden. Dann aber haben sich unter einem konservativen Direktorat die alten Mechanismen einer autoritären Schulführung mit Zucht und vaterländischer Ideologie wieder durchgesetzt. Man verwendete beispielsweise noch alte kaiserliche Lehrbücher, sodass von dem Gedankengut der Reformschule, wie es zur gleichen Zeit an anderen Orten in Dresden, etwa an der Dürerschule, praktiziert wurde, nicht die Rede sein konnte. Der Text von Ullrich Amlung arbeitet diesen Sachverhalt deutlich heraus. Für die Landesschule Dresden ist der Mythos Reformpädagogik, der ja im Übrigen durch den luftigen, modernen architektonischen Habitus der Schule leicht zu assoziieren war, also schlicht falsch.

Mithin war auch der Bruch von 1934 nicht so gravierend, wie bislang angenommen. Zucht und Ordnung gingen weiter, aus dem Vaterländischen wurde das Völkische und die Knabenschule hatte mit ihrem Ideal von Kameradschaft und Körperertüchtigung unverändert fatale Faszination für die Heranwachsenden. Diese besondere Variante von »Gleichschaltung« diente freilich der Erziehung von »Kampfmaschinen«, wie ein ehemaliger Schüler in einer schmerzlichen späten Einsicht formulierte. So genau wie in dem vorliegenden Text von Hanka Blesse wurde dieser unheilvolle Mechanismus an einem Dresdner Beispiel bislang selten beschrieben.

Despite these objectives, the school's conservative directors actually returned to the old mechanisms of an authoritarian method based on discipline and patriotic ideology. The continued use of imperial textbooks, for example, meant that there was no question of the reformist school ideas already being implemented at other Dresden schools (e.g. the Dürerschule) being put into practice at the Landesschule. This issue is dealt with clearly in the contribution made by Ullrich Amlung. Though its airy, modern architecture may have suggested otherwise, the myth which defined the Landesschule Dresden as a seat of progressive learning was simply false.

The upheaval of 1934 was consequently not as significant to the school as previously presumed. Strict discipline was retained, the patriotic became the nationalistic and the tenets of comradeship and physical training held to by the school continued to generate fateful fascination amongst its young charges. As the painful recollections of one former pupil put it, this special type of "enforced conformity" was of course designed to train the boys into "fighting machines". This sinister process has rarely been as accurately described on the basis of an example from Dresden as in the piece by Hanka Blesse featured in this volume.

The essay on the decades of Soviet Army usage of the site is also unique. This is due in particular to the fact that there is generally only scarce knowledge available on the internal affairs of occupying forces in what began as the Soviet Zone and went on to become the GDR. Visits to occupied areas tended to be full of formalities and rituals, and were restricted to the exchange of military tactics between the "brother armies". Details of what actually went on in the lives of the GDR's Soviet "friends" (a characteristically double-edged term) never saw the light of day. The illuminating text contributed by Götz Krüger therefore does pioneering work in an unfamiliar field.

Aber auch der Aufsatz über die Jahrzehnte währende Nutzung des Geländes durch die Sowjetarmee ist ein Unikat. Tatsächlich ist über die inneren Verhältnisse der Besatzungsmacht in der Sowjetischen Besatzungszone und späteren DDR generell sehr wenig bekannt. Besuche waren in aller Regel formelhaft und rituell und meist auf militärtaktischen Austausch der »Bruderarmeen« begrenzt. Vom wirklichen Leben der »Freunde« (bezeichnender Doppelklang) drang nichts nach außen. So leistet der anschauliche Text von Götz Krüger gleichsam Pionierarbeit in einem unbekannten Feld.

Auf ihre Weise bringen auch die beiden Bauberichte dieses Bandes von Ulrike Hübner-Grötzsch und Ullrich Hübner und von Michael Bartsch nützliche Aufklärung zur regionalen Geschichte. Wichtig ist z. B. die Rollenverteilung für die beiden 1925 beauftragten, eigentlich ganz gegensätzlich gestimmten Architekten Heinrich Tessenow und Oskar Kramer, der zunächst die Grundentwürfe lieferte. Ihre Symbiose ist nicht nur architekturgeschichtlich aufschlussreich. Wie schließlich ja auch die lange Geschichte des Wiederaufbaus nach 1994, die vor allem einen Kompromiss zwischen Belangen des Denkmalschutzes und Effizienzpflicht des Bauherrn suchen musste, als gelungenes Beispiel von Interessenausgleich für das Allgemeinwohl gelten kann.

So präsentiert sich dieses Buch in der Vielfalt der beschriebenen Phänomene aus Architektur, Pädagogik und Politik insgesamt als ein höchst originärer Beitrag zur Dresdner Kulturgeschichte.

Hans-Peter Lühr

The accounts provided by Ulrike Hübner-Grötzsch and Ullrich Hübner on the construction of the Landesschule and Michael Bartsch on the reconstruction of the complex provide useful insights into regional history. One important issue now clarified is the division of responsibilities between the two architects commissioned in 1925 to design and build the Landesschule, Heinrich Tessenow and Oskar Kramer (the designer of initial plans for the complex). Despite the two men being entirely different in their approaches, their symbiosis nevertheless throws light on more than just architectural history. The same can effectively be said of the events of 1994 onwards which eventually led to the reconstruction of the complex. Not only was the project characterised by compromise between the interests of monument protection and the new site owner's need for efficiency, but it can also be seen as a successful example of the balancing of interests in order to benefit the greater good.

All in all, the wide variety of architectural, educational and political phenomena described in this book makes it a highly original contribution to cultural history in Dresden.

Hans-Peter Lühr

links / left
Blick über den Campus nach Nordosten.
View north-east across the campus.

rechts / right
Pergola als verbindendes
Element zwischen den Gebäuden.
Pergola as a connecting element
between buildings.

16

Details in Haus 1, dem ehemaligen Lehrgebäude.
Details in building 1 (the former classroom building).

Deckenelemente im Foyer von Haus 1.
Ceiling details in the foyer of building 1.

Blick vom Dach des Akademiehotels nach Nordwesten.
View north-west from the roof of the Academy Hotel.

Fassadengliederung durch Schiefer, Sandstein und verschiedene Fensterformen.
Façade design featuring slate, sandstone and various window types.

Landesschule Dresden – Entstehung, Konzeption und Praxis (1920 – 1933)

The Landesschule Dresden – establishment, concept and practices (1920 – 1933)

ULLRICH AMLUNG

Die 1920 gegründete Landesschule Dresden gehört aufgrund ihres unverwechselbaren pädagogischen Profils und der mit diesem eng korrespondierenden einzigartigen Schularchitektur zweifellos zu den bemerkenswerten Bildungsanstalten der Weimarer Republik in Sachsen. Zahlreiche Delegationen aus dem In- und Ausland, die sich mit Fragen neuzeitlicher Schulgestaltung beschäftigten, kamen seinerzeit nach Dresden, um an diesem außergewöhnlichen Internatsschulmodell zu hospitieren.[1] In auffälligem Kontrast zur Ausnahmestellung der Landesschule Dresden in der sächsischen Schullandschaft steht ihre bis heute anhaltende nahezu vollständige Vernachlässigung durch die historische Bildungs- und Schulforschung. Damit teilt sie das Schicksal ihrer unmittelbaren Vorgängerinstitution, des 1920 aufgelösten Königlich-Sächsischen Kadettenkorps, auf dessen mehr als 200-jähriger Tradition die Landesschule Dresden hinsichtlich Programmatik und pädagogischer Praxis vielfach fußt.

Das Königlich-Sächsische Kadettenkorps in Dresden (1692 – 1920)

Im Jahre 1692 hatte der Kurfürst von Sachsen, Johann Georg IV. (1668 – 1694), eine »Kompagnie adliger Kadetten« in Dresden gegründet, aus der der zukünftige Offiziersstand der sächsischen Armee rekrutiert werden sollte.[2] Das Kadettenkorps bestand aus 125 Zöglingen, die in verschiedenen Unterrichtsfächern, darunter vorzüglich Französisch und Mathematik, geschult und in militärischen Übungen ausgebildet wurden. Die Kadetten waren zu dieser Zeit während ihrer Ausbildung noch nicht einkaserniert, sondern »zur Hebung des Wohlstandes der abgebrannten Stadt bei den [Dresdner] Bürgern«[3] kostenpflichtig einquartiert.

Fechtunterricht auf dem Sportgelände der Landesschule Dresden in Klotzsche, um 1930.
Fencing lessons on the sports field at the Landesschule Dresden in Klotzsche, circa 1930.

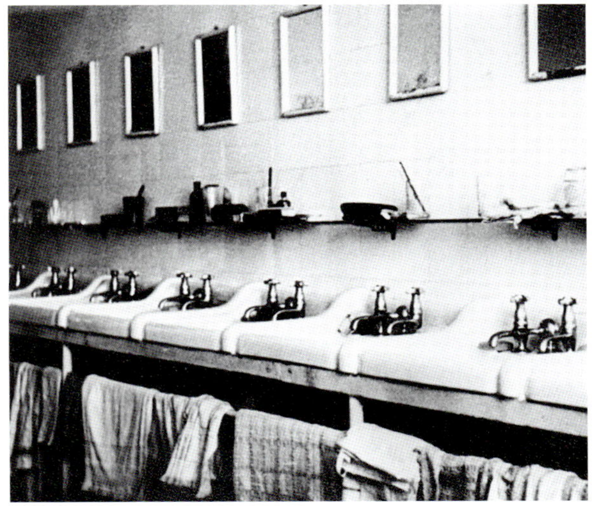

Gemeinschaftswaschräume in einem Schülerheim.
Communal washing facilities in a boarding house.

Founded in 1920, the unmistakable pedagogical profile and closely related, unique architecture of the Landesschule Dresden[1] place it amongst the most remarkable Saxon educational establishments of the Weimar Republic era. A great many delegations from Germany and beyond came to Dresden to observe its exceptional boarding school model as part of their research into modern school design.[2] To date, and in conspicuous contrast to its special position in the Saxon school landscape, the Landesschule Dresden has been continually and almost completely neglected by historical research into education and schools – a fate it shares with its immediate predecessor, the Königlich-Sächsisches Kadettenkorps[3]. The scholastic programme and educational methods employed at the Landesschule Dresden were founded to a large extent on the traditions developed over the course of the 200-year history of the Kadettenkorps, which closed its doors for the final time in 1920.

Nach Vorschlägen und auf Veranlassung des Reichsgrafen und Feldmarschalls Christoph August von Wackerbarth (1662 – 1734) zur Gründung einer militärischen Bildungsanstalt für junge Adlige wurde in den Jahren von 1723 bis 1726 in Dresden eine Ritter- und Militärakademie errichtet, die nach ihrem Initiator »Wackerbarth'sches Palais« genannt wurde. 1725 begann der Unterricht in dem noch unvollendeten Kadettenhaus, in dem die Zöglinge ab 1731 auch wohnten. Der nach Plänen des Barock-Architekten Johann Christoph Knöffel (1686 – 1752) erbaute Gebäudekomplex enthielt Wohnräume für Offiziere, Kadetten und Lehrer, Hörsäle, ein Reithaus mit Stallungen und über der Reitbahn einen großen Turn- und Tanzsaal. Nach sechsjährigem Fachunterricht und militärischer Ausbildung an der Ritterakademie legten die Kadetten die Fähnrichsprüfung vor der preußischen Ober-Militär-Examinations-Kommission ab, die sich hierfür extra nach Dresden begab.

Besonders in den 1820er Jahren entwickelte sich das Königlich-Sächsische Kadettenkorps unter seinem Kommandeur General Carl Friedrich Wilhelm von Gersdorff (1764 – 1829) zu einer »mustergültigen« militärischen Lehranstalt zur Ausbildung zukünftiger Offiziere aller Waffengattungen, die auch auf die Kadettenausbildung in anderen Ländern ausstrahlte.

Nach 1867 begann unter der Leitung des Generalstabchefs Georg Friedrich Alfred Graf von Fabrice (1818 – 1891) eine Reorganisation der sächsischen Armee, die eine Verlegung der militärischen Einrichtungen aus der Inneren Neustadt an den Rand der Dresdner Heide zur Folge hatte. Im neu errichteten Kasernenbezirk in der Albertstadt fanden auch die Kadetten eine neue Heimstatt: Sie bezogen dort 1878 einen Gebäudekomplex auf der Marienallee, bestehend aus Wohn- und Lehrgebäude (Kadettenhaus), einer Exerzier- und Turnhalle, einem Wirtschaftsgebäude mit Speisesaal, Billard- und Lesezimmer sowie mehreren Tanzsälen und einem sich daran anschließenden Stallgebäude. Das Hauptgebäude war das dreistöckige Kadettenhaus, das u. a. Hörsäle, ein Physikzimmer und ein Laboratorium, eine Bibliothek sowie Wohn- und Schlafstuben für die Kadetten, Unterhaltungszimmer, einen großen Fahnensaal und im

The Königlich-Sächsisches Kadettenkorps in Dresden (1692–1920)

The year 1692 saw Johann Georg IV (1668–1694), elector of Saxony, establish a "company of noble cadets" in Dresden. Future Saxon army officers were to be recruited from amongst their number.[4] The Kadettenkorps consisted of 125 pupils schooled in various subjects (French and mathematics were of exceptional quality) and trained in the art of military drills. At that point the cadets were not yet kept in barracks during their training, and were billeted at their own expense with residents of Dresden "in order to raise the prosperity of the burnt-out city".[5]

Between the years of 1723 and 1726, a military school for young noblemen was erected in Dresden at the instigation of Count of the Reich Field Marshall Christoph August von Wackerbarth (1662–1734). The resultant academy of chivalry and military training was named the "Wackerbarth'sches Palais" in honour of the man who had brought about its creation. 1725 witnessed the start of lessons in the as-yet-unfinished "Kadettenhaus", which from 1731 onwards was also used to accommodate cadets. Built according to plans by the Baroque architect Johann Christoph Knöffel (1686–1752), the building complex comprised living quarters for officers, cadets and teachers, lecture halls, an indoor riding school with stables and a large gymnasium and dancing hall above the riding arena. Cadets completed six years of specialist lessons and military training at the academy of chivalry before taking the officer-cadet test in front of the Prussian Upper Military Examination Commission, which travelled to Dresden especially for the occasion.

In the 1820s in particular, the Königlich-Sächsisches Kadettenkorps under the command of General Carl Friedrich Wilhelm von Gersdorff (1764–1829) became an "exemplary" seat of military training for future officers of all types, and also influenced cadet training practices in other countries.

The reorganisation of the Saxon army – which began in 1867 under the leadership of the Chief of the General Staff Georg Friedrich Alfred Graf von Fabrice (1818–1891) – resulted in the movement of military facilities from the Innere

3. Stock ein Lazarett umschloss. Das Hauptgebäude war mit den Nebenbauten durch überdachte Glasgänge verbunden, sodass die etwa 6000 Quadratmeter bedeckende Gebäudeanlage ein geschlossenes Ganzes bildete.[4] Zur Kadettenschule gehörte ein großes parkartiges Gelände zwischen Marienallee und Prießnitzgrund.

Umfasste das Kadettenkorps im Jahr seines Umzuges 160 Kadetten, so stieg ihre Zahl in den 1890er Jahren kontinuierlich an, auf zunächst 200 und schließlich auf 224 Kadetten im Jahre 1906. Entsprechend stark wuchsen auch der Lehrkörper und die anderweitige Beamtenschaft an der Kadettenanstalt. 1906 waren dort beschäftigt: ein Studiendirektor als Leiter der Schule, ein Stabsarzt, zwölf Offiziere, drei Militärlehrer, 14 Zivillehrer, fünf Ober- und 21 Unterbeamte und verschiedene Hilfslehrer, darunter Religionslehrer, Zeichen- und Tanzlehrer.

Um dem gestiegenen Raumbedarf Rechnung zu tragen, wurden zahlreiche, z. T. umfängliche Baumaßnahmen ergriffen. So wurden u. a. ein eigenes Lehrgebäude, ein separates Lazarett und ein Hallenschwimmbad errichtet. Die Primaner erhielten zum altersgerechten geselligen Umgang zwei eigene Kasino-Räume.[5]

Der Unterrichtslehrpan der Kadettenschule richtete sich bis zur Jahrhundertwende nach demjenigen einer achtstufigen Realschule I. Ordnung mit drei obligatorischen Fremdsprachen, darunter Latein. Um 1900 entsprach der fünf- bzw. siebenjährige Lehrgang im Allgemeinen demjenigen eines neunstufigen Realgymnasiums (grundständiges Latein, Französisch ab Quarta, Englisch ab Obertertia), mit dem das Kadettenkorps gleichgestellt war. Der militärische Unterricht bestand im Wesentlichen aus Exerzieren, Turnen, Fechten. Hinzu kamen Übungen in Schießen, Reiten, Felddienst und Gefecht.

Die Aufnahme in das Kadettenkorps erfolgte nach bestandener Prüfung, wenn der Aspirant im zwölften bis 14. Lebensjahr war, in der Regel in die Quarta, in Ausnahmefällen auch in die Unter- oder Obertertia. Die Aufnahmeprüfung erstreckte sich auf die Fächer Religion, Deutsch, Latein, Rechnen, Geschichte, Erdkunde und Naturgeschichte. Die zugelassenen Kadetten mussten Pensionsgelder und

Neustadt district to the edge of Dresden Heath. The newly-erected barracks in the Albertstadt district was also to become the cadets' new home, and in 1878 they moved into a complex opposite the building which was to go on to house the Saxon State Library from 1947 onwards. The new premises comprised a residential/teaching building (the Kadettenhaus), an exercise and gymnastics hall, a management building featuring a dining hall, a billiards/reading room and numerous dance halls and an adjoining stable building. The three-storey Kadettenhaus represented the main building, and housed lecture halls, a physics room and laboratory, a library, living and sleeping quarters for the cadets, common rooms, a large flag hall and a third-storey infirmary. Porched, glazed passages connected the main building to ancillary buildings, and thereby created a cohesive building complex with a combined area of around 6,000 square metres.[6] A large, park-like site between the Marienallee and the floor of the Prießnitz Valley also belonged to the cadet school.

Having numbered 160 cadets in the year of its relocation, the Kadettenkorps steadily grew in size during the 1890s, and initially reached a membership of 200 before eventually rising to a total of 224 cadets in 1906. Corresponding increases were also witnessed where teaching staff and other officials at the cadet school were concerned. By 1906 the Kadettenkorps employed the following staff: a director of studies (also the headmaster of the school); a medical officer; twelve officers; three military instructors; fourteen civilian teachers; five senior and twenty-one junior civil servants; and various assistant teachers for subjects such as religious education, drawing and dance. A wide range of construction measures, some of them substantial, were carried out in order to keep pace with the increasing amount of space required. These measures saw the erection of a dedicated classroom building, a separate infirmary and an indoor swimming pool. The two mess rooms made available to pupils in the top two years were intended to foster social behaviour typical to their age group.[7]

Up to the turn of the century the lesson timetable for the cadet school orientated itself on that of an eight-year secondary school of the first order. Three foreign languages

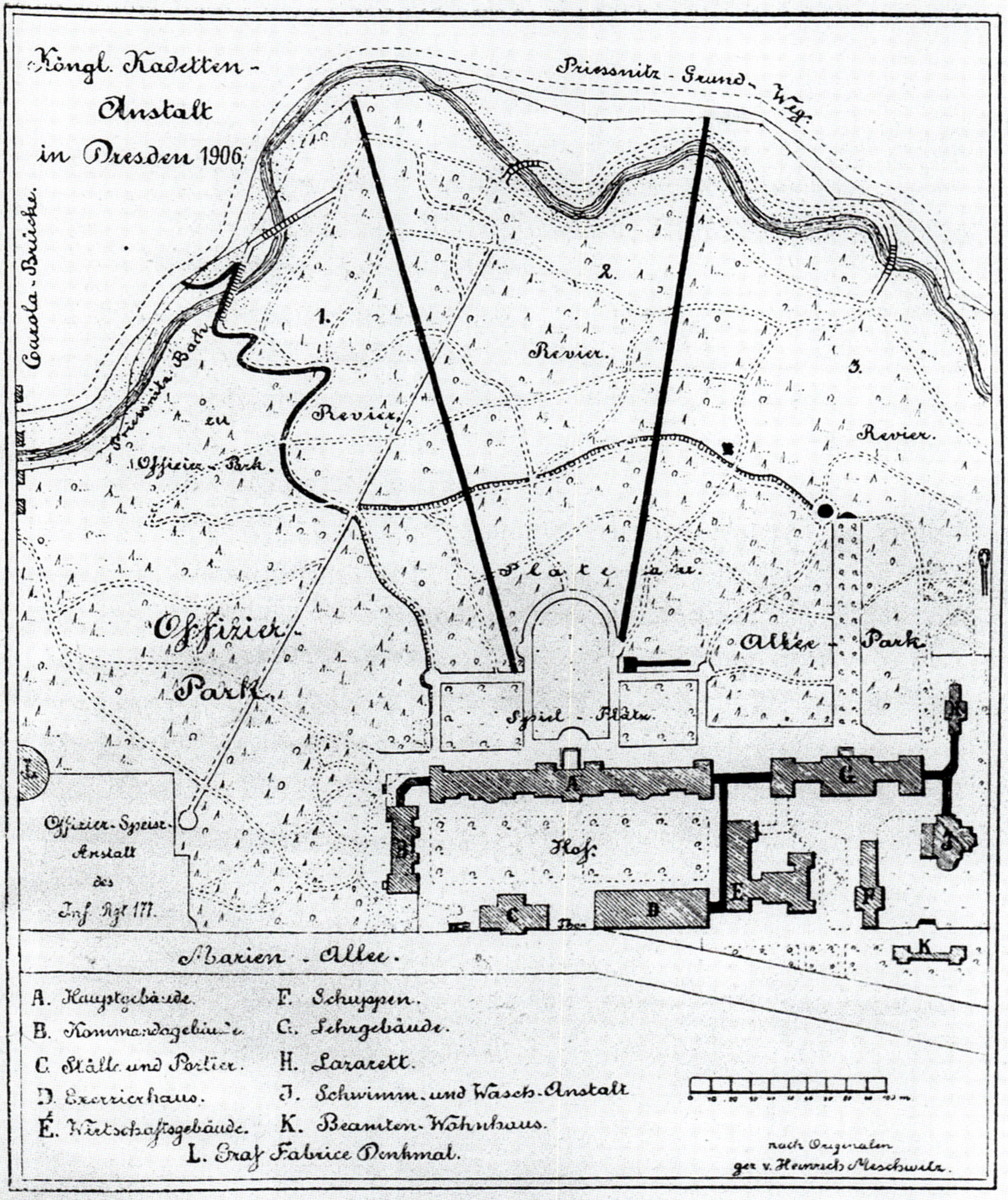

Grundriss der Königlichen Kadettenanstalt in Dresden, 1906.
Layout of the Royal Kadettenkorps complex, 1906.

Kostenbeiträge entrichten, allerdings kam immer jeweils die Hälfte von ihnen in den Genuss von Freistellen. Die Kadetten waren Internatsschüler. Tagesschüler waren die Ausnahme und bedurften der ausdrücklichen Genehmigung durch das Kriegsministerium. Sämtliche Kadetten waren in zwei Kompagnien eingeteilt mit je einem Kadetten als Kompagnieältesten. Die 1. Kompagnie wurde aus den Kadetten der Prima, Sekunda und einem Teil der Obertertia, die 2. aus den übrigen Zöglingen gebildet. Jede Kompagnie bestand ihrerseits aus mehreren Abteilungen, zunächst drei, später fünf, denen je ein Offizier als Erzieher zugeordnet war. Die Abteilungen wiederum waren in Korporalschaften gegliedert, die identisch mit der jeweiligen Schlafraumbelegung mit sechs bis acht Kadetten pro Stube waren. Jeweils an der Spitze der 26 Korporalschaften stand ein Primaner als Stubenältester. Daneben gab es für verschiedene Funktionen, die für die Organisation des Gemeinschaftslebens notwendig waren, sogenannte »Kadetten vom Dienst«.

Der typische Tagesablauf im Sommerhalbjahr sah etwa folgendermaßen aus: 5.30 Uhr Wecken (im Winter: 6.15 Uhr), 6 Uhr: Abmarsch zum 1. Frühstück mit anschließender Arbeitsstunde, 6.50 Uhr: Stundenappell; montags fand danach regelmäßig eine kurze Morgenandacht mit dem Hausgeistlichen im Fahnensaal statt. Die Unterrichtsstunden begannen um 7 Uhr und dauerten 50 Minuten, unterbrochen wurden sie von drei kleinen und einer größeren Frühstückspause. Der Vormittagsunterricht endete um 12.10 Uhr (im Winter um 13 Uhr); 12.55 Uhr: Kompagnie-Appell, 13 Uhr: Abmarsch zum Mittagessen. Die Nachmittage dienten der Erledigung der Hausaufgaben, militärpraktischen Übungen oder der aktiven Freizeitgestaltung; 19.30 Uhr: Abmarsch zum Abendessen. Bis 21.40 Uhr mussten sämtliche Kadetten zu Bett sein.[6]

Lazarettgebäude der neuen Kadettenanstalt an der Marienallee.
Infirmary building at the new Kadettenkorps complex on the Marienallee.

(including Latin) were therefore compulsory. Around 1900 the five- to seven-year course effectively corresponded with the education offered by the nine-year grammar schools with which the Kadettenkorps was equated (foundation Latin, French from year seven upwards, English from year nine upwards). Military instruction essentially consisted of drills, gymnastics, fencing and additional training in the arts of shooting, riding, field duty and battle.

Applicants of between twelve and fourteen years old who successfully negotiated the entrance test tended to be accepted into year seven, however pupils were also taken on in years eight and nine in exceptional cases. The entrance test covered the subjects of religion, German, Latin, arithmetic, history, geography and natural history. Although successful candidates were obliged to pay boarding fees and other contributions towards costs, around half of their number benefitted from free places.

The cadets were boarders; day pupils were the exception to the rule and required express permission from the War Ministry. All enrolled cadets were divided into two companies, each of which featured a cadet in the role of company elder. The first company consisted of years ten to thirteen and some of year nine. The remaining pupils formed the second company. Each company comprised numerous sections (initially three and later five), each of which had an officer allocated to it as a tutor. These sections were divided into "squad" groups identical in their makeup to the groups of six to eight cadets allocated to each dormitory room. Each of the 26 squads elected a top-year pupil as their room elder. So-called "cadets on duty" also performed various functions necessary to the organisation of communal cadet life.

A typical day in the summer term was timetabled as follows: 5:30 – wake-up call (6:15 during the winter term); 6:00 – march to the first breakfast break, followed by work; 6:50 –role call (on Mondays the Kadettenkorps chaplain then led a regular morning service in the flag hall); 7:00 – lessons begin, each lasting 50 minutes, the morning sessions was divided up by three shorts breaks and a longer breakfast break; 12:10 – morning lessons end (13:00 during the winter term); 12:55 – company role call; 13:00 – march to lunch; afternoons were used for the completion of homework tasks, practical military exercises or active leisure pursuits; 19:30 – march to dinner; 21:40 – bed curfew for all cadets.[8]

Between 1876 and 1906 the Kadettenkorps was attended by a total of seven princes, 574 titled boys and 808 untitled boys. They all took the officer-cadet test simultaneous to successful completion of year eleven, and a small proportion of

Zwischen 1876 und 1906 haben das Kadettenkorps insgesamt sieben Prinzen, 574 adlige und 808 bürgerliche Söhne besucht. Sie alle legten gleichzeitig mit der erfolgreichen Absolvierung der Obersekunda die Fähnrichprüfung ab, ein geringerer Teil von ihnen ging mit diesem Patent in der Tasche anschließend zur Armee. Das Fähnrichexamen galt zugleich als Voraussetzung für den Besuch der Unterprima. Ostern 1903 bestanden neun Kadetten vor einer aus Lehrern des Kadettenkorps und auswärtigen Beisitzern zusammengesetzten Prüfungskommission erstmals die Reifeprüfung eines sächsischen Realgymnasiums. Dem Abitur folgte in der Regel der Eintritt in die Armee, dem sich alsbald der Besuch der Kriegsschule anschloss.

Schwimmhalle in der neuen Kadettenanstalt an der Marienallee.
Indoor swimming pool at the new Kadettenkorps complex on the Marienallee.

Die Geschichte des Königlich-Sächsischen Kadettenkorps in Dresden endete im 228. Jahr seines Bestehens mit seiner Auflösung am 10. März 1920 im Gefolge von Auflagen zur Entmilitarisierung, die sich aus dem Versailler Friedensvertrag (Artikel 176) nach dem Ende des Ersten Weltkrieges ergaben.

Bereits am 3. Juli 1919 hatten sich Lehrer und Beamte des Kadettenkorps an das sächsische Kultusministerium gewandt mit dem Ersuchen, »das Kadettenkorps in seiner bisherigen Form (Realgymnasium mit Internat) als Zivilanstalt zu übernehmen und weiterzuführen«[7]. In der Begründung ihres Antrages kommen drei Grundgedanken zum Ausdruck:

1. Eine realistische Bildungsanstalt würde den wachsenden Erfordernissen einer modernen Gesellschaft entgegenkommen und wäre zugleich eine gute Ergänzung zu den beiden humanistischen Fürsten- und Landesschulen in Meißen und Grimma.
2. Die neue Einrichtung sollte den Charakter einer Reformschule haben, die neuzeitliche pädagogische Konzeptionen, wie sie in Ansätzen bereits vor dem Weltkrieg in den von Hermann Lietz gegründeten Landerziehungsheimen[8] und freien Schulgemeinden erprobt worden waren, weiterführt.
3. Die neue Schule sollte eine soziale Funktion erfüllen, als sie vorzüglich begabte Volksschüler, Kinder von Kriegsgefallenen, Schwerkriegsbeschädigten und Vertriebenen aufnehmen sollte.[9]

In einer zweiten Eingabe an das sächsische Kultusministerium vom 31. Oktober 1919 präzisierten die Antragsteller ihren Vorschlag dahingehend, »daß die neue Schule die Klassen Untertertia bis Oberprima eines Reformrealgymnasiums und von Obersekunda an aufwärts auch einen Oberrealschulzug umfassen sollte, dazu neben den planmäßigen Klassen Untertertia und Obertertia Förderklassen, in denen vorzüglich begabte Volksschüler in zwei Jahren so weit gebracht werden sollten, daß sie in die Untersekunda eintreten und so rechtzeitig das Ziel der Reife erreichen könnten. Gleichzeitig wurde angeregt, bei Gemeinden, Bezirksverbänden und anderen Körperschaften aller Art für die Stiftung von Freistellen für begabte Söhne unbemittelter Eltern zu werben.«[10]

Das sächsische Kultusministerium, das diesen Plänen zur Erhaltung und Umgestaltung der ehemaligen militärischen Bildungsanstalt durchaus wohlwollend gegenüberstand,

them pocketed this commission and went straight into military service. The officer-cadet test was also a prerequisite for acceptance into year twelve. The Easter of 1903 saw an examination panel comprising Kadettenkorps teachers and external observers award nine cadets their school leaving certificates, thereby making them the first pupils to be issued with such certificates by a Saxon grammar school. Holders of a school leaving certificate tended to go into the army, which began with a period at military school.

The history of the Königlich-Sächsisches Kadettenkorps in Dresden came to a conclusion in the 228th year of its existence. The conditions of demilitarisation set out in Article 176 of the Treaty of Versailles after the end of the First

Fahnensaal in der neuen Kadettenanstalt an der Marienallee.
Flag hall at the new Kadettenkorps complex on the Marienallee.

beschloss am 9. Februar 1920 die Übernahme des ehemaligen Kadettenkorps in den Verwaltungsbereich des höheren Schulwesens in Sachsen. In einer weiteren Besprechung mit der Lehrer- und Beamtenschaft des Kadettenkorps am 4. März 1920 im Anschluss an eine Besichtigung des Kadettenhauses wurde der Name »Landesschule Dresden« gewählt. Am 31. März 1920 erging eine Ministerialverordnung, die besagte, dass das Ministerium die vormalige Kadettenanstalt nach ihrer Umwandlung in ein Realgymnasium mit Oberrealschulzug und Internatsbetrieb vom 1. April 1920 an vorläufig für ein halbes Jahr seiner Aufsicht unterstellte. Mit der kommissarischen Leitung wurde der letzte Kommandeur des Kadettenkorps beauftragt.

World War brought about its closure on the 10th of March 1920. As early as the 3rd of July 1919, the teachers and civil servants attached to the Kadettenkorps had contacted the Saxon Ministry of Culture in order to request permission to "take over the Kadettenkorps in its present form (a grammar school with boarders) and continue to operate it as a civilian establishment"[9]. Their justification of the request included three fundamental points:

1. An upper-secondary type educational establishment would both comply with the increasing demands being placed on schools by modern society and represent a positive addition to the humanist, state-run Fürstenschulen[10] in Meißen and Grimma.
2. The new establishment was to be in the mould of a progressive school which continued to develop the modern educational concepts tested prior to the war in both the national community homes founded by Hermann Lietz[11] and independent school districts.
3. The new school was to serve a social purpose by primarily taking in talented state-school pupils and the children of those killed, severely disabled or displaced during the war.[12]

The applicants refined their proposal in a second submission made to the Saxon Ministry of Education and Culture Affairs on the 31st of October 1919, stating that "the new school would comprise years eight to thirteen of a progressive grammar school and an upper secondary section from year eleven upwards. In addition to the planned eighth and ninth years it would also feature accelerated learning classes designed to take talented pupils far enough in two years to enable them to pass into year ten and achieve their certificate in good time. It has also been suggested that attempts be made to enlist communities, district associations and other authorities of all types as sponsors of free places for the talented sons of penniless parents."[13]

On the 9th of February 1920, the Saxon Ministry of Education and Cultural Affairs – which saw these plans for the retention and restructuring of the former military school in

Gründung, Auf- und Ausbau der Landesschule Dresden in den 1920er Jahren

Am 14. April 1920 wurde die Landesschule Dresden im ehemaligen Kadettenhaus in der Albertstadt mit 74 Schülern, von denen 65 alte Kadetten waren, eröffnet.[11] Vorausgegangen war die Billigung der von der Lehrerschaft eingereichten »Grundsätze und Richtlinien« für den Schul- und Internatsbetrieb durch das sächsische Kultusministerium.

Am 3. September 1920 beschloss die sächsische Regierung die endgültige Übernahme der Schule in staatliche Verwaltung. Zuvor hatte das Kultusministerium bereits die Ablösung des Kommandeurs des ehemaligen Kadettenkorps durch einen fachlich ausgewiesenen zivilen Studiendirektor in der Leitung der Landesschule beschlossen, Haushaltspläne waren aufgestellt, notwendige Umbaumaßnahmen für das Kadettenhaus ausgearbeitet und potentielle Stifter von Freistellen angeschrieben.

Am 28. Oktober 1920 stimmte auch die Volkskammer der Regierungsvorlage zu mit der Auflage, dass die für die vormaligen Offiziere vorgesehenen Sonderstellen gestrichen würden.[12] Die SPD äußerte in der kontrovers geführten Debatte durch ihren Fraktionsvorsitzenden Arthur Arzt starke Vorbehalte gegen Konzept und Lehrpersonal der Landesschule.[13]

Zu Beginn des Schuljahres 1921/22 wurde an der Landesschule Dresden die erste Untertertia als Aufbauklasse aufgenommen. Deren Schüler sollten allerdings nicht, wie ursprünglich geplant, in einem zweijährigen Förderlehrgang für den Übertritt in die Realgymnasialuntersekunda vorbereitet werden, sondern »den Stamm bilden für die als Aufbauschule einzurichtende [lateinlose] Oberrealschulabteilung, die gleichzeitig mit einer Obersekunda eröffnet wurde«. Parallel zu den ersten Oberrealschulklassen wurde auch mit dem Aufbau des Realgymnasiums begonnen. Eine neu eingerichtete Untertertia wurde erstmalig nach dem Dresdner Reformplan[14] unterrichtet. Gleichzeitig fing man, so die Worte des Schulleiters, damit an, »unter Schonung bewährter militärischer Formen auch das Erziehungsheim innerlich neu aufzubauen«[15].

Landesschule Dresden in Klotzsche:
Schüler vor dem Eingang des Lehrgebäudes, um 1930.
Links im Bild: Schüler in Kadettenuniform.
Landesschule Dresden in Klotzsche:
pupils in front of the entrance to the classroom building.
Left of shot: pupil in Kadettenkorps uniform.

a perfectly benevolent light – took the decision to take the former Kadettenkorps into the administration of the Saxon secondary school system. A visit to the Kadettenhaus on the 4th of March 1920 was followed by a meeting with the teachers and civil servants who worked there. It was during that meeting that the name "Landesschule Dresden" was selected. A ministerial decree issued on the 31st of March 1920 stated that, subsequent to its conversion to a grammar school with an upper secondary section and boarding facilities, the ministry would be taking temporary control of the former cadet school for half a year from the 1st of April 1920 onwards; the last commander of the Kadettenkorps was put in temporary charge.

Rektorat mit Wohnung des Rektors, heute Haus 3.
Headmaster's building featuring headmaster's apartment, now building 3.

Der Aufbau der Landesschule Dresden war Ostern 1923 formal vollendet, nachdem sowohl die Reformrealgymnasialals auch die Oberrealschulabteilung die noch fehlenden Klassen aufgesetzt hatten und damit die höchstmögliche Schülerzahl von 236 erreicht war.[16] In die Unterterzen von Reformrealgymnasium und Oberrealschule wurden seit Ostern 1921 jährlich zwischen 51 und 57 neue Schüler aufgenommen, die sich ungefähr zu gleichen Teilen auf die beiden Schultypen verteilten. Auch das »Erziehungsheim« bekam mehr und mehr den angestrebten »familienhaften Charakter«, seitdem neben den unverheirateten Erziehern acht verheiratete Lehrer mit ihren Familien in das umgebaute Lehrerwohnhaus eingezogen waren und dort fortan mit ihren Zöglingen zusammenlebten.[17]

The foundation, setting up and expansion of the Landesschule Dresden under the Weimar Republic

The Landesschule Dresden opened in the former Kadettenhaus in the Albertstadt district on the 14th of April 1920; 65 of its 74 pupils had previously been enrolled at the Kadettenkorps.[14] The "principles and guidelines" submitted by teaching staff for the operation of the school and its boarding facilities had already been approved by the Saxon Ministry of Education and Cultural Affairs.

On the 3rd of September 1920 the Saxon government decided to take the school under state control on a permanent basis. This was prefaced by the replacement of the head of the Landesschule by the Ministry of Education and Cultural Affairs, which removed the former commander of the Kadettenkorps and appointed a specialist, certified civilian director of studies in his place. Budgetary plans were drawn up, conversion work required at the Kadettenhaus identified and potential sponsors for free places written to. On the 28th of October 1920 the People's Parliament also approved the government bill on the condition that special posts earmarked for former officers were axed.[15] The controversial debate which ensued saw the SPD (in the shape of its local party chairman, Arthur Arzt) express serious misgivings regarding the concept and teaching staff which were to be employed at the Landesschule.[16]

The beginning of the school year 1921/22 saw the Landesschule Dresden admit pupils into year eight, which was set up as a class for accelerated learning. Although the original plans for the school indicated otherwise, the pupils in this class were not to be pushed forward at pace for two years in order to prepare them for the move into the tenth year of

Landesschule Dresden in Klotzsche im Bau, um 1926. Pergolen und Sportplätze sind noch nicht fertiggestellt.
The construction of the Landesschule Dresden in Klotzsche, circa 1926. The pergolas and sports pitches have not yet been completed.

Turnhalle von Osten, um 1930.
Gymnasium viewed from the east, circa 1930.

The foundation of the Landesschule Dresden was formally completed in the Easter of 1923, by which point both the grammar and upper secondary sections had added any years still missing and therefore reached their highest possible pupil population of 236.[19] From the Easter of 1921 onwards the year eight classes of both the progressive grammar and upper secondary sections had registered an annual intake of between 51 and 57 new pupils. These new pupils were spread fairly evenly across the two school types. The arrival of eight married teachers and their families into the converted teachers' accommodation building not only supplemented the staff of unmarried tutors already at the school, but also saw the boarding section move ever closer to the "family atmosphere" that was aspired to.[20]

This setup phase at the Landesschule Dresden took place against a backdrop of difficult negotiations between the state of Saxony and the various ministries of the Reich which owned the site and all its buildings and facilities. These negotiations finally came to a conclusion immediately after the Beer Hall Putsch of 1923, when the Reich Ministry of Defence not only decided to move its central infantry school from Munich to Dresden, but also to use the former Kadettenkorps building as the school's new headquarters from the 1st of April 1926 onwards. This obliged the Landesschule to look for new premises. One option to be discussed was the purchase of the School of Rhythm in Hellerau, which led architect Heinrich Tessenow to draw up plans for the conversion of Hellerau Festival Hall (which he himself had designed) to suit the requirements of the school. His plans were never realised due to the high purchase price involved.

In February 1925 the Saxon Ministry of Finance was tasked with the drawing up of plans for the construction of a new school. An initial design had already been created

grammar school. Instead, they were "to form the backbone of the upper secondary school, which was to be set up in the style of an accelerated learning school [without Latin] and opened simultaneously [to the grammar school] with a year eleven intake". The setting up of the grammar school began at the same time as the establishment of the first upper secondary classes. The classes of the newly founded year eight were the first to see pupils taught according to the Dresden School Reform Plan.[17] In the words of the school's director, this period also witnessed the start of "the internal restructuring of the boarding school with the retention of tried and trusted military methods".[18]

Begleitet wurde die Aufbauphase der Landesschule Dresden durch schwierige und langwierige Verhandlungen des Landes Sachsen mit verschiedenen Ministerien des Reiches, das Eigentümer des Grundstücks mit allen Gebäuden und Einrichtungen war. Diese endeten schließlich mit der Entscheidung des Reichwehrministeriums unmittelbar nach dem fehlgeschlagenen Hitler-Putsch im Jahre 1923, die Infanterieschule von München nach Dresden zu verlegen und dort das Gebäude der ehemaligen Kadettenanstalt ab 1. April 1926 als neuen Standort zu nutzen. Das bedeutete, dass für die Landesschule eine neue Unterkunft gesucht werden musste. Zur Diskussion stand zunächst der Kauf der

Blick vom Lehrgebäude zum Wirtschafts- und Verwaltungsgebäude.
View from the classroom building towards the management and administration building.

Bildungsanstalt in Hellerau: Der Architekt Heinrich Tessenow entwarf einen Plan für den Umbau des einst von ihm selbst entworfenen Hellerauer Festspielhauses für die Bedürfnisse der Schule, die Realisierung scheiterte jedoch an dem zu hohen Kaufpreis.

Im Februar 1925 wurde das sächsische Finanzministerium mit der Erarbeitung eines Neubauprojekts beauftragt. Nach einem ersten Entwurf von Ministerialrat Oskar Kramer wurde der Architekt Heinrich Tessenow, damals Professor an der Dresdner Kunstakademie, hinzugezogen. In gemeinsamer Arbeit entstand bis zum Juli des Jahres der Plan für den gewaltigen Schulneubau. Bis zuletzt hatte es nicht nur »Auseinandersetzungen hinsichtlich der Verteilung der Baukosten und des Schulprogramms«, sondern auch einen erbitterten Streit um das Projekt überhaupt gegeben. »Während die Vertreter von KPD und SPD ihre Ablehnung zum Ausdruck brachten, befürworteten die bürgerlichen Parteien den Neubau.«[18]

Als Bauplatz stand ein etwa 14 Hektar großes staatliches Forstrevier der Dresdner Heide zwischen Thümmelsberg und Schänkhübel zur Verfügung. Das bewaldete Gelände grenzte an die damalige Dresdner Vorortgemeinde Klotzsche. Man hatte damit, so die offizielle Verlautbarung, »einen Platz gefunden, der für die Landesschule hervorragend geeignet ist und sie insbesondere in die Lage setzt, das ihr von vornherein gesteckte Ziel weiterzuverfolgen, nämlich die Vorzüge eines Landeserziehungsheimes mit den Bildungsmöglichkeiten der nahen Großstadt zu vereinigen.«[19]

Die Landesschule an der Königsbrücker Straße war mit Gesamtkosten von über fünf Millionen Reichsmark der wohl teuerste Schulneubau in Dresden in der Weimarer Republik. In eineinhalbjähriger Bauzeit entstand ein großzügig angelegter Gebäudekomplex mit sechs Internatsbauten (je drei vis-à-vis), einem Schulgebäude und einem diesem direkt gegenüberliegenden Wirtschafts- und Verwaltungsgebäude, in dem sich im Erdgeschoss der Speise- und im 1. Stock der Festsaal (Aula) befanden – alle symmetrisch um einen Gartenhof gruppiert, durch Laubengänge (Pergolen) verbunden, mit Gärten, Spiel- und Sportstätten im Freien sowie einer Turnhalle.

Anfang November 1926 konnten die ersten Schüler, die alle nach der Räumung der alten Kadettenanstalt im Sommer 1926 für einige Monate in verschiedene benachbarte Schulen ausquartiert werden mussten, in das neue Landesschulgebäude einziehen. Bis Ende 1926 war der Umzug aller Schüler und Lehrer abgeschlossen.

by Undersecretary Oskar Kramer when architect Heinrich Tessenow, then a professor at the Dresden Academy of Arts, was brought in to participate in the project. Working in partnership, they had finalised a plan for the immense new school complex by the end of July that year. Until the very end there were not only "arguments regarding the distribution of construction costs and the school syllabus", but also an embittered dispute surrounding the project as a whole. "Whilst representatives of the KPD and the SPD voiced their disapproval, the non-Socialist parties endorsed the new complex."[21]

oben/above
Blick in die Turnhalle, 1931.
View into the gymnasium, 1931.

rechts/right
Lehrerwohnhaus
an der Königsbrücker Straße.
Teachers' residence
on the Königsbrücker Straße.

Im Frühjahr 1927 legte der »Jahrgang 1921«, der erste der Landesschule überhaupt, seine Reifeprüfung ab. Alle 37 Kandidaten bestanden das Abitur: 19 Realgymnasiasten, 18 Oberrealschüler.[20] Das erste Schuljahr nach dem Umzug in den Klotzscher Neubau begann Ostern 1927 mit insgesamt 269 Schülern, davon 250 Heim- und 19 Tagesschüler.[21]

Bei der Einweihungsfeier für die neue Landesschule am 15. Oktober 1927 überreichte die Lehrerschaft der Schülervertretung die neue Schulfahne: blaues Tuch mit weiß-grün paspeliertem Rand, Schrift und Wappen. Dieselben Farben trugen auch die Schülermützen.

A 14 hectare section of state forest between Thümmelsberg and Schänkhübel on Dresden Heath was made available for the construction of the school. This forested site abutted Klotzsche, which at that time was a suburb of Dresden. The official project announcement stated that a space had been found "which is excellently suited to the Landesschule, and in particular puts it in a position to pursue the goal which has been set for it right from the beginning, namely the marriage of the advantages of a national community home with the educational opportunities of the nearby city."[22]

Total costs of over five million Reichsmarks are certain to have made the Landesschule on the Königsbrücker Straße the most expensive new school to be built in Dresden under the Weimar Republic. A construction period of one-and-a-half years created a generously proportioned building complex with six boarding houses, (two sets of three opposing buildings), a school building and a management and administration building. The latter was located directly opposite the school building, and housed a dining hall on its ground floor and a banqueting and assembly hall on its first floor. All buildings were arranged symmetrically around a lawned courtyard and connected by pergolas, with gardens, playgrounds, open-air sports facilities and a gymnasium also created.

Having been placed in temporary accommodation at various neighbouring schools further to the vacation of the former Kadettenkorps site in the summer of 1926, the first pupils of the new Landesschule were able to take up residence at the new complex at the beginning of November 1926. By the end of 1926 all pupils and teachers had moved into the new school.

In the spring of 1927 the first crop of pupils to attend the Landesschule – the "class of 1921" – took their leaving exams. All 37 candidates (19 from the grammar school section, 18 from the upper secondary section) gained their Abitur and were therefore entitled to study at university.[23] The first school year after relocation to the new complex in Klotzsche began in the Easter of 1927, and was attended by a total of 269 pupils (250 boarders, 19 day pupils).[24]

The new school flag was presented to pupils' representatives by the teaching staff on the occasion of the opening ceremony on the 15th of October 1927. Its white and green writing, insignia and piping were set against a blue cloth background. School caps also followed this colour scheme.

The educational profile of the school and its boarding facilities

As expressed at the time by Prof. Dr. Curt Fischer, the school's long-serving headmaster and senior director of studies, the Landesschule Dresden was "a state institute of education and upbringing designed to prepare talented boys of all social classes who could not be brought up in their parents' homes for an active role in the cultural life of our nation – and in particular for a continuative academic career – by giving them a thorough all-round education and an upbringing which fosters a strictly moral mentality and disposition. The school and its boarding houses work hand in hand to achieve this goal, this bringing up of boys to be complete human beings."[25]

Each year eight pupil would go on to attend the school for a total of six years. Those who did not reach the required standard for the respective year would generally be obliged to leave the school. The pass certificate awarded to successful year ten pupils also acted as an intermediate secondary school certificate.

Monthly school and boarding fees were kept relatively low in order to ensure that the school selected "the most gifted pupils" and facilitated the "social advancement of the less well-off".[26] This saw the establishment of free places for half of the pupils at the school. 125 of an average pupil population of 250 were awarded scholarships, with 62 places sponsored by the state of Saxony, 25 by the city of Dresden and the remaining quantity by public bodies, other towns in Saxony, Amtshauptmannschaften[27] and other organisations.[28]

STUNDENTAFELN

A. REFORMREALGYMNASIUM

Fächer	UIII A	OIII A	UII A	OII	UI	OI	
				A) Sprachl.-histor. Abteilung B) Mathem.-naturw. Abteil.			
Religionskunde	2	2	2	2	—	2	
Philosophie . .	—	—	—	—	2	—	
Deutsch . . .	3	3	3	4	4	4	
Lateinisch . .	9	9	5	4	4	A) 5 B) 3	
Englisch	—	—	5	A) 5 B) 3	4	A) 5 B) 2	
Französisch od. Spanisch*)	6	4	2	A) 3 B) 2	2	A) 3 B) 2	
Geschichte . .	3	3	3	3	3	3	
Erdkunde . .	2	2	2	2	2	2	
Mathematik	4	4	5	A) 4 B) 5	4	A) 3 B) 5	
Darst. Geom.	—	—	—	A) — B) 1	1	A) — B) 2	
Physik	—	—	2	2	3	3	
Chemie	—	—	—	2	2	2	
Naturkunde .	2	2	2	—	1	A) 1 B) 2	
Gesang u. Musik	1	—	—	1	1	1	u. 1 Chorsingstunde
Turnen	2	2	2	2	2	2	
Zeichnen . . .	2	2	2	wahlfr.	wahlfr.	wahlfr.	
Spiele	2	2	2	2	2	2	

B. OBERREALSCHULE MIT AUFBAUKLASSEN

Fächer	UIII C	OIII C	UII C	OII	UI	OI	
	Aufbauklassen			C) Neusprachliche Abteilung D) Mathem.-naturw. Abteil.			
Religionskunde	2	1	2	2	—	2	
Philosophie . .	—	—	—	—	2	—	
Deutsch	5	4	4	4	4	4	
Englisch	6	5	4	C) 4 D) 2	C) 4 D) 2	C) 4 D) 2	
Französisch . .	6	6	4	C) 5 D) 3	C) 4 D) 2	C) 4 D) 2	
Geschichte . .	3	3	3	3	3	3	
Erdkunde . . .	2	2	2	2	2	2	
Mathematik u. Darst. Geom.	5	5	6	C) 5 D) 7	C) 5 D) 7	C) 5 D) 7	
Kaufm. Rechnen	—	1	2	—	—	—	
Physik	—	2	3	3	C) 2 D) 3	C) 2 D) 3	
Chemie	—	1	2	2	C) 2 D) 3	C) 1 D) 2	
Naturkunde . .	3	1	1	2	C) 1 D) 2	C) 1 D) 2	
Gesang u. Musik	1	—	—	1	1	1	u. 1 Chorsingstunde
Turnen	2	2	2	2	2	2	
Zeichnen . . .	2	2	2	wahlfr.	wahlfr.	wahlfr.	
Spiele	2	2	2	2	2	2	

*) Auf Wunsch der Mehrheit der Klasse kann nach Ministerialverordnung Nr. II, 2851 B vom 14. 12. 1923 von O II an Spanisch an Stelle des Französisch treten; es beginnt dann mit 4 Wochenstunden; Französisch wird Wahlfach.

WAHLFREIER UNTERRICHT

1. Lateinisch (2): OICD; UICD; OIICD
2. Griechisch (2): UIA–D
3. Französisch (2): OIAB
4. Spanisch (2): OICD; UIA–D; OIIA–D
5. Italienisch (2): OIAB; OIIAB
6. Biologische Uebungen (1 oder 2): OIA; OICD; UIA–D; OIIAB; OIICD
7. Chemische Uebungen (2): OIA–D; UIA–D
8. Physikalische Uebungen (2): OIA–D; OIIA–D
9. Zeichnen (2): OIA–D; UIA–D; OIIA–D
10. Kunstgeschichte (1): OIA–D; UIA–D
11. Kurzschrift (2 bzw. 1): UIIIAC; OIIIAC; UIIC
12. Werkunterricht (mindest. 2 Stdn.): alle Klassen.

Amtliche Lehrpläne der Landesschule Dresden.

Official teaching plans for the Landesschule Dresden.

Pädagogisches Profil von Schule und Internat

Die Landesschule Dresden war, wie der langjährige Schulleiter, Oberstudiendirektor Prof. Dr. Curt Fischer programmatisch formulierte, »eine staatliche Unterrichts- und Erziehungsanstalt, dazu bestimmt, begabte Knaben aus allen Schichten des Volkes, die nicht im Elternhaus erzogen werden können, durch allseitige gründliche Schulung und durch eine zu sittlich ernster Denk- und Sinnesart führende Erziehung zur Mitarbeit am Kulturleben unseres Volkes, insbesondere zu einer weiteren wissenschaftlichen Laufbahn vorzubereiten. Im Dienste derselben Aufgabe, der Erziehung zum ganzen Menschen, arbeiten Schule und Erziehungsheim Hand in Hand.«[22]

Die Schulzeit für jeden der Untertertia angehörenden Schüler betrug sechs Jahre. Wer das Klassenziel nicht erreichte, musste in der Regel die Schule verlassen. Mit dem Versetzungszeugnis der Untersekunda erlangte der Schüler zugleich das »Zeugnis der mittleren Reife«.

Um den Funktionen der »Begabtenauslese« und des »sozialen Aufstiegs Minderbemittelter« gerecht zu werden, wurde das monatliche Schul-, Wohnungs- und Kostgeld vergleichsweise niedrig gehalten[23], für die Hälfte der Schüler wurden Freistellen eingerichtet. Bei einer durchschnittlichen Schülerzahl von etwa 250 waren dies 125 Stipendien, von denen 62 vom Land Sachsen, 25 von der Stadt Dresden und die übrigen von öffentlich-rechtlichen Körperschaften, anderen sächsischen Städten und Amtshauptmannschaften usw. gestiftet wurden.[24]

Die Landesschule Dresden war eine Internatsschule, die die beiden Schulformen eines Reformrealgymnasiums und einer Oberrealschule umschloss.

Das Reformrealgymnasium umfasste die Klassen Untertertia (U III) bis Oberprima (O I) – es fehlte also der Unterbau von Sexta (VI) bis Quarta (IV) – und arbeitete nach dem Curriculum des Dresdner Reformplans, d. h.: Für die Aufnahme in die Untertertia wurde Französisch ab Sexta vorausgesetzt, Latein wurde ab Untertertia, Englisch ab Untersekunda unterrichtet. Die Reihenfolge der beiden modernen Fremdsprachen änderte sich erst ab dem Schuljahr 1928/29, als mit der Neuordnung des höheren Schulwesens in Sachsen nunmehr Englisch als erste und Französisch als zweite Fremdsprache für diesen Schultyp verfügt wurden.[25] Jeder Aspirant hatte eine Aufnahmeprüfung in Deutsch, Französisch, Rechnen mit Raumlehre und ab 1928 in Englisch abzulegen. Bei der Beurteilung der Kandidaten wurden auch soziale Aspekte der Herkunftsfamilie berücksichtigt, so z. B. Kinder von Kriegsgefallenen, Schwerkriegsbeschädigten und Auslandsdeutschen. Die Bewerber, die aus allen Teilen Sachsens kamen, hatten in der Regel zuvor bereits eine höhere Schule besucht.

Aufgrund der Mehrheit einer Klasse konnte seit dem Schuljahr 1924/25 von Obersekunda (O II) an bis zum Abitur Spanisch statt Französisch als Pflichtfach unterrichtet werden. Der Spanischunterricht begann mit vier Wochenstunden, Französisch wurde dann obligatorisch Wahlfach.[26] Englisch und ab 1928 Französisch konnten ebenso wie Griechisch oder Italienisch wahlfrei betrieben werden. Fanden sich genügend Schüler eines Jahrgangs, trat in der Oberstufe von O II an eine den wissenschaftlichen Neigungen und Begabungen der Schüler entgegenkommende Spezialisierung in einen sprachlich-historischen (A) oder einen mathematisch-naturwissenschaftlichen Zweig (B) ein.

Die Oberrealschule war als sechsstufige Aufbauschule verfasst. Sie nahm ausschließlich besonders begabte Volksschüler aus allen Teilen Sachsens, die das 7. oder 8. Schuljahr beendet und die Aufnahmeprüfung in Deutsch und Rechnen bestanden hatten[27], in ihre unterste Klasse (U III) auf. Die U III und Obertertia (O III) waren als Aufbauklassen (Förderklassen) konzipiert und hatten einen eigenen Lehrplan. Alle weiteren Klassen ab Untersekunda (U II) orientierten sich am Lehrplan für sächsische Oberrealschulen. Zu den Pflichtsprachen gehörten für die 14-Jährigen ab Klasse U III Englisch und Französisch. Als Wahlfächer konnten ab der Klassenstufe O II Latein, Spanisch und Italienisch gewählt werden. In der Oberstufe der Oberrealschule fand eine Gabelung statt in eine neusprachliche (C) und eine mathematisch-naturwissenschaftliche (D) Abteilung.

Sportunterricht auf dem Gelände der Landesschule Dresden. Physical education on the grounds of the Landesschule Dresden.

The Landesschule Dresden was a boarding establishment which featured both a progressive grammar school and an upper secondary school.

The progressive grammar school comprised years eight to thirteen, and therefore lacked the foundation of years five to seven. It was operated according to the Dresden School Reform Plan, which dictated that French from year five upwards was a prerequisite for acceptance into year eight. Latin and English were taught from years eight and ten upwards respectively. The order of the two modern foreign languages did not change until the 1928/29 school year, when Saxon secondary school reforms reclassified English and French as the first and second languages respectively for schools of this type.[29] Each prospective pupil

Schlafraum im ersten Stock eines Schülerheimes.
Dormitory on the first floor of a boarding house.

In der Oberstufe beider Schulformen gab es zahlreiche wahlfreie Unterrichtsangebote und praktische Übungen, in denen die Schüler neben der wissenschaftlich-geistigen Kompetenzerweiterung auch in den Bereichen musisch-ästhetischer und körperlich-sportlicher Bildung gefördert wurden.

Der Neubau der Landesschule in Klotzsche bot mit seinen hell und freundlich eingerichteten Klassenräumen, modernen naturwissenschaftlichen Hörsälen und Laboratorien, wozu auch eine Sternwarte gehörte, sehr gute äußere Lernbedingungen: Für den Zeichen- und Kunstunterricht standen ein großer Zeichensaal mit Nebenräumen, ein Raum für Linol-, Zink- und Kupferdruckübungen sowie die Schülerwerkstätten zu Verfügung.

had to take entrance exams in German, French and arithmetic (including geometry), with English added to this list from 1928 onwards. Candidates were also assessed according to social aspects relating to their family background, for example whether or not their parents had been killed or severely disabled during the war or were German expatriates. Applicants came from all over Saxony, and tended to have already attended another secondary school.

From the 1924/25 school year onwards it was possible to teach Spanish rather than French as a compulsory subject from year eleven upwards due to the ability shown in the subject by the majority of the class. Spanish was initially introduced on a four-hours-per-week basis, with French automatically demoted to the rank of optional subject.[30] It was possible to offer English, and from 1928 onwards French, on an optional basis along with other languages such as Greek and Italian. If a year group had enough pupils with similar academic tastes and abilities a corresponding specialisation would be introduced from year eleven upwards. Pupils had the choice between a language and history path (A) or a mathematics and natural sciences path (B).

The upper secondary school was set up as a six-year accelerated learning school. The only pupils it accepted into its lowest year group (the eighth) were especially talented state school pupils from around Saxony who had both completed their seventh or eighth year of school and passed an entrance test in German and arithmetic.[31] The eighth and ninth years were conceived as accelerated learning years and had their own curricula. All other years from the tenth upwards followed the curriculum set for upper secondary schools in Saxony. English and French were amongst the compulsory languages for fourteen-year-olds from year eight upwards. From year eleven upwards they could choose between optional Latin, Spanish and Italian. Pupils in the last three years of the upper secondary school had the choice between a modern languages path (C) and a mathematics and natural sciences path (D).

Für den Musikunterricht gab es einen Musiksaal für Gesang und Orchester, zwei Konzertflügel, vier Übungsklaviere und ein Pedalharmonium. In der Aula befanden sich eine Bühne und eine zweimanualige Orgel. Die Schule verfügte über ein Schulorchester und einen Schulchor sowie einen eigenen Spielmannszug.

Für den Werkunterricht konnten Schülerwerkstätten für Papier-, Holz- und Metallarbeiten sowie zum Modellieren genutzt werden. Darüber hinaus besaß die Landesschule eine Druckerei und eine Buchbinderei, in denen u.a. die von Studienrat Edgar Herzog angeregte und zwischen 1928 und 1934 halbjährlich erschienene Schulzeitschrift hergestellt wurde.

Geradezu ideale Bedingungen galten für den Sportunterricht: Die Schule verfügte nicht nur über eine geräumige Turnhalle, sondern auch über ein Stadion mit einer 400-Meter-Aschenbahn, Rasen- und Kiesplätze für Sport und Spiel sowie einen Tennisplatz. All das lag innerhalb des riesigen Schulareals mitten in der Dresdner Heide. Die überragende Bedeutung des Sports an der Landesschule Dresden kommt nicht nur dadurch zum Ausdruck, dass über den täglichen Frühsport und die zwei lehrplanmäßigen Turnstunden am Vormittag hinaus an zwei Nachmittagen Sport- und Kampfspiele stattfanden, zusätzlich im Frühjahr und im Herbst Waldläufe sowie regelmäßige Besuche im Friedrich-August-Schwimmbad an der Prießnitz bzw. in einem Dresdner Hallenbad, sondern vor allem auch dadurch, dass die Leistungen in den Leibesübungen bei der Gesamtbeurteilung eines Schülers das gleiche Gewicht hatten wie diejenigen in den wissenschaftlichen Fächern. Sportcracks genossen das höchste Prestige bei Schülern und Lehrern.

Die Landesschüler waren Heimschüler, d.h. sie lebten und wohnten im schuleigenen Internat. Tagesschüler, sogenannte Externe, bildeten die absolute Ausnahme, die der Sondergenehmigung durch das Volksbildungsministerium – zuständig Geheimrat Dr. Menke-Glückert – bedurfte. Die meisten von ihnen kamen aus den Nachbargemeinden Klotzsche und Hellerau.

Landesschüler beim Aufräumen.
Landesschule pupils tidying up.

The top three years of both school types offered pupils a wide range of optional lessons and practical exercises which supported them not only in the expansion of their academic and intellectual ability, but also in their pursuit of artistic and sporting interests. The bright, welcomingly furnished classrooms, modern, science-focused lecture theatres and laboratories (which included an observatory) at the Landesschule in Klotzsche served to create an outwardly excellent learning atmosphere.

Lessons in drawing and art were held in a large art room with ancillary rooms, a room for linoleum printing, zincography and copperplate engraving practice and studios where pupils could go about their work on their own.

Music lessons made use of a music room for vocal and orchestral music, two concert pianos, four practice pianos and a pedal harmonium. The assembly hall featured a stage and a dual manual organ. The school had its own orchestra, choir and marching band.

Das Internat der neuen Landesschule in Klotzsche bestand aus sechs Doppelhäusern, die sich an den Längsseiten des Innenhofes zwischen dem Schulgebäude auf der einen und dem Wirtschaftsgebäude mit der Aula auf der anderen Seite befanden, und bot Platz für insgesamt 253 Schüler. Im Parterre jedes Hauses lagen die Arbeitsräume mit Tischen und Pulten zur Erledigung der Hausaufgaben, im 1. Stock die Schlafräume und ein gemeinsamer Waschraum mit Duschen. Das Alumnat gliederte sich in Ober- und Unterhaus: Das »Oberhaus« umfasste im Allgemeinen die Klassen O II bis O I, das »Unterhaus« die von U III bis U II. Ausschlaggebend für die Zuteilung war nicht die Klassenstufe, sondern die »Altersreife«. Die gesamte Internatsschülerschaft war in zwölf Abteilungen, sogenannte Familien, zu je 21 Mann aufgegliedert. Jeweils zwei Abteilungen bewohnten eines der erwähnten sechs Häuser. Jede Abteilung hatte die gleichen Räume, die spiegelgleich in den einzelnen Häusern sich gegenüberlagen. Lediglich ein gemeinsamer Spiel- und Aufenthaltsraum bzw. Leseraum, in dem wechselnde Tageszeitungen auslagen, diente beiden Abteilungen. Jede Abteilung wurde von einem »Erzieher« betreut, der gleichzeitig Lehrer an der Schule war und mit seiner Familie im Doppelhaus seiner Abteilung wohnte. Auf diese Weise waren zwölf Lehrer der Schule in ständigem und engstem Kontakt von früh bis abends mit den Schülern verbunden. Jede Abteilung bestand aus zwei Stuben zu zehn bzw. elf Mann unterschiedlichen Alters. Jedes Jahr wurden die Abteilungen je nach Wahl der Schüler neu zusammengesetzt. Die Erzieher führten von jedem ihrer Schüler einen Beurteilungsbogen, der diesen durch die gesamte Landesschulzeit begleitete.

An der Spitze jeder Stube stand ein Stubenältester, zu denen die Primaner der Schule berufen waren. Sie wurden jeweils fürs nächste Schuljahr von den amtierenden Stubenältesten gewählt, wobei der Erzieherschaft ein gewisses Vorschlags- und auch Einspruchsrecht zustand. Einer der beiden Stubenältesten jeder Abteilung war deren Abteilungsältester. Stuben- und Abteilungsälteste waren u.a. für die Einhaltung der Hausordnung verantwortlich und

Lesezimmer, um 1931.
Reading room, circa 1931.

unterstützten die Arbeit der Erzieher. Aus ihrer Mitte wählten alle 24 Stubenältesten den Hausältesten, der als Vertrauensmann der Gesamtschülerschaft dem Internatsleiter, der wiederum aus den Reihen der Erzieher gewählt wurde, zur Seite stand. Aufgrund seiner exponierten Stellung bewohnte der Hausälteste als einziger der Schüler ein Einzelzimmer. Er stand der Schülervertretung vor, die über Einrichtung und Ausstattung des Internats, über Ausgestaltung von Schulfeiern und Schulaufführungen sowie über Wünsche und Beschwerden allgemeiner Art zu beraten hatte. Zusammengesetzt war die Schülervertretung aus je zwei gewählten Mitschülern aus jeder Schulklasse.

Workshops for paper-, wood- and metalwork were available for the purposes of handicrafts lessons and model making. The Landesschule also had a print shop and bookbinders which, amongst other projects, were used to produce the school gazette set up by graduate secondary school teacher Edgar Herzog and published on a half-yearly basis between 1928 and 1934.

Conditions for sport lessons were almost perfect. The school not only had its own spacious gymnasium, but also boasted a stadium with a 400-metre cinder track, a tennis court and grass and gravel pitches for various other sports and games. All of these facilities were located within the boundaries of the school's enormous site on Dresden Heath. The exceptional significance of sporting endeavour at the Landesschule was not only reflected in the manifold physical activities its pupils engaged in – early-morning exercise, two timetabled hours of gymnastics each morning, matches and contact sports two afternoons a week, cross-country runs through the forest in spring and autumn and regular visits to the Friedrich-August swimming pool on the Prießnitz or an indoor swimming pool in Dresden – but also, and in particular, in the fact that pupils' performances in physical education carried the same weight as their performance in academic subjects. This saw sports jocks enjoy the highest degree of prestige amongst their fellow pupils and the teaching staff.

The pupils of the Landesschule were boarders, and therefore lived and resided within the school's own boarding facilities. Day pupils – nicknamed "outsiders" – were a rare exception, and required special permission to attend the school on that basis from privy councillor Dr. Menke-Glückert at the Ministry of Popular Education. The majority of them came from the neighbouring communities of Klotzsche und Hellerau.

The boarding facilities at the new Landesschule in Klotzsche provided accommodation for a total of 253 pupils, and consisted of six semi-detached houses located on the longer sides of the inner courtyard which stretched between the school building on one side and the management

a) an Wochentagen außer Mittwochs:

6.00	Uhr:	Wecken, Morgenturnen, Duschen, Waschen, Ankleiden.	
6.40	„	1. Frühstück.	
7.15—1.00	„	Unterricht.	
1.15	„	Mittagessen, darnach Freizeit.	im Sommerhalbjahr
2.30—4.30	„	Arbeitsstunde.	im Sommerhalbjahr
4.30—5.00	„	Vesper.	im Sommerhalbjahr
5.00—7.15	„	wahlfreier Unterricht, Uebungen, Spiel.	im Sommerhalbjahr
2.30—4.45	„	wahlfreier Unterricht, Uebungen, Spiel.	im Winterhalbjahr
4.45—5.15	„	Vesper.	im Winterhalbjahr
5.15—7.15	„	Arbeitsstunde.	im Winterhalbjahr
7.30	„	Abendbrot, darnach Freizeit.	
9.00	„	Schlafengehen der U III bis O III.	
10.00	„	Schlafengehen der U II bis O I.	

b) Mittwochs:

Bis zum Mittagessen wie an den anderen Wochentagen, dann

bis 7.00	Uhr:	allgemeiner Urlaub.
7.00	„	Abendbrot.
7.30—9.00	„	Arbeitsstunde.

c) Sonntags:

7.30—8.15	Uhr:	Aufstehen, Duschen, Waschen, Ankleiden.
8.15	„	1. Frühstück.
8.30—12.00	„	allgemeiner Urlaub.
12.00 oder 1.30	„	Mittagessen.
12.30 (2.00) —7.30	„	allgemeiner Urlaub.
7.30	„	Abendbrot.
10.20	„	Schlafengehen.

Nähere Bestimmungen über Urlaub und Empfang von Besuchen enthält die „Hausordnung", die jedem Neueintretenden eingehändigt wird; von den Erziehungsberechtigten wird erwartet, daß sie auch ihrerseits diesen Bestimmungen Rechnung tragen.

Tagesablauf im Sommer- und Winterhalbjahr.
Daily schedule during the summer and winter term.

Das gemeinsame Leben im Internat war nach strengem Reglement, wie es in der vom sächsischen Ministerium für Volksbildung genehmigten Haus- und Schulordnung von 1925, mit kleineren Nachträgen von 1928 und 1930, niedergelegt war, straff organisiert. Täglich wiederkehrende Handlungsabläufe, insbesondere die Mahlzeiten, die Ordnung in den gemeinsamen Räumen, den Abendurlaub usw. überwachte jeden Tag ein Erzieher vom Dienst (EvD), unterstützt von Funktionsträgern aus den Reihen der Schüler: Warte, z. B. Gerätewarte in der Turnhalle, Ordner bei größeren Veranstaltungen, Obmänner etwa zur Ausgabe von Werkzeugen in den Schülerwerkstätten oder bei Arbeiten im Schulgarten, oder Tagesdienste, wie Hausdienst oder Tischdienst im Speisesaal.

Innerhalb des Schul- und Internatsgeländes war jede politische Betätigung verboten. Die Teilnahme an politischen Versammlungen außerhalb der Schule musste dem Rektor angezeigt und von diesem genehmigt werden. Ebenfalls genehmigungspflichtig war die Teilnahme an externen öffentlichen Tanzvergnügen, musikalischen oder theatralischen Aufführungen. Nikotin- und Alkoholgenuss waren strikt untersagt, lediglich im Primaner-Kasino durfte zu festgelegten Zeiten geraucht werden.

building with assembly hall on the other. The ground floor of each house featured workrooms with tables and desks, and it was here that pupils would go to do their homework. The first floor comprised sleeping quarters and a communal washroom with showers. Pupils were divided into upper and lower houses, with years eleven to thirteen generally belonging to the "upper house" and years eight to ten the "lower house". It was maturity and not the year in which the pupils were currently attending classes which determined the house they were allocated to. The entire boarding population was divided into twelve groups – or "families" – of 21 pupils each, with two groups allocated to each of the above-mentioned houses. The rooms on one side of a house were a mirror-image of those on the other, therefore each group had the same rooms as the next. The only space in the building that was shared by both groups was a recreation, games and reading room stocked with a regularly updated selection of daily newspapers. Each

Routine und Höhepunkte im Schul- und Internatsleben der Landesschüler

Der Tagesablauf im Sommerhalbjahr[28] sah wie folgt aus: 6 Uhr Wecken, anschließend zehn Minuten Frühsport im Freien bei jedem Wetter, anschließend kalt abbrausen sowie Schlaf- und Waschraum in Ordnung bringen (Bettenbau usw.); 6.40 Uhr Abmarsch zum Frühstück; 7.05 Uhr Appell; 7.15 bis 13 Uhr Schulunterricht, das Betreten der Heime war in dieser Zeit untersagt; 13.15 Uhr Abmarsch zum Mittagessen mit Postausgabe, Telefonieren beim Pförtner erlaubt; 14.30 bis 16.30 Uhr Arbeitsstunde, in der die Schulaufgaben zu erledigen waren (die Stuben durften in dieser Zeit nur aus zwingenden Gründen verlassen werden; betrat ein Lehrer die Stube, hatte der Stubenälteste Meldung zu machen); 16.30 Uhr Vesper; 17 bis 19.15 Uhr Sport und wahlfreie Unterrichtsfächer, drei mal 45 Minuten, Konfirmandenunterricht, Klavierstunden usw.; 19.30 Uhr Abmarsch zum Abendbrot; danach Freizeit, Aufenthalt u. a. in Lesezimmer, Billard- und Rundfunkzimmer, die bis 21.45 Uhr geöffnet waren; für das »Unterhaus« (Untertertia bis Untersekunda) galt Nachtruhe ab 21 Uhr, für das »Oberhaus« (Obersekunda bis Oberprima) ab 22 Uhr.

Jeden Montagmorgen fand vor Unterrichtsbeginn eine zehnminütige Morgenfeier auf freiwilliger Basis statt, bei der Lehrer und ihre Frauen sowie Schüler im Sologesang oder Instrumentalspiel auftraten, häufig auch Schulchor oder -orchester mitwirkten.

Stadturlaub war lediglich am Mittwochnachmittag, der von sonstigen Verpflichtungen frei war, zwischen 14 und 19 Uhr möglich, sowie sonntags. Sonderurlaub konnte gewährt werden, z. B. zum Haareschneiden. Etwa alle drei bis vier Wochen gab es Heimurlaub, in dem die Schüler über das Wochenende nach Hause fahren konnten. Jeder Internatsschüler hatte ein Urlaubsbuch in Form eines Oktavheftes, in dem Urlaubsanträge vom Erzieher genehmigt werden mussten. Der Pförtner zeichnete diese beim Passieren des Tores ab.

Landesschüler bei einem Ausflug in die Sächsische Schweiz.
Landesschule pupils during an excursion into Saxon Switzerland.

Zu den Höhepunkten im Schul- und Internatsleben zählten, wenn man den Berichten und Nachrichten folgt, die in den zwölf Heften der Schülerzeitschrift »Mitteilungen aus der Landesschule« (1928–1934) abgedruckt sind, vor allem die zahlreichen größeren und kleineren Feste und Feiern: Geburtstage, glückliche Genesung, erster und letzter Tag im Schülerheim, Elterntag, Semesterabschluss, Fastnachtsfeier, Weihnachtsfeier usw. Auch kulturelle Veranstaltungen, wie Theateraufführungen, Kabarett, Schulkonzerte und Kammermusikabende, Vorträge und Filmvorführungen, gehörten dazu, ebenso Wander- und Kletterfahrten in die Sächsische Schweiz oder Wintersportaufenthalte im Erzgebirge, Reisen nach Weimar, Naumburg, Schulpforte und Jena, nach Berlin und Potsdam mit Museumsbesuchen,

rechts / right
Schulball 1928. The 1928 School Ball.

group had two dormitories housing ten or eleven pupils of varying ages. The makeup of the groups changed on an annual basis according to the wishes of the pupils. Each group was supervised by a "tutor", who was also a teacher at the school and lived with his family in his group's boarding house. This meant that twelve of the school's teachers were in constant, close contact with the pupils from morning until evening. The assessment log kept by the tutors on each of their pupils would accompany the latter throughout their time at the Landesschule.

One top year pupil per dormitory was appointed dormitory elder. The elder for the following year was chosen by the acting dormitory elder, whereby tutors also had a certain right to make proposals or voice objections. One of the two dormitory elders in each group was made group elder. Amongst other things, dormitory and group elders were responsible for ensuring adherence to house rules and supporting the work of the tutors. The dormitory elders elected a senior elder, who was then available to the tutor-elected boarding house leader in his capacity as the boarders' representative. His prominent role made the senior elder the only pupil to be given a single room. He presided over the pupils' representation board (which deliberated on the furnishing and equipment of the boarding houses), organised school functions and performances and dealt with any general requests or complaints. Each class elected two of its fellow classmates to the pupils' representation board.

As laid out in the house and school regulations approved by the Saxon Ministry of Popular Education in 1925 and minor amendments added to them in 1928 and 1930, communal boarding life was tightly organised according to strict rules. Events which were repeated on a daily basis, and in particular meals, the tidying of shared spaces, evening free time, etc. were supervised by a duty tutor, who in turn was

Landesschule Schulball 1928.

supported by special prefects selected from the ranks of the pupils. Their roles included those of monitor (e.g. equipment monitor in the gymnasium), steward (at large events) or representative in charge of the allocation of tools in the various workshops, work in the school garden or daily chores such as cleaning or table duty in the dining hall.

No political activity was permitted within the confines of the site on which the school and boarding houses were situated. Any involvement in political gatherings outside of school was to be reported to the rector, who had the power to permit or forbid such involvement. Participation in external, public dances and musical or theatrical performances also required permission. Smoking and the consumption of alcohol were strictly forbidden, though smoking was permitted at specified times in the year twelve and thirteen mess.

Routines and highlights in the school and boarding life of Landesschule pupils

The daily timetable for the summer term[32] looked like this: 6:00 – wake-up call followed by ten minutes of early-morning exercise (outdoors and in any weather), cold showers and tidying of dormitories and washrooms (bed-making, etc.); 6:40 – march to breakfast; 7:05 – role call; 7:15 to 13:00 – school lessons, during which time pupils were not permitted to access their boarding houses; 13:15 – march to lunch, distribution of post, telephone calls from the porter's lodge permitted; 14:30 to 16:30 – homework time, during which pupils could only leave their dormitories if absolutely necessary, the entrance of a teacher into a dormitory was to be announced by the dormitory elder; 16:30 – vespers; 17:00–19:15 – 3 x 45 minutes of sport and optional subjects, confirmation classes, piano lessons, etc.; 19:30 – march to supper, then free time, for instance in the reading room or billiards and radio room, which were open until 21:45; years eight to ten were subject to a curfew of 21:00, the respective time for years eleven to thirteen was 22:00.

A voluntary ten-minute morning assembly took place before lessons on Monday mornings, and featured solo vocal or instrumental performances by the teachers and their wives or pupils. The school choir or orchestra also often took part.

Pupils only had leave to go into town on Wednesday afternoons (which were free of other obligations) and Sundays. Special leave could also be arranged, for example for the purpose of going to the barbers. Home leave was scheduled every three to four weeks, and allowed pupils to go home for the weekend. Each boarder had a leave logbook in the form of an octavo notebook, with leave requests in that logbook to be submitted to the respective tutor for approval and then initialled by the porter as the pupil passed through the school gates.

According to the reports and announcements included in the twelve issues of the school gazette ("Mitteilungen aus der Landesschule", 1928–1934) to be printed, the numerous parties and celebrations both great and small which took place at the Landesschule were amongst the highlights of school and boarding life. Birthdays, successful recovery from illness, first and last days as a boarder, parents' evening, the last day of term, Shrove Tuesday and Christmas were all celebrated. Cultural events such as theatrical performances, cabaret, school concerts and chamber music evenings, lectures and films also had a part to play, as did other pursuits further afield including walking and climbing in Saxon Switzerland, winter sports in the Ore Mountains, trips to Weimar, Naumburg, Schulpforte and Jena, tours of Berlin and Potsdam and their museums and year thirteen exchanges with the state schools in Potsdam and Vienna. Notwithstanding this wealth of activities, there were two absolute cultural and social highlights at the Landesschule. One of those highlights was the school of

Nach dem Tanzstundenball.
After the Dancing Class Ball.

Klassenaustausche der Primen mit den staatlichen Bildungsanstalten in Potsdam und Wien. Die absoluten Highlights im kulturellen und gesellschaftlichen Leben der Landesschüler aber waren die Tanzschule mit ihren Hausbällen in der Aula der Landesschule[29] und die Sportwettkämpfe unterschiedlichster Disziplinen, bei denen die Landesschüler fast immer Spitzenplätze erzielten. Bei den Reichsjugendfestspielen auf der Ilgenkampfbahn in Dresden »sahnten« sie regelmäßig ab. Sie wurden jahrelang Handballmeister unter den höheren Schulen Dresdens und gewannen reihenweise die Pokale bei den traditionellen Staffelläufen im Großen Garten und beim Tauziehen.

Resümee

Die Landesschule Dresden war kein reformpädagogisches Schulmodell. Über diese Feststellung kann auch nicht der suggestive Charme einer phantastischen Architektur à la Tessenow hinwegtäuschen. Das Bild von der Landesschule als einer Reformschule ist ein Mythos, an dem die ehemaligen Lehrer[30] und Schüler selbst maßgeblich mitgewirkt und den sie durch nostalgisch-verklärende Aktivitäten im Stile der »Feuerzangenbowle« in ihrem »Traditionsverband ehemaliger Landesschüler« gern aufrecht erhalten haben. Wer wollte es ihnen verdenken?

Doch Reformschulen sahen anders aus. Man denke nur an die Dürerschule (Staatliche Höhere Versuchsschule) auf der Silbermannstraße in Dresden oder an die 46. Volksschule am Georgplatz und ihr Versuchsschul-Pendant in Hellerau. Dort stritten innovationsfreudige Lehrerinnen und Lehrer, Eltern- und Schülerschaften in öffentlichen Versammlungen und in der Tagespresse gemeinsam um das »richtige« reformpädagogische Konzept, man beteiligte sich aktiv an den aktuellen erziehungswissenschaftlichen Diskursen, wie sie auf Tagungen und in Fachzeitschriften geführt wurden, oder kämpfte über Standes- und Interessenverbände für die schulpolitische Durchsetzung seiner pädagogischen Positionen.[31]

dance, which held house balls in the Landesschule assembly hall[33]. The other was sporting competitions in various disciplines, which invariably saw Landesschule pupils take podium places. The school also regularly swept the board at the Reich Youth Games on the Ilgenkampfbahn track in Dresden. They were serial winners of the Dresden Secondary School Handball Championship, and won trophy after trophy in the traditional relay races in the Großer Garten and tug-of-war contests.

Résumé

Not even the suggestive charm of Tessenow's fantastic architecture can obscure the fact that the Landesschule Dresden was not the model of a progressive school. The notion of the Landesschule as a progressive school is a myth which former teachers[34] and pupils not only played a significant role in creating, but also sought to maintain by way of the nostalgic-idealistic activities of their "Traditional Association of Former Landesschule Pupils". Who could blame them?

No, a progressive school was something entirely different. One only has to think of the Dürerschule[35], the 46th state school on the Georgplatz and its pilot school counterpart in Hellerau. These establishments saw innovative teachers (both male and female), parents and pupils seek to establish the "correct" progressive educational concept by engaging in common debate at public meetings and in the daily press. They played an active part in contemporary pedagogical discourse at conferences and in specialist journals, and used pressure groups and professional associations to fight for the realisation of their educational policies.[36]

One did not come across this type of enthusiasm for reform and educational development at the Landesschule. Its teachers were characterised by scepticism, reluctance and even hostility in the face of reform, and were supporters of both a bygone era and a school model which was on its way out. Whilst elsewhere impassioned debate deliberated

Diese Art von Reformenthusiasmus und pädagogischer Aufbruchstimmung begegnet einem in der Landesschule nicht. Hier wirkten eher reformskeptische, -unwillige oder gar innovationsfeindliche Pädagogen, Anhänger einer vergangenen Epoche und eines auslaufenden Schulkonzepts. Während anderswo leidenschaftlich über Themen wie »Arbeitsschule contra Drill- und Paukschule«, »schülerorientierter versus Frontalunterricht« oder »Schülermitbestimmung«, von »Gemeinschaftserziehung« und »Koedukation« ganz zu schweigen, diskutiert wurde, hielt man in der Landesschule unbeirrt am überkommenen autoritären Erziehungskonzept der alten Kadettenschule fest. In diese ideologische Linie gehören der nationalistisch-vaterländische, militärerzieherische, d. h. auf kriegerische Erfolge ausgerichtete Unterricht in den Fächern Deutsch[32] und Geschichte, der Gebrauch von Lehrbüchern aus der Kaiserzeit, die unverhohlene Ablehnung des Arbeitsunterrichts und die offene Sympathie des Schulleiters mit dem pädagogischen und schulpolitischen Programm des reformfeindlichen nationalkonservativen Sächsischen Philologenverbandes. Die soziale Öffnung der Schule, sicherlich ein wichtiger Schritt in die richtige Richtung, wirkt vor diesem Hintergrund eher wie eine unvermeidliche Teilkonzession an den ungeliebten republikanischen Zeitgeist.[33]

Die Traditionen des Kadettenkorps waren mittels Übernahme eines Großteils seiner Lehrer und Schüler in das Schul- und Internatsleben der Landesschule transplantiert und übten dort während der gesamten Weimarer Zeit einen dominierenden Einfluss auf das Schulklima aus. Selbst im Einweihungsjahr des neuen Landesschulgebäudes 1927 stammte noch immer knapp die Hälfte des ständigen Lehrerkollegiums, darunter die gesamte Schul- und Internatsleitung um Oberstudiendirektor Curt Fischer, aus der Zeit der Königlich-Sächsischen Kadettenanstalt. So gesehen ist es wohl auch kein Zufall, dass bei der Einweihungsfeier für die neue Landesschule im Oktober 1927 der sächsische Landeskommandant Oberst Fischer, ein Namensvetter des Schulleiters, sprach und die besten Glückwünsche der Reichswehr überbrachte.

issues such as "continuative learning schools as opposed to 'drill and cram' schools", "pupil-orientated or class teaching" and "community education", not to mention "coeducation", the Landesschule stuck stubbornly to the obsolete authoritarian educational concept of the old Kadettenkorps. The features of this ideological direction included nationalist-patriotic, militarily influenced (i.e. focused on military success) teaching in the subjects of German[37] and history, the use of textbooks from the imperial period, the undisguised rejection of continuative learning and clear directorial support for the pedagogical and school-related aims of the anti-reformist, nationalist-conservative Association of Teachers of Language and Literature in Saxony. Against this backdrop, and despite certainly being a step in the right direction, the social opening-up of the school appears to have simply been an unavoidable part-concession to the republican zeitgeist its officials despised.[38]

The integration of a large section of Kadettenkorps teachers and pupils into school and boarding life at the Landesschule meant that the traditions of the former were not only transplanted into the latter, but also continued to have a dominating influence on the atmosphere at the school throughout the Weimar era. As late as 1927 – the year in which the new Landesschule building was opened – almost half of the permanent teaching staff had also taught at the Königlich-Sächsisches Kadettenkorps. This included senior director of studies Curt Fischer and the senior teaching and boarding staff around him. Seen in this light, it is probably no coincidence that the opening ceremony of the new Landesschule in the October of 1927 saw the best wishes of the Reichswehr extended to the school by its director's namesake, Saxon state commander Colonel Fischer.

The soldierly way and its specific attributes, for example conciseness, austerity, punctuality, objectivity, subordination, obedience, discipline and a sense of honour and duty, had not only held sway over the cadet school for the previous two hundred years, but also represented the inherited virtues which were to characterise teaching practice at the Landesschule. Hierarchical organisational structure, boarding-style pedagogical concepts, masculine bonding rituals,

Soldatische Zucht mit den ihr eigenen Attributen wie Straffheit, Knappheit, Pünktlichkeit und Sachlichkeit, Unterordnung und Gehorsam, Disziplin, Ehr- und Pflichtbewusstsein waren die tradierten Tugenden, die die pädagogische Praxis der neuen Landesschule – genauso wie die der Kadettenanstalt zwei Jahrhunderte lang zuvor – prägten. Hierarchische Organisationsstruktur und pädagogisches Konzept des Internatslebens, männerbündlerische Rituale und elitärer Habitus der Alumni, die Beibehaltung soldatischer Umgangsformen zwischen Lehrer und Schüler und unter den Schülern selbst, die Weiterverwendung der militärischen Terminologie sowie die nahezu identischen Tagesabläufe offenbaren ungebrochene Kontinuitätslinien zwischen Kadettenanstalt und Landesschule. Affinitäten zum monarchischen Militär- und Obrigkeitsstaat waren auffälliger als zur freiheitlich-demokratischen Republik von Weimar. Vereinzelt wurden von Landesschülern noch bis Ende der 1920er Jahre weiße Drillichhosen und blaue Kadettenröcke getragen, um damit ihre Verbundenheit mit der alten Institution zu demonstrieren.[34]

1932 beantragten Einwohner von Klotzsche und Hellerau, unterstützt von den Gemeinderäten, die Zulassung von Mädchen als Tagesschülerinnen an der Landesschule. Sie beriefen sich dabei zu Recht auf einen Grundsatz im sächsischen Schulgesetz. Ihr Anliegen wurde zurückgewiesen, weil »erzieherische Gründe« es – nach vermeintlichen »Erfahrungen an den Lietzschen Internaten« vor dem Weltkrieg – »nicht als unbedenklich« erscheinen ließen, »Mädchen zum Besuch der Schule zuzulassen«.[35]

Der »Charakter der Schule als eines ausgesprochenen Jungeninternats«[36] blieb auch nach 1934 erhalten, als die Landesschule Dresden eine Staatliche Nationalpolitische Erziehungsanstalt (NPEA) wurde. Im selben Jahr verabschiedete sich der 1869 geborene Studiendirektor Curt Fischer in den altersbedingten Ruhestand. Am 20. November 1933 hatte er noch den Reichssportführer Hans von Tschammer und Osten (1887–1943), seit 1930 SA-Führer von Dresden, begeistert empfangen, der ein alter Schüler von ihm am Königlich-Sächsischen Kadettenkorps gewesen war.[37] Damit schließt sich der Kreis, Vergangenheit und Zukunft wurden eins.

an elitist disposition amongst alumni, the maintenance of soldierly relations between teachers and pupils and amongst pupils themselves, the continued use of military terminology and the almost identical daily routines of the two establishments reveal the unbroken continuity between them.

Affinities towards a state which was monarchic, authoritarian and military in style were more obvious than any exhibited towards the liberal-democratic Weimar Republic. A few Landesschule pupils even demonstrated their bond with the old school by continuing to wear white dungarees and blue cadet's jackets right until the end the 1920s.[39]

In 1932 the residents of Klotzsche and Hellerau petitioned for the admission of girls to the Landesschule as day pupils. This move was not only supported by local councillors, but also correctly referred to a precept in the Saxon Education Act. The request was denied, as "educational issues" supposedly based on "experiences at the Lietz boarding schools" prior to the First World War indicated that the "admission of girls to the school" would "not be without cause for concern".[40]

The "school's distinctive boys' boarding school character"[41] continued to prevail after the transformation of the Landesschule Dresden into a State National Political Educational Institution[42] in 1934. A child of 1869, the advancing years of director of studies Curt Fischer saw him enter retirement that same year. This still gave him time to give an enthusiastic reception to one of his former Kadettenkorps pupils on the 20th of November 1933. The visitor was Hans von Tschammer und Osten (1887-1943), who had been head of the SA in Dresden since 1930 and recently appointed to the position of "Reichssportführer".[43]

The circle of history closed, and the past and future became one and the same.

Anmerkungen

1 U. a. hospitierte auch Prof. Dr. Peter Petersen mit Studierenden des von ihm geleiteten Pädagogischen Instituts der Universität Jena an der Landesschule.

2 Bei den Ausführungen in diesem Kapitel stütze ich mich wesentlich auf folgende Quellen: SHD 11344; Meschwitz 1907; Meschwitz 1913; Jubelfest 1825.

3 Scharfenort 1906, hier S. 849.

4 Vgl. ebd.

5 Vgl. Meschwitz 1907, S. 382.

6 Vgl. Meschwitz 1913, S. 32f.

7 Fischer 1927, S. 3.

8 Die Schöpfer des Schulprogramms berufen sich hier auf den Gründer der deutschen Landerziehungsheime für Jungen, Hermann Lietz, einen kaisertreuen Monarchisten, dessen Erziehungskonzept stark völkisch-elitäre und militaristische Züge trug.

9 Vgl. SHD 17745, Bll. 1ff.

10 Fischer 1927, S. 3f.

11 Vgl. ebd. S. 4.

12 Vgl. ebd. S. 5.

13 Vgl. SHD 17745.

14 Der Dresdner Reformplan bezieht sich auf die Fremdsprachenfolge: ab Sexta 1. moderne Fremdsprache, ab Untertertia Latein, ab Untersekunda 2. moderne Fremdsprache. Vgl. Amlung 2006, S. 167 – 173 sowie Amlung 2007, S. 165 – 198.

15 Fischer 1927, S. 6.

16 Vgl. ebd., S. 7. Tatsächlich stieg die Zahl der Schüler bis zum Schuljahr 1926/27 noch auf 276.

17 Vgl. ebd.

18 Starke o. J.

19 »Dresdner Anzeiger« vom 14. Mai 1925.

20 Vgl. Fischer 1927, S. 49.

21 Vgl. Fischer 1927, S. 49.

22 Fischer 1929, S. 3 (ähnlich formuliert in der vom sächsischen Volksbildungsministerium genehmigten »Schul- und Hausordnung« von 1925).

23 In den Jahren nach 1927 lag es bei ca. 50 RM im Monat.

24 In den Genuss kamen nur Schüler, deren Fleiß- und Betragenszensuren nicht dagegen sprachen und deren Durchschnittsnoten nicht unter 2- lagen.

25 Vgl. Denkschrift 1926.

26 Vgl. Dresdner Lehrerverein 1929, S. 92 – 95.

27 Die Zahl der Bewerbungen war meist wesentlich höher als die Zahl der Aufgenommenen. So konnten etwa 1927 von 100 Kandidaten nur 30 genommen werden.

28 Im Winter gab es einen etwas abgewandelten Nachmittagsablauf.

29 Vgl. die amüsanten Erinnerungen von Christa Hahn in Hahn 2001, S. 49 – 55.

30 Vgl. Schmidt 1978.

31 Vgl. Amlung 2009, S. 16 – 35.

32 Vgl. die Aufsatzthemen in Deutsch im Schuljahr 1928/29 in: Fischer 1929, S. 22f.

33 Diese soziale Öffnung wurde aber zugleich wieder eingeschränkt durch den Zusatz, dass Kriegswaisen, Kriegsbeschädigten- und Vertriebenensöhne bevorzugt in die Landesschule aufgenommen werden sollten.

34 Vgl. Burkhardt 1973.

35 SHD 21361.

36 Ebd.

37 Nachzulesen in dem vom »Traditionsverband ehemaliger Landesschüler« gern verschwiegenen Heft 12 der Landesschul-Mitteilungen vom Februar 1934, das auf der Titelseite geradezu programmatisch die Hakenkreuzfahne zeigt. Vgl. SHD 12506.

Notes

1 The Landesschule Dresden was a boarding establishment which featured both a progressive grammar school and an upper secondary school.

2 Amongst those to visit and observe the Landesschule were Prof. Dr. Peter Petersen and students studying at the pedagogical institute he led at the University of Jena.

3 English translation: the Royal Saxon Cadet Corps.

4 My remarks in this chapter are essentially based on the following sources: SHD 11344; Meschwitz 1907; Meschwitz 1913; Jubelfest 1825.

5 Scharfenort, 1906, here p. 849.

6 See ibid.

7 See Meschwitz, 1907, p. 382.

8 See Meschwitz, 1913, p. 32f.

9 Fischer, 1927, p. 3.

10 A "Fürstenschule" was a state boarding school for the fostering of upper-level civil servants and clergy.

11 In making this point, the creators of the school programme were invoking Hermann Lietz, the founder of German national community homes for boys and a monarchist loyal to the emperor. His notion of education bore strongly national-elitist and military characteristics.

12 See SHD 17745.

13 Fischer 1927, p. 3f.

14 See ibid. p. 4.

15 See ibid. p. 5.

16 See SHD 17745.

17 The Dresden School Reform Plan was based on the sequence in which foreign languages were integrated into the curriculum: first modern language from year five upwards, Latin from year eight upwards, second modern language from year ten upwards. Also see Amlung, 2006, p. 167 – 173 and Amlung, 2007, p. 165 – 198.

18 Fischer, 1927, p. 6.

19 See ibid, p. 7. The number of pupils actually continued to rise until reaching 276 in the school year of 1926/27.

20 See ibid.

21 Starke (n.d.)

22 "Dresdner Anzeiger" dated the 14th of May 1925.

23 See Fischer, 1927, p. 49.

24 See Fischer, 1927, p. 49.

25 Fischer, 1929, p. 3 (this is expressed in a similar way in the "Schul- und Hausordnung" of 1925, which was approved by the Saxon Ministry of Popular Education).

26 In the years after 1927 this stood at around 50 Reichsmarks per month.

27 The Amtshauptmannschaften were a type of lower administrative district specific to Saxony.

28 Scholarships were only awarded to pupils who exhibited appropriate application and disciplinary conduct and had an average grade of no less than 2.

29 See the memoirs of 1926.

30 See Dresdner Lehrerverein, 1929, p. 92 – 95.

31 The number of applications was usually significantly higher than the number of pupils admitted. Of the 100 that applied in 1927 only 30 could be taken on.

32 The afternoon schedule was somewhat different in the winter.

33 See the entertaining recollections of Christa Hahn in Hahn, 2001, p. 49 – 55.

34 See Schmidt, 1978

35 The Dürerschule was a state secondary pilot school on the Silbermannstraße in Dresden.

36 See Amlung, 2009, p. 16 – 35.

37 See the essay topics for the subject of German in school year 1928/29 as listed in: Fischer 1929, p. 22f.

38 This social opening-up was nevertheless restricted by the decision to favour the admittance of war orphans and the children of those who had lost their lived or been displaced during the war.

39 See Burkhardt, 1973.

40 SHD 21361.

41 Ibid.

42 The "Nationalpolitische Erziehungsanstalten" were a type of educational establishment set up under National Socialism, and were also known by the abbreviations "NPEA" or, more colloquially, "NAPOLA". In this case the school also bore the name of the "Rudolf-Schröter-Schule".

43 Available to read in issue 12 (February 1934) of the Landesschule gazette, which displays the swastika flag in an almost programmatic way on its title page and is eagerly forgotten by the "Traditional Association of Former Landesschule Pupils". See SHD 12506.

5

Moderne Interpretation des historischen Pergolamotivs.
Modern interpretation of the historic pergola motif.

Ein eingehängtes Zwischendach bietet Schutz vor Regen.
An integral intermediate roof provides protection from the rain.

Pergola als verbindendes Element.
Pergola as a connecting element between buildings.

links / left
Lernräume im Freien.
Outdoor learning spaces.

rechts / right
Blick von der Aula zum Biergarten.
View from the auditorium towards the beer garden.

58

Blick vom Akademiehotel auf Haus 1.
View of building 1 from the Academy Hotel.

Kramer und Tessenow – Bau und Architektur der Landesschule (1925 – 1927)

Kramer and Tessenow – the construction and architecture of the Landesschule (1925 – 1927)

ULRIKE HÜBNER-GRÖTZSCH
UND ULRICH HÜBNER

»Ein Werk, das seine Meister lobt, nicht nur zweckmäßig errichtet, sondern mit der Freude am Schönen«, pries Oberstudiendirektor Prof. Dr. Curt Fischer den Neubau der Landesschule Dresden in Klotzsche anlässlich seiner Eröffnung im Oktober 1927.[1] Er hatte gemeinsam mit den Lehrern und 250 Schülern bereits Gelegenheit gehabt, die Neubauten der größten Internatsschule Sachsens mit Leben zu füllen und ihre Qualität zu prüfen, denn die Bewohner waren während der noch andauernden Bauarbeiten bereits ab Herbst 1926 eingezogen und hatten die Schule sukzessive in den ersten Monaten des Jahres 1927 in Betrieb genommen. Die Landesschüler genossen ihre neue Heimat nach einer ermüdenden Interimszeit, die sie seit der Räumung der alten Kadettenanstalt im Sommer 1926 an verschiedenen Notstandorten von Strehlen über Hellerau bis nach Bischofswerda verbracht hatten.

Die Schule

Die neue Landesschule lag in den Ausläufern der Dresdner Heide auf der Klotzscher Höhe. Von einem Ausflug in die nahe Kunst- und Kulturstadt Dresden kommend, konnte sie der Landesschüler in einer halben Stunde mit der Straßenbahn erreichen. Bei den ersten Häusern des Villenvorortes bot ihm auf der östlichen Seite der Landstraße ein kleines Pförtnerhaus mit der Pförtnerwohnung Einlass in das umfriedete Gelände. Ein alter Forstweg legte sich den Höhenlinien entsprechend nach rechts um den Hügel und führte durch ein Kiefernwaldstück, das die Schulanlage von der Straße abschirmte. Am Ende des Weges erreichte der Landesschüler über eine große Freitreppe den Haupteingang des auf dem Hügel liegenden, zweistöckigen Schulgebäudes.

Blick durch die nördliche Pergola nach Westen zum Lehrgebäude.
View west through the northern pergola to the classroom building.

Eingangshalle im Lehrgebäude, um 1931.
Entrance hall in the classroom building, circa 1931.

“A work which extols its foremen, and one which has been built not simply to serve a purpose, but to take delight in all that is beautiful.” These were the words used by Prof. Dr. Curt Fischer, senior director of studies at the Landesschule Dresden in Klotzsche[1], to praise the school’s new complex on the occasion of its opening in the October of 1927.[2] Together with the school’s teachers and 250 pupils, Fischer had already taken the opportunity to both fill the school’s new buildings with life and examine the quality of what was now the largest boarding school in Saxony. Despite ongoing construction work, the school’s residents had begun to move in from the autumn of 1926 onwards, and gradually restarted normal school activity during the first few months of 1927. Having vacated the old Kadettenkorps[3] site in the summer of 1926, the pupils found their new home a welcome change from the temporary accommodation

Durch eine vordachähnliche Pergola und eine der drei Flügeltüren betrat er die lichte Eingangshalle. Ihre Stützen mit ornamentalen Kapitellen waren in gleichmäßigem Raster gesetzt, dazwischen schmückten dekorative runde Scheiben die Decke des schlichten Raumes. Gegenüber dem Eingang öffneten sich drei weitere Flügeltüren zum Innenhof des Gebäudes. Über der Mittleren versinnbildlichte das Relief eines Knaben über einem Männerkopf die Jugend, die aus dem Alten schöpft.[2] Den rechteckigen Rasenhof umgaben die kleinen Fensterbänder der Flure, aufgelockert durch runde Bullaugenfenster.

Der Landesschüler wandte sich nach rechts zu einem der drei kleinen, dezentral angelegten Treppenhäuser, dessen Stützen wiederum stilisierte Ornamentik schmückte.[3] Rote klinkerverkleidete Wände und mit gelbem Klinker ausgelegte Fußböden waren strapazierfähig und vermittelten einen warmen Eindruck. An den langen, vom Hof belichteten Fluren reihten sich die hellen Klassenzimmer. Zu den zahlreichen Fachräumen mit Spezialausstattungen und umfangreichen Vorbereitungs-, Sammlungs- und weiteren Nebenräumen gehörten auch Zeichensäle und verschiedene Werkstätten. Diese Raumvielfalt entsprach den anspruchsvollen Forderungen an damalige moderne Schulen und wurde in den meisten Neubauten der Zeit mehr oder weniger verwirklicht. Wiederum rechts gelangte der Landesschüler auf die Terrasse des Biologieflügels, die für Freiluftunterricht, Experimente und Ähnliches vorgesehen war und deren Ende eine kleine Sternwarte krönte. Mit der Eingangstreppe im Rücken hatte er von hier aus einen weiten Ausblick auf das Elbtal mit der Stadt Dresden und auf das gesamte Gelände der Landesschule vor sich.

Die Anlage war vollständig von dichtem Kiefernwald umgeben. Die natürliche Umgebung entsprach einem pädagogischen Leitgedanken der Landerziehungsheime, an deren Erziehungsstruktur sich die Landesschule orientieren wollte. Mit diesen Schulgemeinden, die noch vor dem Ersten Weltkrieg oft aus Umnutzungen alter Burg- oder Schloss-, Rittergut-, Mühlen- oder Klosteranlagen mit heimatstilistisch angepassten Erweiterungsbauten entstanden waren, hatte sie auch die offene, siedlungsartige Struktur gemeinsam.

where they had spent the tedious intervening period. This accommodation was provided for them at various emergency locations anywhere from Strehlen and Hellerau all the way to Bischofswerda.

The school

The new Landesschule was situated in the elevated Klotzsche area on the fringes of Dresden Heath. By taking the tram, a Landesschule pupil returning from an excursion to see the artistic and cultural sights of nearby Dresden could be back at the school within half an hour. One of the first buildings that greeted him as he arrived into the residential suburb of Klotzsche was the school porter's lodge and apartment, which was located on the eastern side of the Königsbrücker Straße and represented his point of entry into the enclosed site. Following an old foresters' path which extended to his right along the contours of the hill, he passed through the section of pine forest which screened the school complex from the road. At the end of the path he ascended a large flight of steps up to the main entrance of the two-storey school complex on top of the hill. Continuing through a porch-like pergola and one of three sets of double doors, he would then enter the well-lit, simple entrance hall. The hall's pillars were arranged in a regular grid pattern and featured ornamental capitals; decorative circular bezants adorned the ceiling sections between them. Another set of three double doors opposite the entrance provided access to the building's inner courtyard. The relief of a boy above a man's head which was positioned above the middle set of doors symbolised youth and the way it draws on the old.[4] The small rows of windows which lined the corridors around the rectangular, lawned courtyard were interspersed by round bulls-eye windows.

Treppenhaus im Lehrgebäude.
Stairwell in the classroom building.

Flur mit Fenstern zum Innenhof im Lehrgebäude.
Classroom building corridor featuring windows to the inner courtyard.

Der Landesschüler blickte von der Terrasse auf einen großen, parkartigen Rasenhof mit einzelnen Birken, den Rest einer früheren Waldlichtung auf der langgestreckten Hügelkuppe. Um diesen parkähnlichen Mittelpunkt gruppierten sich symmetrisch und pavillonartig die übrigen Bauten. Gärten und Wiesen wechselten mit den zweistöckigen Häusern ab, deren Mittelkörper flache Walmdächer, die Flügelbauten Flachdächer aufwiesen. Sandsteinmauern und ein Wandelgang, der in Höhe der Traufgesimse mit einer Pergola überspannt war, gaben dem zentralen Rasenplatz eine feste Kontur und verbanden die Gebäude zu einer optischen Einheit. Den flach und breit gelagerten Häusern verlieh die Höhe und Leichtigkeit der Pergola eine gewisse Großzügigkeit und sogar Monumentalität. Um den Anbau mit der Dachterrasse, auf dem der Landesschüler stand, führte der Weg von der Eingangstreppe in den Rasenhof, und mit einer flachen Pergola überspannt, zum Haus des Rektors, das auf der Nordseite der Anlage durch das Konrektorhaus gespiegelt wurde. Zwischen beiden hatte der Rasenhof eine Breite von über hundert Metern, danach verengte er sich durch Sandsteinmauern und die anschließenden sechs Schülerheime auf weniger als die Hälfte. Vermittelnd waren die Flügel der ersten beiden Heime zum Schulgebäude hin geöffnet, während sich die der anderen zum Gartenhof hin streckten. Die Pergola, die auf jeder Seite drei Schülerheime verband, leitete perspektivisch zum Flucht- und Höhepunkt der Anlage, dem Aula- und Wirtschaftsgebäude über. Als Antipode zum breit gelagerten Schulgebäude im Westen schloss es den Rasenhof mit den basilikalen Proportionen eines langgestreckten Mittelsaales und zweier flach gedeckter Seitenflügel im Osten ab. Die graugrüne Schieferdeckung der geneigten Dachflächen und der hellgrün gefärbte Putz der Häuser waren gut auf das dunkle Kieferngrün des Waldes abgestimmt.

Turning right, our Landesschule pupil approached one of three small, off-centre stairwells, which again featured pillars with stylised ornamentation.[5] Red clinker-clad walls and yellow clinker floors were hard-wearing and conveyed a feeling of warmth. Bright classrooms were arranged along corridors flooded with light from the courtyard. The school boasted numerous subject rooms fitted with specialist equipment, as well as an extensive range of other rooms used for preparation, storage or other ancillary purposes such as drawing and workshop-based activities. This variety of different rooms reflected the exacting demands placed on modern schools of that era, and was featured to at least some extent at the majority of new schools built at

Die Anlage erinnerte an die Bildungsanstalt für Rhythmus in der benachbarten Gartenstadt Hellerau, die der Landesschüler von Sommerlagern der Wandervögel kannte. Ihr großes Festspielhaus stand in der Mitte eines großen Platzes. Die Schauseite mit ihrer monumentalen, die ganze Fassade zusammenfassenden Säulenfront unter dem Dreiecksgiebel und den breit gelagerten, kontrastierend flächigen Seitenflügeln war beeindruckend. Die Hoffassade des Aulagebäudes in der Landesschule war ähnlich, obwohl der vorgezogene Mittelrisalit lediglich sechs hochrechteckige Fenster in der schlichten Wandfläche unter dem fliehenden Walmdach aufwies. In der symmetrischen Anlage in Hellerau umgaben kleine, durch Pergolen miteinander verbundene Pavil-

Chemieunterricht: letzte chemische Übung des Schuljahres 1932.
Chemistry lesson: the last chemical experiment of school year 1932.

the time. Another right-hand turn took our pupil onto the terrace of the biology wing, which was used for open-air lessons, experiments and such like. The end of the terrace was rounded off by a small observatory. With his back to the entrance stairwell the pupil had a panoramic view of the Elbe Valley, the city of Dresden and the entire Landesschule site.

Surrounded as it was by thick pine forest, the Landesschule had natural surroundings which corresponded with a central pedagogical principle of the national community homes upon whose educational structure it sought to base itself. The school's open, estate-like structure was another characteristic it shared with these community homes, which

lonbauten das Festspielhaus. Die Landesschule war komplexer, offener und lockerer mit dezentralen Eingängen und Wegen ausgestattet. Hier waren die umgebende Natur und die durch Sandsteinmauern gefassten Gärten und Wiesen bewusst in die Gestaltung einbezogen worden, die vom »bewegten Waldcharakter des Bauplatzes«[4] beeinflusst war. Diese zunehmende Bedeutung des Außenraumes ist auch bei einigen Hellerauer Siedlungshäusern zu sehen, die hinter ihre Gärten zurückgesetzt sind und damit den Straßenraum in eine Gartenlandschaft auflösen. Der fließende Raum ist ein wichtiges Charakteristikum der Moderne und tritt seinen Siegeszug nach dem Zweiten Weltkrieg in der Auflösung des Stadtgefüges in eine Stadtlandschaft an.

had often been created by the conversion and expansion of forts, castles, manors, mills and monasteries to include buildings deemed to portray a Heimat style. The pupil's view from the terrace took in a large, lawned, park-like courtyard with solitary birch trees which had originally been a clearing on the elongated hilltop. The other structures were grouped symmetrically in a pavilion style around this landscaped hub, and gardens and meadows alternated with two-storey buildings with hipped roofs on their central sections and flat roofs on their wings. Sandstone walls and a walkway covered by a pergola which extended up to eaves cornice height gave the central lawned area a distinct outline and formed the buildings into a single optical unit. The height and delicate form of the pergola lent the flat, broad-based buildings a certain sense of spatial generosity and even monumentality. The path from the entrance stairway into the lawned courtyard led around the biology wing and its roof terrace before continuing under a flat pergola to the headmaster's house. The deputy headmaster's house on the northern side of the complex was a mirror image of the latter building. The lawned area between the two houses reached a width of over one-hundred metres before being narrowed to less than half this distance by sandstone walls and the six adjoining boarding houses. The wings of the first two boarding houses opened out welcomingly towards the classroom building, whilst the wings of the other boarding houses extended out towards the courtyard. In terms of perspective, the pergola which grouped together three boarding houses on each side of the courtyard led towards the vanishing point and highlight of the complex: the assembly hall and management building. Acting as a counterweight to the broad-based class-

Blick über den Wirtschaftsweg nach Südosten
auf Wald und Schülerheim B, heute Haus 7.
View south-east over the goods access road to woods
and boarding house B, now building 7.

Die lockere Massenverteilung des großen Bauvolumens der Landesschule über die gesamte Hügelkuppe war sinnvoll, da sie Schülern, Lehrern und Personal, die die Anlage selten verließen, als Lebensraum für Arbeit und Freizeit, geistige und körperliche Ausbildung und nicht zuletzt als Zuhause dienen sollte. Die dezentrale Anlage entsprach auch dem zeitgenössischen Trend im Schulbau, der die großen kasernenartigen Blöcke der Vorkriegszeit (Gründerzeitschulen und Erlweinschulen in Dresden) in mehrere Flügel auflöste und um Höfe gruppierte, idealerweise sogar Flachbauschulen mit Gartenzugang wie die Waldschule am Fischhaus des Dresdner Stadtbaurates Paul Wolf favorisierte.[5] Der Landesschüler wandte seinen Blick von der Terrasse nach Südosten über das Rektorenhaus. Hinter den drei südlichen Schülerheimen erstreckten sich großzügige Sportanlagen: eine Turnhalle mit zwei Turnplätzen, ein »Ball-« und ein »Netzspielplatz« und eine »Kampfbahn« mit Zuschauerrampe. Die »starke Betonung der körperlichen Ertüchtigung«[6] als Erbe der Vorgängerinstitution der Landesschule, der Kadettenanstalt, brachte häufige Siege der Landesschüler bei Schulwettbewerben ein.

Der heutige Blick von der wieder sanierten Terrasse unterscheidet sich von dem des Landesschülers erheblich: An Stelle der Sportanlagen entstanden eine Straße und Parkplätze, den Waldbestand ersetzten große Fabrikhallen und die Turnhalle ein langgestreckter Hotelneubau.

Setzen wir den Rundgang mit dem Landesschüler fort. Kam er aus dem Unterricht, verließ er das Schulgebäude durch einen der beiden Ausgänge im Ostflügel in Richtung der Schülerheime. Über beiden Türen zeigten und zeigen Reliefs in antiker Manier Schüler und Lehrer als Reminiszenz an die Wurzeln des Gymnasiums im alten Griechenland.[7]

Blick über den Rasenhof nach Osten
zum Wirtschafts- und Verwaltungsgebäude.

View east over the lawned courtyard
towards the management and administration building.

room building to its west, the basilican proportions of its elongated central hall and two flat-roofed wings closed off the eastern edge of the lawned courtyard. The grey-green slate which covered its sloping roof surfaces and the light-green colour of its rendered walls were a suitable contrast to the dark green of the surrounding pine forests.

The complex was reminiscent of the School of Rhythm in the neighbouring garden city of Hellerau, which was a location our Landesschule pupil knew well from summer camps with the Wandervogel youth rambling club. The school included a large festival theatre standing at the centre of a large square. The front side of the building was characterized by a monumental line of pillars extending along its entire façade, a central triangular gable and contrasting, flat wings – all of which combined to create an impressive ensemble. Though the courtyard-side façade of the assembly hall building at the Landesschule exhibited some similarities with the front of the festival theatre, it only featured six tall, rectangular windows in the plain wall surface under the receding hipped roof of its protruding central section. Whereas the symmetrical Hellerau site used pergolas to connect the pavilion buildings which surrounded the festival theatre, the Landesschule was more complex, more open and less strict in its layout, which included off-centre points of access and paths. Its natural surroundings and the gardens and meadows enclosed by its sandstone walls were consciously integrated into its design, which was influenced by the "emotionally moving forest character of the construction site"[6]. This evidence of the growing importance of outdoor spaces can also be observed on the Hellerau housing estate, where the setting back of some homes behind their gardens turns the roadside environment into a garden landscape. The notion of fluid space is a significant feature of the modern age, and has achieved a series of triumphant successes since the Second World War by taking the concept of an urban structure and turning it into that of an urban landscape.

The pupils, teachers and other school staff at the Landesschule rarely left the complex, which not only provided a variety of spaces for work, leisure activities and intellectual and physical training, but also served as their home. This made the loose distribution of the Landesschule's substantial structural volume across the entire hilltop a sensible choice. The decentralised complex followed contemporary school-building fashions, which saw the large, barrack-like blocks of the pre-war period (in Dresden: late

Die breit hingestreckte Hofseite der Schule, im Mittelteil mit den Direktions- und Lehrerzimmern im ersten Stockwerk etwas vorgezogen, belebten quadratische Fenster in der Fassade und kleine spitze Gauben im Walmdach. Der Landesschüler ließ das Rektorhaus rechts und das Konrektorhaus links hinter sich. Die beiden Wohn- und Verwaltungshäuser unterschieden sich einzig durch die Anordnung ihrer Balkone und Pergolen, die zusammen mit den Fensterläden einen wohnlichen Eindruck vermittelten. Ganz ähnlich waren auch die Turnhalle mit vorgesetzten Pergolen und die als Straßenbahn- und Pförtnerhäuschen genutzten Gebäude an der Königsbrücker Straße gestaltet, ebenso wie die sogenannte Vierhäusergruppe, in der drei Lehrer und der Hausmeister mit ihren Familien wohnten.

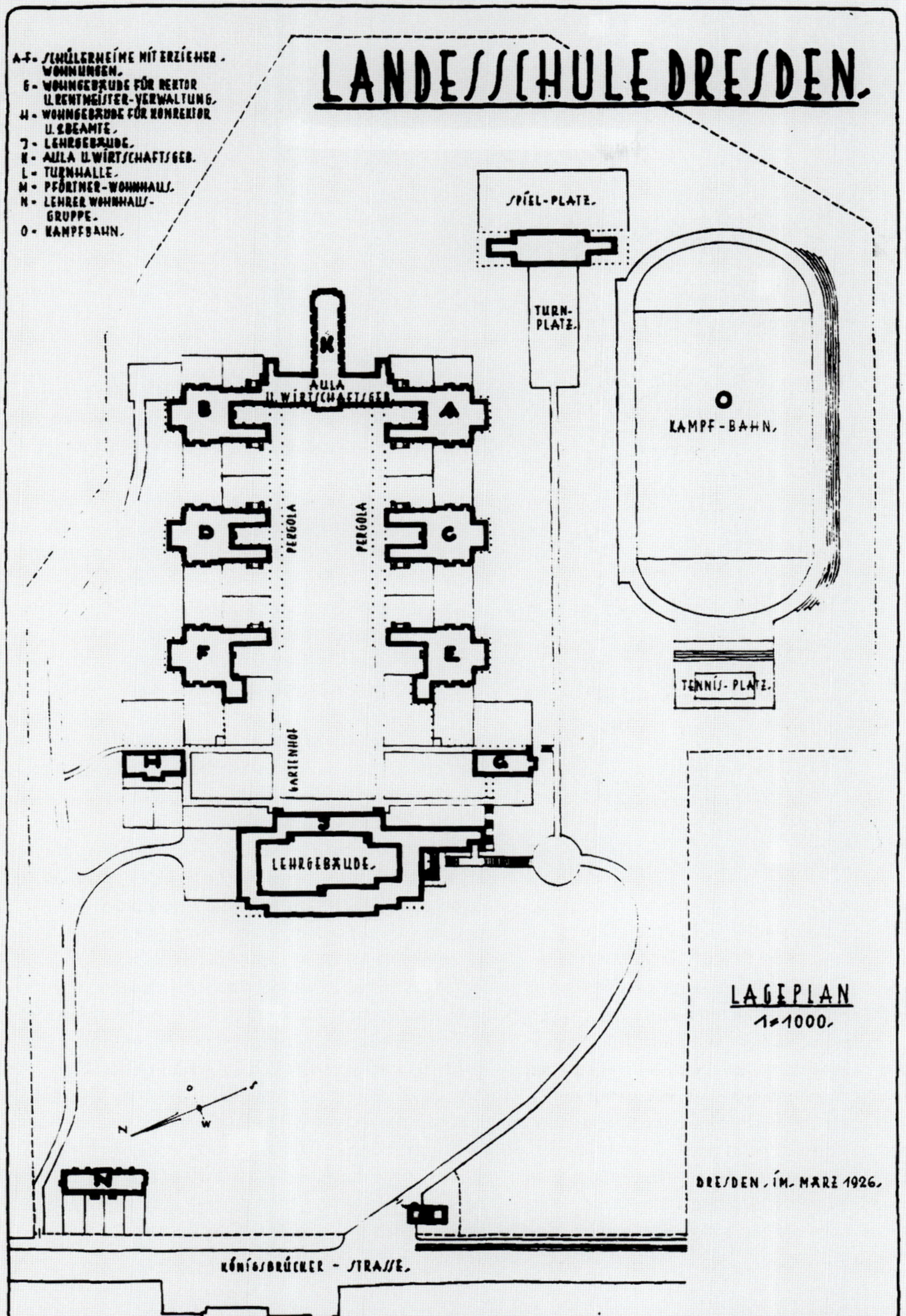

Lageplan, 1926.
Site plan, 1926.

Sie stand an der Wirtschaftszufahrt, die vom nördlichen Geländeeingang an der Königsbrücker Straße zum Kohlenhof an der Nordfassade des Lehrgebäudes und zum Wirtschaftshof am Aulagebäude führte.

Der Landesschüler ging über den weiten Rasenhof zum ersten Schülerheim. Erst bei genauerer Betrachtung wurde deutlich, dass sich die Schülerheime und die Aula vor ihm von Rektoren- und Schulhaus hinter ihm unterschieden. Trotz der einheitlichen Wirkung der Gesamtanlage mit flachen Walmdächern, schlichten Fassaden und Pergolen an allen Häusern wirkte die Schule mit dem vorgezogenen Dach und den bis fast darunter reichenden Fenstern anders als die flächigen Fassaden mit der sparsamen Fenster- und Türverteilung und dem Raster der Pergolen, das alle vor ihm liegenden Gebäude zusammenfasste. Tatsächlich war die Landesschule von zwei sehr unterschiedlichen Architekten entworfen worden, dem Ministerialrat Dr. Oskar Kramer und dem Architekturprofessor Heinrich Tessenow. Beide Architekten trugen die Verantwortung für den künstlerischen Entwurf und die Realisierung der Gesamtanlage gemeinsam. Die Sächsische Staatsregierung hatte dieses sicherlich nicht einfache Konstrukt gewählt, da der Neubau unter großem zeitlichen und finanziellen Druck entstehen musste.[8] Die Landesschule war 1920 als Nachfolgeinstitution der Kadettenanstalt im Dresdner Militärgelände gegründet worden. Sie nutzte zunächst deren Gebäude, was mit schwierigen Verhandlungen zwischen Reich und Land verbunden war. Bereits im März 1923 beanspruchte das Reichswehrministerium das Gebäude für die aus München verlegte Infanterieschule zurück. Noch während des Kampfes gegen die Räumungsdrohung bis Ende 1924 zerschlug sich das Projekt, das Hellerauer Festspielhaus für

19th-century and Erlwein schools) split into numerous wings and grouped around courtyards, ideally in the form of low buildings with access to gardens. This style can be observed in the form of the Waldschule am Fischhaus[7] constructed by Paul Wolf in his capacity as head of Dresden's Municipal Planning and Building Control Authority.[8]

Shifting his view towards the south-east, the Landesschule pupil's gaze passed over the top of the headmaster's house and lingered on generously proportioned sports facilities behind the three southern boarding houses. These facilities included a gymnasium with two gymnastics practice areas, a "ball games" court, a "net games" area and a stadium with a running track and spectator stand. Having inherited a "heavy emphasis on physical training"[9] from its predecessor (the Kadettenkorps), the Landesschule saw its pupils enjoy frequent success in inter-school competitions.

The view from the now-renovated terrace is considerably different to that which greeted our Landesschule pupil: a road and parking spaces have been created where the sports facilities once stood, the forest has given way to large factory buildings and the gymnasium has been replaced by the long structure of a new hotel.

Let us rejoin our Landesschule pupil on his way around the site. Coming out of class, he left the classroom building through one of the two exits from the east wing and aimed towards the boarding houses. Reliefs above both doors depicted – and indeed still depict – pupils and teachers in classical style as a memento of grammar schools' ancient Greek roots.[10] The wide expanse of the courtyard side of the school protruded slightly in the area of first-floor headmaster's and teachers' rooms, and included design features such as square windows in its façade and small, pointed dormer windows on its hipped roof. Walking on, our pupil left the houses of the headmaster and deputy headmaster behind him to his right and left respectively. The only difference between these two split-usage buildings (residential/administration) was the layout of their balconies and pergolas, which worked in combination with window shutters to create a homely impression. The gymnasium with its protruding pergolas and the buildings used as tram stop and porter's lodge on the Königsbrücker Straße were also similar in terms of design. The same applied to the so-called "group of four" buildings which accommodated three teachers, the caretaker and their respective families. These buildings were located next to the goods access road which led from the north site entrance on the Königsbrücker Straße to the coal yard on the north façade of the teaching building and the utility yard next to the assembly hall building.

Continuing over the broad, lawned courtyard, the Landesschule pupil arrived at the first of the boarding houses. The fact that the boarding houses and assembly hall building in front of him were different from the headmaster's house and classroom building behind him only became apparent upon closer inspection. Despite the impression of uniformity made by the flat hipped roofs, simple façades and pergolas which characterised the complex as a whole, the classroom building, its protruding roof and the windows which almost reached up to it deviated from the pergola grid patterns and expansive façades with sparingly distributed windows and doors featured by all the buildings laid out before it. The Landesschule had in fact been designed by two entirely different architects: Undersecretary Dr. Oskar Kramer and professor of architecture Heinrich Tessenow. The two architects bore joint responsibility for the artistic design and realisation of the entire complex. Though this setup was certainly not entirely free of difficulties, it remained the first choice of the Saxon state government due to the time pressure and financial constraints under which the new school was to be built.[11] Having been founded in 1920 as the successor to the Kadettenkorps, the Landesschule initially used the military build-

Oskar Kramer (1871 – 1946).

die Landesschule umzubauen, am hohen Kaufpreis. Dem Räumungsbeschluss Ende 1924 folgten im Januar 1925 die Ortswahl für den Neubau und der Streit um die Entschädigungssumme des Reiches, die mit einem Zehntel der Neubaukosten von fünf Millionen Mark letztlich gering ausfiel. Im Februar erarbeitete die Hochbaudirektion im sächsischen Finanzministerium unter Oskar Kramer einen Vorentwurf. Anfang März wurde Heinrich Tessenow hinzugezogen, der sich sowohl theoretisch als auch praktisch mit seinen Meisterschülern an der Kunstakademie mit dem Schulbau aus-

rechts / right
Festspielhaus Hellerau, 1911,
Architekt Heinrich Tessenow, Foto 1936.
Hellerau Festival Hall, built 1911,
architect Heinrich Tessenow, photo
dated 1936.

ings in Dresden which had housed its predecessor. This led to awkward negotiations between the Reich and the state of Saxony, and as early as March 1923 the Ministry of the Reichswehr demanded that the buildings be returned to them for the purposes of the relocation of their central infantry school from Munich to Dresden. The Landesschule's fight against eviction from these premises not only continued until the end of 1924, but also coincided with the abandonment of plans to convert Hellerau Festival Hall into its new home (the purchase price was too high). The serving of an eviction notice at the end of 1924 was followed in January 1925 by the selection of a new location for the school and disputes over the compensation to be paid to it by the Reich. The sum eventually paid out was fairly low at a tenth of total construction costs of five million marks. The February of that year saw the board of construction at the Saxon Ministry of Finance draw up a preliminary design under the supervision of Oskar Kramer. Heinrich Tessenow was integrated into the project from the following March onwards, and deliberated both the theoretical and practical aspects of the new complex with his master-class students at the Academy of Arts. He had already drawn up plans for the conversion of the Hellerau Festival Hall (which he himself had designed) to fit the purposes of the Landesschule, and had qualified for the perceptive, cost-effective construction of the new school by proving himself to be a subtle master of his art with an eye for simple, pleasing aesthetics. Despite the project still being under discussion in the state parliament during the month of May, a new construction authority for the Landesschule was founded during the preceding April and commenced site survey and deforestation work.[12] Though plans for the project were finalised by the beginning of July that year, a construction workers' strike dictated that construction work could only begin in the September of 1925.

Heinrich Tessenow (1876 – 1950).

einandergesetzt, bereits den Umbau seines Hellerauer Festspielhauses für die Landesschule projektiert und sich als sensibler Baukünstler mit seiner schlichten Ästhetik für einen sowohl einfühlsamen als auch sparsamen Schulbau qualifiziert hatte. Im April wurde das Neubauamt für die Landesschule gegründet, das Geländevermessungen und Abholzungen durchführte, während das Projekt im Mai noch im Landtag verhandelt wurde.[9] Anfang Juli war die Planung fertig, die Bauarbeiten konnten aber wegen eines Bauarbeiterstreiks erst im September 1925 beginnen.

The architects

The architects came to a mutual agreement on the overall concept. From today's perspective it is no longer possible to determine whether it was based on Kramer's preliminary design – which was the first to be drawn up and is of unknown whereabouts – or whether Tessenow was able to use his artistic weight to ensure that a general plan of his own was also drawn up.[13] The latter assumption is supported by the similarity between plans for the Landesschule, the design of the Hellerau Festival Hall complex and the master plan published by Tessenow.[14] Once a basic structure had been settled on, the architects divided the buildings amongst themselves "in order to allow [their] artistic idiosyncrasies the greatest possible room to manoeuvre".[15] The fact that this compromise was not without its difficulties is exhibited by Kramer's conspicuously terse acknowledgements of Tessenow's buildings in the "Bauzeitung" construction gazette and Tessenow's commitment to his own, unrealised master plan – even after the project had been completed.[16] Though Kramer himself noted that the pair were at pains to achieve "both the utmost in objectivity and as consistent a design as possible whilst safeguarding individual styles"[17], their architectural language is easy to read, classify and interpret.

Oskar Kramer (1871–1946) was an experienced state architect. Having graduated from Dresden College of Advanced Technology in around 1890, he went on to enter the civil service as a state building inspector in 1924. The regional court building erected on the Münchner Platz in Dresden between 1902 and 1907 represents his most important work. Despite the historical motifs communicated by this impressive example of monumental reform architecture (for example its fort-like character), the fluid organisation of its structural volume and layout lend it a symbolic and urban landscape-defining

Modell der Landesschule von Osten.
Model of the Landesschule, viewed from the east.

Die Architekten

Die Architekten sprachen die Gesamtkonzeption gemeinsam ab. Aus heutiger Sicht lässt sich nicht mehr feststellen, ob sie auf Kramers zeitlich vorhergehendem Vorentwurf basierte, der nicht mehr auffindbar ist, oder ob Tessenow sein künstlerisches Gewicht einsetzte, um eine eigene Grundplanung aufzustellen.[10] Für letztere Annahme spricht die Ähnlichkeit des Landesschulplanes mit der Anlage des Hellerauer Festspielhauses ebenso wie der von Tessenow veröffentlichte Gesamtplan.[11] Nach der Festlegung der Grundstruktur teilten die Architekten die Ausführungsplanungen der einzelnen Gebäude untereinander auf, »um der künstlerischen Eigenart [eines jeden] am besten Spielraum zu lassen«[12]. Dass dieser Kompromiss nicht problemfrei war, zeigen die auffällige Knappheit, mit der Kramer Tessenows Bauten in der Bauzeitung würdigte, und Tessenows Festhalten am eigenen, nicht ausgeführten Gesamtplan noch nach der Fertigstellung.[13] Und obwohl beide nach Kramers Worten um »größte Sachlichkeit und zugleich – bei Wahrung ihrer Eigenart – möglichst einheitliche Gestaltung«[14] bemüht waren, lässt sich ihre Formensprache klar ablesen, zuordnen und herleiten.

Oskar Kramer (1871 – 1946) war ein erfahrener Amtsbaumeister. Er hatte um 1890 ein Studium an der Technischen Hochschule in Dresden absolviert und 1894 als Landbauinspektor den Staatsdienst angetreten. Sein Hauptwerk ist das 1902 bis 1907 am Münchner Platz in Dresden errichtete Landgericht. Dieses beeindruckende Beispiel für den Monumentalstil der Reformarchitektur vermittelt zwar historische Motive wie den burgartigen Charakter, erlangt aber durch die freie Gliederung der Baumasse und des Grundrisses eine zeichenhafte und stadtraumbildende Eigenschaft.[15]

Als Leiter des Hochbauamtes im Finanzministerium ab 1920 verwirklichte Kramer – meistens gemeinsam mit seinem Amtskollegen Ernst Dutzmann – viele öffentliche Gebäudekomplexe in einigen sächsischen Städten, zum Beispiel das Braunkohlenforschungsinstitut in Freiberg (1919 – 1924), mehrere medizinische Instituts- und Klinikbauten in Leipzig (bis 1928) und das Amtsgericht in Auerbach/Vogtland (1925 – 1927). Diese großen Bauaufgaben setzte er weiterhin mit monumentalen und geschlossenen Formen um, ergänzte sie aber durch kleinteilige Elemente, wie Schmuckreliefs und horizontale Fenstergliederungen und reduzierte ihre Formensprache der allgemeinen Stilentwicklung entsprechend. Seine leitende Amtsposition erlaubte seiner Architektur weder Experimente noch ausgeprägte individuelle Äußerungen, sondern forderte solide und der regionalen Eigenart angepasste Bauten. Kramer war aktives Mitglied im Landesverein Sächsischer Heimatschutz und publizierte Grundwerte wie »Heimischfühlen«, Gemütlichkeit und Wirtschaftlichkeit in dem großformatigen »Atlas für freistehende kleine Wohnhäuser in Stadt und Land«.[16] Sein traditionsbewusstes Herangehen an die Baukunst wurzelte in der Heimatschutzarchitektur bzw. dem Traditionalismus, Teilen der umfangreichen Reformbewegungen um 1900, die sich gegen die als kulturellen Niedergang begriffene Industrialisierung und ihre negativen Folgen wie historistischen Formenwildwuchs und ungesunden Mietskasernenbau wendeten.[17]

quality.[18] Kramer was head of the board of construction at the Ministry of Finance from 1920 onwards, and generally worked in partnership with his colleague Ernst Dutzmann. He realised a large number of public buildings in a variety of Saxon towns, including the Brown Coal Research Institute in Freiberg (1919 – 1924), a number of medical institutes and clinics in Leipzig (up to 1928) and the County Court in Auerbach/Vogtland (1925 – 1927). Though monumental, cohesive forms were a feature of his participation in these large construction projects, he supplemented them with elements of fine detail such as ornamental reliefs and horizontal window layouts. He also limited the use of form in order to correspond with contemporary trends. As a result of his leading position in the civil service his architecture could neither afford to experiment nor make clear individual statements, and therefore focused on sturdy structures which reflected the regional style. Kramer was an active member in the State Society for the Preservation of Saxon Heimat, and wrote on fundamental values such as "a feeling of homeliness", cosiness and economic efficiency in the large-format "Atlas of detached small residential buildings in urban and rural settings".[19] His tradition-conscious approach to his art was rooted in the architecture of the Heimat preservation movements, traditionalism and some sections of the reform movements which came into being around 1900. These movements were a reaction to industrialisation – which was seen as a cause of cultural decline – and its negative consequences, for example the proliferation of historicist forms and unwholesome tenement block developments.[20]

The planning and construction of the Landesschule was one of numerous large projects taken on by Kramer during the 1920s. As a man conscious of the need to integrate each of his designs into its respective urban landscape, he not only reacted in a professional manner to the dominance of Tessenow's plans, but also used the project to create some of the most modern constructions to grace his own oeuvre. He was also successful in asserting his own architectural ideas on building ornamentation – an element he saw as an important part of the identity of the complex. His previ-

Die Konzeption und der Bau der Landesschule waren in den 1920er Jahren eine von vielen großen Aufgaben Kramers. Da er seine Entwürfe in den jeweiligen städtebaulichen Charakter einzufügen verstand, reagierte er professionell auf den dominanten Tessenowschen Entwurf und schuf hier den modernsten Bau innerhalb seines eigenen Œuvres. Doch behauptete er seine Auffassung in der Verwendung von Gebäudeschmuck, der für ihn als Teil der Identität des Bauwerks ein wichtiges Anliegen war. Er hatte schon bei seinen vorangegangenen Arbeiten eng mit bildenden Künstlern zusammengearbeitet.[18] In der Landesschule interpretieren die figürlichen Reliefs den Schulalltag in antiker Manier und mit historischem Hintergrund. Die mit stilisierten Pflanzenmotiven verzierten Kapitelle im Lehrgebäude[19] sollten der Strenge des Baus entgegenwirken, die runden Deckenelemente im Foyer schwächten die schwere und geradlinige Struktur ab und der runde Brunnen im Innenhof des Lehrgebäudes sollte zur scharfen Kontur des Bauwerks vermitteln und der natürlichen Lebendigkeit des Hofes als Treffpunkt und Kommunikationsraum dienen.

Landgericht am Münchner Platz in Dresden, 1902 – 1907, Architekt Oskar Kramer, Foto 1921.
Regional court on the Münchner Platz in Dresden, built 1902-1907, architect Oskar Kramer, photo dated 1921.

ous work had already seen him collaborate closely with artists[21], and the figurative reliefs realised at the Landesschule interpreted everyday school life against a historical backdrop and in a classical style. The capitals in the teaching building were decorated with stylised plant motifs[22], and were designed to counteract the austerity of the building. The bezants on the ceiling of the foyer were intended to soften its heavy, straight-edged structure, whilst the round fountain on the inner courtyard of the teaching building was to both provide a mediative counterpoint to the sharp contours of the building and support the naturally lively character of the courtyard as an area of interpersonal contact and communication. The setting of door jambs with clearly protruding beading against broad, smooth door leaves created the type of delicate feature which engenders a sense of harmony within human beings. Kramer also used this door design in the house he built for himself in Langebrück in 1933.

Despite the fact that the career path followed by Tessenow (1876 – 1950) took him in an entirely different direction to Kramer, his architecture actually developed from highly similar roots. They were to be found in the craftsman's values of his father (a carpenter) and his training and initial teaching posts at various vocational schools, which included the Saaleck establishment run by Paul Schulze-Naumburg, a leading champion of reformist and Heimat-preserving architecture. This architectural style took its cues from the traditions of pre-industrial rustic and civic building in its various regional forms, which were documented in numerous books. Inspired by the simple architecture of his north German homeland, Tessenow went one step further and identified architectural "archetypes" arrived at by stripping away all superfluous and arbitrary elements to reveal a type of shared fundamental principle. To do so, he pared structures down to a few traditional elements such as basic geometric forms, simple cubic constructions with pitched or hipped roofs, roof dormers and plain, flat façades (often with symmetrical designs). In spite of this search for simplicity, his buildings are never boring, and often appear upmarket or even exclusive. This impression is created by

the clever proportioning of their structural components, the flatness of their façades (emphasised using windows which are flush with wall surfaces), well-balanced but intriguing ratios between windows and doors in façades and the hidden symmetries of his compositions. Tessenow enlivened these simple elements through the use of repetition: a group of houses aligned into a row of gables might feature wood siding, front steps, arbours vaulted by overhanging roofs, pergolas or trellises. The integration of these elements into his building designs illustrates how garden architecture and landscapes were incorporated into his work.[23]

Tessenow supported his designs by publishing what were in some cases successful theoretical essays on small houses, residential construction and the social design of a guild of craftsmen – an idea he attempted to develop further after the Second World War within the framework of the garden city project in Hellerau. It was there, as part of a model estate which reflected the architectural and social reform movements of the pre-war period, that he had designed Hellerau Festival Hall and both small and country houses. Even before the first shot had been fired in the First World War, the simple styling which characterised these buildings had already contributed to the eventual division and breakup of the garden city concept. The guild of craftsmen, which was designed to cure society through the means of "healthy, creative work" and community life, also failed due to its utopian nature and the difficult economic situation which prevailed during the post-war period. Individual houses and some groups of residential buildings remained unfinished. Though similar guilds of craftsmen existed at various locations around Germany at the start of the 1920s, the Bauhaus was the only to survive.[24] This illustrates just how similar the roots of the increasingly polarised architectural trends of the late 1920s actually were. The founder of the garden city of Hellerau, Karl Schmidt, had already combined artistic design with the industrial production of machine-made furniture and houses prior to the First World War, and though Tessenow himself lacked the euphoria of the technically-enthused supporters of the

Landesschüler vor dem Eingang zum Aulagebäude (links), im Hintergrund Schülerheim A, heute Haus 6.
Landesschule pupils in front of the entrance to the assembly hall building (left of shot), boarding house A (now building 6) to the rear of shot.

Die Türgewände mit deutlich hervortretenden Rundstäben im Gegensatz zum flächigen, glatten und undurchbrochenen Türblatt sind Beispiele für eine dem menschlichen Wesen harmonisch erscheinende Kleinteiligkeit. Die gleiche Türform setzte Kramer auch in seinem eigenen, 1933 erbauten Wohnhaus in Langebrück ein.

Heinrich Tessenow (1876–1950) ging einen ganz anderen Weg als Kramer, obwohl sich seine Architektur aus ganz ähnlichen Wurzeln entwickelte. Sie lagen in den handwerklichen Werten seines Zimmerervaters und seiner Ausbildung und ersten Lehrtätigkeiten an verschiedenen Gewerbeschulen u.a. bei Paul Schulze-Naumburg in Saaleck, einem wichtigen Protagonisten der Reform- und Heimatschutzarchitektur. Diese fand ihre Vorbilder in der vorindustriellen Tradition ländlichen und bürgerlichen Bauens und deren regional ausgeprägten Formen, die in zahlreichen Büchern publiziert wurden. Angeregt durch die schlichte Architektur seiner norddeutschen Heimat ging Tessenow noch einen Schritt weiter und suchte nach den »Urformen« der Architektur, die er aus dem Weglassen alles Überflüssigen und der Eliminierung alles Beliebigen als eine Art gemeinschaftliches Grundgesetz kristallisierte. Entsprechend reduzierte er die Vorbilder auf einige traditionelle Elemente: geometrische Grundformen, einfache kubische Baukörper mit Sattel- oder Walmdächern und Dachgauben sowie schmucklose, flächige Fassaden in oft symmetrischen Gestaltungen. Seine Bauten wirken trotzdem nie langweilig, sondern oft anspruchsvoll, ja sogar vornehm. Dieser Eindruck entsteht aus ausgeklügelten Proportionen der Bauteile, der durch mauerbündige Fenster betonten Flächigkeit der Fassaden, dem ausgewogenen, aber spannungsvollen Verhältnis der Fenster und Türen

New Objectivity movement, he certainly recognised the advantage of serial mass production: the true-to-design, cost-effective manufacture of simple forms. The harshness or lack of form which Theodor Fischer feared automated production would bring to modern architecture was a danger avoided by Tessenow thanks to his architectural "Bildungskraft", his feel for proportion and composition and, above all, his use of "finely nuanced irregularities".[25]

The simplicity and lack of any ornamentation which characterised Tessenow's forms saw them become a part of the New Objectivity movement, with Tessenow hailed as one of its pioneers. For his own part he felt a sense of attachment towards rational architecture, as is testified to by his membership of such progressive architects' associations as the "November Group" and "The Ring", his planned participation in the "Weißenhofsiedlung" project in Stuttgart and his close contact with Bruno Taut, Hans Poelzig and Ludwig Mies van der Rohe. The increasing polarisation of the architectural community and the severity of the disputes within it during the late 1920s led Tessenow to withdraw from the field of conflict. "Tessenow rejected revolutionary change. The inventorisation and critical examination of the existent and the possible must take place first. He was an advocate of the well-founded, continuous renewal of architecture – an advocate of evolution".[26] This spirit characterised his work with his master-class students at the Dresden Academy of Arts from 1920 onwards. Teacher-student relationships were friendly, and work was based on the monthly tasks which had been a key feature of his guild of craftsmen. Tasks followed "themes which were particularly close to his heart, for example the raising of children, and were supposed to identify new solutions in the field of school building."[27] These methods highlight Tessenow's interest in the fundamental contemplation of the structural form of human coexistence, a topic he also reflected upon in his writings. "In 'Handwerk und Kleinstadt' in particular he drew new educational inspiration from the national community home movement".[28] One of that movement's protagonists, Gustav Wyneken, had actually taken part in the planning of the guild of craftsmen in Hellerau during

zueinander und auf der Fassade sowie versteckten Symmetrien, die ihre Spannung aus kleinsten Feinheiten der Komposition erhielten. Er belebte diese kargen Elemente durch Wiederholungen wie in Giebelreihen angeordnete Häusergruppen, teils mit Verbretterungen, Vortreppen, von Dächern überwölbte Lauben, Pergolen und Spaliere, die die Einbeziehung der Gartenarchitektur und der Landschaft in seine Bauten zeigen.[20]

Tessenow untermauerte seine Entwürfe mittels theoretischer Erörterungen in teils erfolgreichen Veröffentlichungen über Kleinhäuser, Wohnungsbau und den gesellschaftlichen Entwurf einer Handwerkergemeinde, mit der er nach dem Zweiten Weltkrieg das Gartenstadtkonzept in Hellerau weiterzuentwickeln suchte. Hier, in einer Mustersiedlung der architektonischen und gesellschaftlichen Reformbewegungen der Vorkriegszeit, hatte er Klein- und Landhäuser und das Festspielhaus realisiert, deren Formreduzierung zur Spaltung und Auflösung der Gartenstadtkonzeption noch vor dem Ersten Weltkrieg beigetragen hatte. Auch die Handwerkergemeinde, die die Gesellschaft durch »gesunde, schaffende Arbeit« und gemeinschaftliches Leben kurieren wollte, scheiterte an ihrem utopischen Charakter und der schwierigen Wirtschaftslage nach Kriegsende. Einzelne Wohnhäuser und einige Wohnhausgruppen blieben Fragment. Ähnliche Handwerkergemeinden gab es Anfang der 1920er Jahre vielerorts in Deutschland, das Bauhaus war die einzige, die überlebte.[21] Dies verdeutlicht, wie ähnlich die Wurzeln der sich Ende der 1920er Jahre immer mehr polarisierenden Architekturströmungen waren. Wie vor dem Ersten Weltkrieg der Gründer der Gartenstadt Hellerau, Karl Schmidt, der künstlerische Entwürfe mit industrieller Produktion von Maschinenmöbeln und Häusern verband, sah auch der Handwerker Tessenow Vorteile in serieller Massenproduktion: die ehrliche und preiswerte Ausführung einfacher Formen, allerdings ohne die Euphorie der technikbegeisterten Vertreter des Neuen Bauens. Der Gefahr der Härte oder Formlosigkeit des Maschinendiktates, die Theodor Fischer an der modernen Architektur fürchtete, entging Tessenow durch die »Bildungskraft« des Architekten, durch seine Sensibi-

the summer of 1918.[29] The construction of the Landesschule was therefore a project for which Tessenow had been preparing himself for some time, and one which would, at least to some extent, perpetuate the community and educational ideals of his guild of craftsmen.

Let us once again seek the company of our Landesschule pupil, who has continued his route towards Tessenow's buildings and stepped into the sandstone-paved courtyard of the first boarding house. Each of the boarding houses was split along its longitudinal axis and designed to accommodate two "Kameradschaft" groups, their tutor-teachers and their families, who lived in the flat-roofed wing buildings. The courtyard was austere and bright, and offered access to the boarding house through a door in a simple façade. Inside the house a generously proportioned stairway provided both "pupil families" with direct access to the first floor. Having reached the top of the stairs, our pupil turned right into the long corridor which led to the staff room, living quarters and work spaces allocated to his "section". The last door in the corridor led to the shared common room, which featured a large, veranda-like extension offering views into adjacent gardens and woods through windows on three of its sides. Whereas living quarters in the three southern houses faced south, the respective areas of the northern houses faced north due to the axial symmetry of the two groups of buildings. Tessenow's decision to favour the design of the overall complex by not positioning living quarters according to the compass direction in which they faced went against modernist methods, which saw buildings developed on the basis of their intended layouts and usages according to the principle of "form follows function". He nevertheless avoided forcing function into form by taking the former into consideration when developing the latter. Basement levels were generally well usable due to the buildings' hillside location, and accommodated workshops and storage rooms, elders' rooms, bathrooms and laundry and shoe-cleaning rooms. Our guide and ten of his fellow pupils shared a first-floor room provided with daylight through a traditional slated window oriel. Two doors – one next to the wardrobe room, one on the ground floor – controlled access

lität für das richtige Maß und die Anordnung der Elemente und vor allem kleine Störungen der Ordnung, »fein nuancierte Unregelmäßigkeiten«.[22]

Das Fehlen jeglicher Ornamentik und die Einfachheit der Formen in Tessenows Bauten bewirkten, dass sie als Teil des Neuen Bauens und Tessenow als einer seiner Vorreiter angesehen wurden. Auch er fühlte sich der rationalen Architektur verbunden, wie seine Mitgliedschaft in progressiven Architektenvereinigungen wie »Novembergruppe« und »Der Ring«, seine geplante Beteiligung an der »Weißenhofsiedlung« Stuttgart und sein enger Kontakt zu Bruno Taut, Hans Poelzig und Ludwig Mies van der Rohe zeigen. Die zunehmende Polarisierung der Architektenschaft und die Härte ihrer Auseinandersetzungen am Ende der 1920er Jahre führten zu Tessenows Rückzug aus diesem Spannungsfeld. »Tessenow lehnte revolutionäre Veränderungen ab. Zunächst muß eine Bestandsaufnahme mit kritischer Sichtung des Vorhandenen und des Möglichen geschaffen werden. Er war für eine fundierte, kontinuierliche Erneuerung der Architektur – für Evolution«.[23] In diesem Sinne arbeitete er mit seinen Meisterschülern ab 1920 an der Dresdner Kunstakademie in einem freundschaftlichen Lehrer-Schüler-Verhältnis nach dem Ideal seiner Handwerkergemeinde an Monatsaufgaben, deren »Themen ihm besonders am Herzen lagen, zum Beispiel zur Erziehung der Kinder, um neue Lösungen im Schulbau zu finden.«[24] Dabei ging es ihm um grundsätzliche Überlegungen über die bauliche Form menschlichen Zusammenlebens, die er auch in seinen Schriften theoretisch reflektierte: »Vor allem in ›Handwerk und Kleinstadt‹ griff er neue pädagogische Impulse der Landerziehungsheimbewegung auf«[25], deren Protagonist Gustav Wyneken im Sommer 1918 an der Planung zur Handwerkergemeinde in Hellerau teilgenommen hatte.[26] So war ihm der Bau der Landesschule ein lange vorbereitetes Anliegen, welches die Gemeinschafts- und Erziehungsideale der Handwerkergemeinde wenigstens ansatzweise weiterführen sollte.

Suchen wir erneut die Gesellschaft des Landesschülers, der seinen Weg zu Tessenows Bauten fortsetzte und in den mit Sandsteinplatten belegten Hof des ersten Schüler-

to the two-storey teacher's apartments, which were positioned in a way which ensured that tutors and pupils lived at close quarters. It is not possible to make an assessment here on whether the intended family-like closeness was achieved, or whether the hierarchical monitoring structures of the old cadet school continued to dominate. Taking country boarding schools as its reference point, the "family structure" had certainly spread during the 1920s, and, to a minor extent, was influencing the architecture of other new school complexes. One example of this influence can be seen in the layouts of the nursing school built by Paul Wolf, the then head of the Municipal Planning and Building Control Authority, on the grounds of the Johannstadt Hospital in Dresden towards the end of the 1920s.

Our Landesschule pupil left his boarding house at supper time. To his right, a roof-height, half-open pergola opened out towards the assembly hall building. His view left passed through its generously spaced pillars, which crossed the entire lawned courtyard. The right-hand side of the pergola was closed off by a latticed trellis fence which blocked the line of sight into the private gardens kept by both teachers and pupils. The "all-embracing green" which was not only to both "cover the pergolas and buildings" and develop into a thick roof which served the "practical purpose of protection from the sun"[30], but would also change the current aesthetically arranged view, had not yet grown into place. Though the pupils would sometimes have welcomed the chance to shelter under them, the pergolas had not been designed as a form of protection from the rain – as was illustrated by their height and lack of a direct point of contact with the school. On the contrary, and according to the same principle as the garden arbours which were never realised at the site due to a lack of resources, the pergolas were to act as meeting places on the boundary between inside and outside areas and as links between public and private spaces. The artistic effect of the pergolas as connecting elements was of even more importance to Tessenow. It was for this reason that he not only used them for this important urbanistic function in the courtyard area, but also applied them as a design feature at regular grid

heimes trat. Jedes war – in der Längsachse geteilt – für zwei »Kameradschaften« mit ihren Erzieher-Lehrern und deren Familien gedacht, die in den flachgedeckten Flügelbauten wohnten. Der Hof war nüchtern und hell, vor ihm die Tür zum Schülerheim in einer schlichten Fassade. Im Haus führte eine großzügige Treppe für beide »Schülerfamilien« gerade ins Obergeschoss. Der Landesschüler wandte sich zunächst nach links, wo vom langen Flur das Lehrerzimmer und die Wohn- und Arbeitsräume seiner »Abteilung« zu erreichen waren. Die letzte Tür führte in den gemeinsamen Gesellschaftsraum, dessen verandaartiger großer Anbau mit drei Fensterseiten Blicke auf die benachbarten Gärten und in den Wald erlaubten. In den drei südlichen Heimen waren die Wohnräume nach Süden ausgerichtet, während sie in den nördlichen wegen der axialsymmetrischen Spiegelung der Bauten nach Norden wiesen. Tessenow hatte die Ausrichtung der Räume nach der Himmelsrichtung zu Gunsten der Gestaltung der Gesamtanlage zurückgesetzt – ein Unterschied zur Moderne, die die Bauten entsprechend dem Leitgedanken »form follows function« aus den Grundrissen entwickelte. Trotzdem zwang Tessenow die Funktion nicht in die Form, sondern dachte sie bei der Formentwicklung mit. Im Untergeschoss, das wegen der Hanglage gut nutzbar war, gab es Bastel- und Abstellräume, Ältestenzimmer, Kleider- und Schuhputzräume und Bäder. Im Obergeschoss teilte sich der Landesschüler mit zehn Mitschülern einen Schlafraum, dessen Licht durch einen traditionell verschieferten Fenstererker fiel. Neben dem Schrankraum lag wie im Erdgeschoss ein Zugang zur zweistöckigen Lehrerwohnung, damit Erzieher und Schüler in einem engen Verhältnis zusammenleben konnten. Ob dabei die postulierte familiäre Vertrautheit erreicht wurde oder noch hierarchische Überwachungsstrukturen der alten Kadettenanstalt dominierten, kann hier nicht beurteilt werden. Die »Familienstruktur« hatte sich – ausgehend von den Landschulheimen – in den 1920er Jahren verbreitet und bestimmte auch die Architektur anderer Neubauten, wenn auch in geringerem Maße, beispielsweise die Grundrisse der Ende der 1920er Jahre errichteten Schwesternschule im damaligen Johannstädter Krankenhaus in Dresden von Stadtbaurat Paul Wolf.

Waschraum in einem Schülerheim der Landesschule Dresden.
Washroom in a boarding house at the Landesschule Dresden.

intervals around all low boarding house sections and the assembly hall building. He reduced them to a type of cornice and a pilaster-like wall protrusion, brought them forward to form porch-like structures on some corners and positioned them all the way around the oriel-like wings on the outer edges of the boarding houses. These usages had no specific purpose, and represented a further deviation from the maxims of modern construction. Though Tessenow's master plan also foresaw the use of these pergolas at the classroom building, Kramer reduced them to pillars set back into the

Zur Abendbrotzeit verließ der Landesschüler das Haus. Nach rechts öffnete sich die Pergola vor ihm als dachhoher, halboffener Raum bis zu den Türen des Aulagebäudes. Nach links ging der Blick durch die weit auseinanderstehenden Stützen über den gesamten Rasenhof, nach rechts verschloss ein Lattengitter in der gesamten Höhe bis zur Dachkante den Blick auf die privaten Gärten der Lehrer und Schüler. Noch fehlte »das alles verbindende Grün, das Pergola und Gebäude überranken« und »zum praktischen Zweck als Sonnenschutz« zu einem dichten Dach wachsen sollte[27] und den jetzigen, ästhetisch gliedernden Anblick verändern würde. Obwohl sich die Schüler das vielleicht manchmal gewünscht hätten, war die Pergola nie als Regenschutz gedacht, wie ihre Höhe und die fehlende Verbindung zur Schule zeigten, vielmehr diente sie ebenso wie die aus Kostengründen nicht ausgeführten Gartenlauben

Lehrerwohnflügel mit Garten und Pergola.
Teachers' accommodation wing feat. garden and pergolas.

wall line. Despite being an indication of their shared will to achieve uniformity across the entire complex, the pergola motif also highlighted the differences between the ideas of the two architects. What Tessenow saw as "an overheight decorative feature which is wonderful in its unification of structural volumes but has outgrown man himself" was described by Kramer as "a thoroughly usable pergola adapted to be true to human scale".[31]

From his first designs onwards, Tessenow consistently returned to the image of rural middle-class houses with loggias or garden arbours. They not only featured in his designs for detached houses, but were also used by him as an urbanistic means of grouping a number of houses on an estate together. The boardhouses around Hellerau Festival Hall are just one example of this. He came upon the intensified monumental form demonstrated by the Landesschule at the 1925 and 1926 annual shows in Dresden, where the tall, slim pergolas of two exhibition structures served as "actual size models"[32]. Tessenow also built a glass-covered version for his highly acclaimed exhibition rooms at the 1926 International Art Exhibition in Dresden. The architecture of the period also featured a wide variety of pergolas, some of which harked back to the covered walkways of 19th-century spa buildings – a trend reflected in Hans Poelzig's pergolas at the 1913 Centennial Exhibition in Breslau, Paul Wolf's urban grouping of individual buildings built at what is now Dresden's Neustadt Hospital from 1928 onwards and the pergolas designed by Oskar Kramer for the Bad Elster spa complex in 1933/34. The monumentality of the motif was further intensified after the Second World War, for example in the student halls of residence built in Chieti by Giorgio Grassi and Antonio Monestiroli during the second half of the 1970s – a major work in Italian

als Aufenthaltsraum auf der Grenze zwischen drinnen und draußen, als Verbindung vom öffentlichem zum privaten Raum. Noch wichtiger war Tessenow die künstlerische Wirkung des Laubenganges als verbindendes Element. Deshalb benutzte er sie nicht nur für die wichtige städtebauliche Funktion im Hofbereich, sondern zog sie als gestalterisches Element in regelmäßigen Rasterabständen um alle Flachbauteile der Schülerheime und des Aulagebäudes herum. Völlig zweckfrei – ein weiterer Unterschied zum Modernen Bauen – reduzierte er sie auf eine Art Gesims und einen lisenenartigen Wandvorsatz, zog sie an einigen Ecken laubenartig vor und ummantelte mit ihr auch die erkerartigen Anbauten auf den Außenseiten der Schülerheime. Auf seinem Gesamtplan hatte er die Pergola auch für das Lehrge-

rationalist architecture.[33] Tessenow's Landesschule pergolas were nevertheless an expensive artistic measure. They not only made a significant contribution to initial construction costs, but were also extremely expensive to maintain in the years that followed.[34] It is therefore unsurprising that some sections of the pergolas were dismantled in 1941/42 as a result of war-related reprioritisation.[35]

Having reached the end of the pergola, our Landesschule pupil now entered the wing of the assembly hall building. The small stairway on the right-hand side of the foyer led up to the infirmary and the medical orderly's quarters, and was laid with stones which retreated or stood out from its surface in a fascinatingly abstract pattern. The pattern also extended up the walls of the stairway. The left-hand stairway

bäude vorgesehen, wo Kramer sie als Stützen reduziert in die Mauerflucht zurücksetzte. Das Pergolamotiv, das vom gemeinsamen Willen zur Einheitlichkeit der Gesamtanlage zeugte, verdeutlicht die Unterschiede in der Auffassung der beiden Architekten: bei Tessenow als »überhohe, die Baumassen wundervoll zusammenziehende, aber dem Menschen entwachsene dekorative Anlage«, bei Kramer als »dem Menschen maßstäblich angepaßter, wirklich nutzbarer Laubengang«.[28]

Tessenow hatte die ländlich bürgerlichen Vorbilder von Laubenhäusern oder Gartenlauben schon seit seinen ersten Entwürfen verarbeitet, nicht nur bei Einzelhäusern, sondern auch als städtebauliches Mittel zur Zusammenfassung mehrerer Siedlungshäuser oder der Pensionshäuser, die das Festspielhaus in Hellerau umgeben. Die monumental gesteigerte Form in der Landesschule fand er Mitte der 1920er Jahre, als ihm die hohen schlanken Pergolen zweier Ausstellungsbauten auf den Jahresschauen in Dresden 1925 und 1926 als »Modelle in natürlicher Größe«[29] dienten. Gleichzeitig baute er eine glasüberdachte Variante in seinen viel gelobten Ausstellungsräumen der Internationalen Kunstausstellung 1926 in Dresden. Auch in der zeitgenössischen Architektur erschienen vielfältige, teilweise an die Wandelgänge von Kurbauten des 19. Jahrhunderts erinnernde Pergolen, beispielsweise Hans Poelzigs Pergolen der Jahrhundertausstellung in Breslau 1913, Paul Wolfs ab 1928 gebaute städtebauliche Zusammenfassung von Einzelgebäuden im heutigen Neustädter Krankenhaus oder Kramers Kurgelände in Bad Elster von 1933/34. Eine weitere Steigerung der Monumentalität erlebte das Motiv nach dem Zweiten Weltkrieg, beispielsweise in einem Hauptwerk des Rationalen Bauens in Italien, dem Studentenwohnheim von Giorgio Grassi und Antonio Monestiroli in Chieti aus der zweiten Hälfte der 1970er Jahre.[30] Allerdings war Tessenows Pergola in der Landesschule ein teures künstlerisches Mittel. Sie trug ganz erheblich zu den Baukosten bei und ihre Unterhaltung in den Folgejahren war sehr aufwendig.[31] So ist es nicht verwunderlich, dass die Pergolen 1941/42 während kriegsbedingter Prioritätenverschiebungen zumindest teilweise abgebaut wurden.[32]

Blick aus dem Hof des Schülerheimes A (heute Haus 6) über den Rasenhof, rechts die Aulafassade, gegenüber Schülerheim B (heute Haus 7). View across the lawned courtyard from the boarding house A (now building 6) courtyard, assembly hall building façade to the right of shot, boarding house B (now building 7) opposite.

with its copper guardrails led up to the large banqueting hall, which featured a stage, organ and film projector and was used for large school celebrations and performances. Smaller concerts and lectures were held in additional music rooms and the lecture room with slide projector directly adjacent to the hall. The foyer's middle door would have taken the pupil into the dining hall, where the school's "families" would have been eating together at twelve large tables. Windows were located in niches behind two rows of slim pillars on both sides of the elongated hall, and created a lively mix of light and shadow. Food for the Landesschule pupils was prepared in the north wing of the assembly hall building, which also housed living quarters for the kitchen staff. Storerooms and the laundry rooms where pupils'

Am Ende der Pergola betrat der Landesschüler den Seitenflügel des Aulagebäudes. In der Foyerhalle führte rechts eine kleine Treppe zur Krankenstation und zur Wohnung des Krankenwärters, die mit einem faszinierenden abstrakten Muster aus leicht vor- und rückspringenden Steinen, das sich an der Wand fortsetzte, verkleidet war. Links führte die große Treppe mit Messinggeländer zum großen Festsaal, der – mit Bühne, Orgel und Filmprojektor versehen – für große Schulfeste und Aufführungen zur Verfügung stand. Für kleinere Konzerte und Vorträge gab es weitere Musikräume und den Vortragssaal mit Lichtbildapparat gleich neben der Halle. Wählte der Landesschüler die mittlere Tür, betrat er den Speisesaal, in dem die Schülerfamilien an zwölf großen Tafeln zusammen aßen. Hinter zwei Reihen aus schlanken Stützen lagen die Fenster zu beiden Seiten des langgestreckten Saales in Nischen und sorgten für ein lebhaftes Spiel aus Licht und Schatten. Das Essen für die Landesschüler wurde im nördlichen Seitenflügel des Aulagebäudes zubereitet, wo das Küchenpersonal auch seine Wohnräume hatte. Ihre Wäsche wurde im Untergeschoss unter dem Speisesaal gewaschen, wo sich auch die Vorratsräume befanden. Der Landesschüler und seine Kameraden waren gut versorgt.

Allerdings war auch im Herbst 1927, zur Zeit der festlichen Einweihung der Landesschule, noch vieles unvollendet. Details wie der runde Brunnen und die Sonnenuhr am Kraftwerksschornstein im Innenhof des Lehrgebäudes wurden bald ergänzt, anderes wie die festliche Ausstattung von Musikzimmer und Festsaal entfielen aus Kostengründen völlig.[33] Mit über fünf Millionen Mark Gesamtkosten war der Bau der wohl teuerste Schulneubau im Dresden der Weimarer Republik.[34] Leider zeigten sich schon im ersten kalten Winter bauliche Unzulänglichkeiten wie der fehler-

clothes and bedclothes were washed were situated underneath the dining hall. Our Landesschule pupil and his "comrades" were certainly well looked after.

This notwithstanding, the Landesschule was still incomplete in many areas on the occasion of its festive opening celebrations in the autumn of 1927. Though some features were added soon afterwards (for example the round fountain and the sun dial on the power station chimney in the inner courtyard of the classroom building), others were dropped entirely as a result of their cost. This included the lavish quipment planned for the music room and the banqueting hall.[36] Despite the fact that construction costs of over five million marks undoubtedly made the project the most expensive construction of a new school in Dresden under the Weimar Republic[37], the first cold winter at the complex unfortunately highlighted structural inadequacies including the ineffective drainage of water away from flat roof surfaces (which led to water damage). Tessenow's prioritisation of aesthetics over practical demands was criticised as the cause of such inadequacies.[38]

The architecture of the Landesschule was nevertheless enthusiastically received, and featured in numerous publications. Though the daily press reacted positively, it was also taken aback: "one feels somewhat wondrous, as if one were North African"[39]. Architectural journals rhapsodised about a "[construction] which corresponds with the most modern in pedagogical, hygienic and architectural standards, and has a wonderfully educational effect on the intellect and disposition of the pupil".[40] This success attracted a large number of experts and students of educational theory and architecture to the school, all of them eager to see the new complex for themselves. The Landesschule made significant contributions to not only the shift from barrack-style school complexes to a looser, more dynamic type of development with internal functional and routing axes, but also to the creation of a new architectural concept with which Wyneken's idea of a friendly communal life could be realised. Together with Hellerau Festival Hall and five other large-scale school and community facilities designed for sites in Kassel and Berlin between 1925 and 1931, the Landesschule ranks amongst Tessenow's greatest achievements[41]. His renown as an architect saw him called upon on a more and more frequent basis to act as a judge and expert in issues of school construction. Tessenow's use of form remains without equal to this day: "No-one else stands so naturally between tradition and the urge to innovate, between past and future".[42] Using the most economical of means, he was able to achieve a quiet monumentality which made "the near-shabby [appear] elegant and almost precious".[43] In the case of the Landesschule, his slender pergola supports combined with the existing inventory of birch and pine trees to create "the formal leitmotif for an exquisitely formalistic work of architecture"[44].

Schüleraufführung im Festsaal.
Pupil performance in the banqueting hall.

hafte Wasserabfluss der Flachdächer, der zu Wasserschäden führte. Als Ursache wurde Tessenows Priorität der Ästhetik vor praktischen Anforderungen kritisiert.[35]

Trotzdem wurde die Architektur der Landesschule enthusiastisch und zahlreich publiziert. Die Tagespresse war positiv, aber auch etwas befremdet, »man fühlt sich etwas wunderlich, nordafrikanisch angemutet«[36]. Die Architekturfachzeitschriften schwärmten von einem »den modernsten pädagogischen, hygienischen und architektonischen Forderungen gerecht werdenden [Bau], der auf Verstand und Gemüt des Schülers wundervoll erzieherisch« wirke.[37] Aufgrund dieses Erfolges besichtigten zahlreiche Fachleute und Studenten der Pädagogik und der Architektur den Neubau. Er war ein wichtiger Beitrag zur Entwicklung des Schulbaus von der Kasernenform zur einer aufgelockerten dynamischen Bebauung mit internen Funktions- und Wegachsen und einer neuen architektonischen Konzeption für die Umsetzung des kameradschaftlichen Gemeinschaftslebens nach Wyneken. Zusammen mit dem Hellerauer Fest-

Development

Fortune sadly did not smile upon the Landesschule. Its initial transformation into a State National Political Educational Institution[45] under National Socialism only led to a limited number of minor structural amendments, for example the addition of a shooting range behind the gymnasium in 1933, the relocation of the infirmary to the ground floor of one of the boarding houses in 1942 and the creation of seven cover trenches around the site in 1943.[46] The latter measure was carried out as an alternative to the cost-intensive conversion of boarding house basements into air-raid shelters. Despite having been timetabled for 1938, plans for the construction of three additional buildings in the woods between the road and the school according to a Tessenow-designed layout never came to fruition. The same fate befell roof conversions which were to accommodate pupils from abandoned elite schools from as late as early 1945 onwards.[47] The site remained entirely free of war damage, and was occupied by Soviet troops in May 1945. Though the school returned to German administration for a brief period during the summer months, the Mayor of Klotzsche (who had assumed responsibility for it) had no means of preventing the devastation exacted upon it by occupying soldiers, with furniture particularly badly affected.[48] Short-

spielhaus und fünf weiteren großen Schul- und Gemeinschaftsanlagen, die Tessenow zwischen 1925 und 1931 für Kassel und Berlin entwarf, gehört die Landesschule zu Tessenows größten Leistungen[38]. Der Architekt wurde zunehmend als Preisrichter und Sachverständiger für Schulbaufragen herangezogen. Tessenows Formensprache sucht bis heute ihresgleichen: »Keiner steht so natürlich da zwischen Überlieferung und Neuerungsdrang, zwischen Vergangenheit und Zukunft«[39]. Mit sparsamsten Mitteln erreichte er eine stille Monumentalität, die »das fast Ärmliche vornehm und beinahe kostbar«[40] erscheinen ließ. In der Landesschule bildeten seine schlanken Pergolapfeiler zusammen »mit den erhaltenen Birken und Kiefern das formale Leitmotiv eines erlesen formalistischen Architekturwerkes«[41].

Die Entwicklung

Leider war der Landesschule kein günstiges Schicksal beschieden. Zunächst erlebten die Gebäude während der Naziherrschaft als nationalpolitische Erziehungsanstalt nur geringfügige bauliche Veränderungen wie die Errichtung eines Schießstandes hinter der Turnhalle 1933, die Verlegung der Krankenstation in das Erdgeschoss eines Schülerheimes 1942 und 1943 die Anlage von sieben Deckungsgräben im Gelände statt des kostspieligen Ausbaus der Wohnheimkeller zu Luftschutzräumen.[42] Die 1938 im Wald zwischen Straße und Schule geplanten drei Erweiterungsbauten nach Tessenowschem Grundriss wurden ebenso wenig ausgeführt wie die Dachausbauten, die noch Anfang 1945 zur Unterbringung von Eliteschülern aus aufgegebenen Schulen geschehen sollten.[43] Das gesamte Gelände blieb von Kriegsschäden verschont. Im Mai 1945 wurde es von der sowjetischen Militäradministration konfisziert. In den Sommermonaten gelangte es kurzzeitig wieder unter deutsche Verwaltung, der zuständige Klotzscher Bürgermeister hatte aber keinerlei Handhabe gegen die von den Soldaten angestellten Verwüstungen vor allem des Mobiliars.[44] Kurz darauf erfolgte die erneute russische Besatzung und das Gelände wurde für die folgenden 47 Jahre hermetisch abgeriegelt. Erst nach dem Abzug der GUS-Truppen 1992 offenbarte sich der Bauzustand der Anlage: Das Aulagebäude, drei Wohnheime und die Turnhalle waren wahrscheinlich in den 1960er Jahren abgetragen worden.[45] Die noch vorhandenen drei Wohnhäuser, die Rektorhäuser und das Lehrgebäude waren in schlechtem baulichem Zustand. Im umgebenden Wald waren mehrere fünfstöckige Plattenbaublocks entstanden. Am Lehrgebäude waren durchaus Erhaltungsversuche unternommen worden, wohl aber hatten nicht nur die nötigen Mittel sondern auch das Interesse an der Gebäudepflege gefehlt.

Nach der Öffnung der Anlage konzentrierte sich das denkmalpflegerische Konzept sowohl auf den städtebaulichen Aspekt als auch auf die Bewahrung der Originalsubstanz. So konnte das Lehrgebäude vollständig und in seiner Ursprünglichkeit wieder hergerichtet werden. Viel schwieriger war der Erhalt der drei ehemaligen Schülerheime, die bis auf die Außenmauern der beiden äußeren südlichen Häuser ebenso wie die Rektorhäuser abgerissen wurden. Die Kompromissfähigkeit der Beteiligten führte dazu, dass das städtebauliche Grundkonzept wiederbelebt und eine den Zusammenhang herstellende Pergola errichtet wurde, die – anders als die Tessenows – eine klare Regenschutzfunktion aufweist. Der Neubau an Stelle des Aulagebäudes wurde mit einem Café zum Rasenplatz geöffnet. Der dahinter liegende Hotelneubau ist Teil des notwendigen Betreiberkonzeptes und vermittelt in seiner Größe zu den benachbarten Fabrikbauten. Das Pförtnerhaus wurde 2002 wegen des Ausbaus der Königsbrücker Straße abgerissen. So finden wir heute eine in ihrer Grundstruktur zum Teil erhaltene Anlage, die mit ihrer hervorragenden Aufenthaltsqualität an das historische Vorbild anknüpft. Die faszinierende Eleganz von Heinrich Tessenows Formensprache ist nicht mehr zu erleben, aber Oskar Kramers Schulgebäude strahlt den ursprünglichen Charakter aus. Das wiedergekehrte öffentliche Leben im Rahmen einer Akademie der Deutschen Gesetzlichen Unfallversicherung ist eine schöne Reminiszenz an den ursprünglichen Zweck – und das nach jahrzehntelanger Unterbrechung.

Innenhof des Lehrgebäudes mit Brunnen und Sonnenuhr. Inner courtyard next at the classroom building feat. fountain and sundial.

ly thereafter the site was re-occupied by the Russians and hermetically sealed for the following 47 years. It was only after the withdrawal of CIS troops in 1992 that the structural condition of the complex was revealed: the assembly hall building, three boarding houses and the gymnasium had all been pulled down, presumably during the 1960s.[49] The remaining three boarding houses, the headmasters' buildings and the classroom building were in a poor state of repair, and a number of five-storey prefabricated blocks had been erected in the surrounding woods. Though attempts had undoubtedly been made to maintain the classroom building, it was apparent that its occupiers had lacked both the necessary resources and an interest in building preservation.

The monument protection concept drawn up after the reopening of the complex focussed on both urban planning aspects and the preservation of the original building fabric. This resulted in the restoration of the entire classroom building to its original form. The preservation of the three

remaining boarding houses and the headmasters' buildings proved more difficult, as all that remained of them were the outer walls of the two southern boarding houses. The ability to compromise exhibited by the parties involved in the regeneration of the site facilitated the return of the original urban planning concept and the erection of a communicating pergola which, unlike the Tessenow version, is designed to perform a weather protection function. The new construction on the site of the assembly hall building features a café which faces onto the lawned courtyard. The large new hotel it stands in front of is a prerequisite of the operator concept, and performs a mediative role between the complex and neighbouring factory buildings. The porter's lodge was demolished in 2002 as part of the widening of the Königsbrücker Straße. What now exists at the site is essentially a partially preserved complex which maintains the atmosphere of its historical model by ensuring outstanding experiential quality. Though the fascinating elegance of Heinrich Tessenow's architectural language is no longer in evidence, Oskar Kramer's classroom building still exudes its original character. The return of public life to the site in the form of an academy specialising in occupational safety and health is a welcome reminder of its original purpose – especially after an intermission which spanned a number of decades.

Anmerkungen

1 Fischer 1927, S. 12.
2 Die Deutung ist eine Vermutung, sehr ausführlich dazu Rother 2001.
3 Vgl. Rother 2001.
4 Conert 1929, S. 98.
5 Hübner-Grötzsch/Hübner 2009, S. 36 – 43.
6 Kramer 1927, S. 817.
7 Genauer siehe Rother 2001, S. 22 f.
8 Nach dem »Anschlag« des Volksbildungsministeriums durch Dr. Kramer für 3 115 000 M erhofften sich der Dresdner Oberbürgermeister Blüher und die sächsischen Minister Dr. Kaiser, Dr. Reinhold und Ministerialdirektor Dr. Woelcker von einem neuen »Anschlag« des Kultusministeriums durch Prof. Tessenow eine Kostenverminderung auf 2,5 Millionen Mark. Vgl. StA 2.3.1.
9 Die Vorlage vom 19. 5. 1925 wurde nach Reduzierung des Vollkrankenhauses in eine Krankenstation im Wirtschaftsgebäude und der Anzahl der Wohnheime von 8 auf 6 bei Erhöhung der Schülerzahl von 15 auf 20 pro Lehrer, dem Abbau von Beamtenpersonal sowie der Vergrößerung der Turnhalle am 29. 5. 1925 einstimmig beschlossen. Vgl. SHD 1306.
10 Stadtbaudirektor Herbert Conert und Regierungsbaurat Thomas, der Leiter des Neubauamtes, schreiben beide, dass die Grundgedanken der Planung der Hochbaudirektion unter Leitung Ministerialrat Dr. Kramers für die gemeinsame Planung Kramers und Tessenows »maßgebend« blieben. Vgl. Conert 1929, S. 98 und Fischer 1927, S. 30.
11 Tessenow legte mehr Wert auf den Zusammenhalt der Gesamtanlage und ihre Symmetrie. Kramer betonte in der Ausführungsplanung eher die Einzelgebäude, gab dem Unterrichtsgebäude eine kleinteiligere Struktur, reduzierte dessen Pergolen und fügte einen zusätzlichen Flügel im Südosten an. »Dass Tessenow die ›künstlerische Leitung‹ übernommen hat und Oskar Kramer sich gekonnt einfügt, legen die fertig erstellte Schulanlage [und] anerkannte eigene Bauten des Ministerialrates nahe.«: Boesch 1997, S. 76 f.
12 Conert 1929, S. 103.
13 Kramer 1927, S. 817 – 828 und Tessenow 1986, (1. Aufl. 1916). Der teilweise nicht ausgeführte Plan erschien auch bei Schmidt 1928, S. 21 und bei Behrendt 1927, S. 668, auf dessen Exemplar der Sächsischen Landesbibliothek Kramer eine Randnotiz zur Nichtausführung hinterließ.
14 Kramer 1927, S. 824.
15 Hübner/Grötzsch/Klatte 2005, S. 15.
16 Kramer 1914.
17 Hübner-Grötzsch/Hübner 2008, S. 135 f.
18 Beispiele siehe Rother 2001, S. 14.
19 Wolfgang Rother erörtert den Gebäudeschmuck sehr ausführlich. Vgl. Rother 2001, S. 3 – 24.
20 Hofer 2005, S. 54.
21 Wangerin/Weiss 1976, S. 37.
22 De Michelis 1991, S. 107.
23 Konrad Wachsmann in: Grüning 1986, S. 123.
24 Wangerin/Weiss 1976, S. 17. Die Schülerentwürfe sind dabei sehr an Tessenows Formensprache orientiert und zeigen mit axialsymmetrischen, einheitlichen Anlagen, die die Umgebung einbeziehen, Ähnlichkeiten zur späteren Landesschule.
25 Wangerin/Weiss 1976, S. 40.
26 Wangerin/Weiss 1976, S. 36 und S. 38.
27 Conert 1929, S. 104.
28 Ebd.
29 Boesch 1997, S. 77.
30 Vgl. Lampugnani 1998, S. 305.
31 Vgl. Conert 1929, S. 104.
32 In der Baumittelbedarfsnachweisung für das Rechnungsjahr 1941 vom 26. 6. 1941 wird die Beseitigung der Pergolen zur Verhütung von Unfällen und zur Herabsetzung des Bauunterhaltungsaufwandes mit der Begründung empfohlen, die »im überreichen Maße errichteten hölzernen Pergolen haben durch eigene rasche Verwitterung und durch Begünstigung der Gebäudedurchfeuchtung ständig erhebliche Unterhaltungskosten ausgelöst«. SHD 496.
33 Fischer 1929, S. 9 f.
34 Amlung 2000.
35 Conert 1929, S. 104; Fischer 1929, S. 10.
36 DN 332, S. 7.
37 Conert 1929, S. 98.
38 Vgl. Rother 2001, S. 6
39 Scheffler 1928, S. 44 und 46.
40 Karl Scheffler, zitiert nach De Michelis 1991, S. 100.
41 Lampugnani 1991, S. 21.
42 Zur Verlegung der Krankenstation vgl. SHD 496; umfangreiche Korrespondenz über Luftschutzkeller und Deckungsgräben vgl. SHD 640.
43 Erweiterungsplan in einer Eingabe des Anstaltsleiters Dr. Barth vom 3. 9. 1937, Ablehnung vom Frühjahr 1938, vgl. SHD 21352; Dachausbauten vgl. SHD 640.
44 Treuhänderische Verwaltung durch den Klotzscher Bürgermeister ab 3. 7. 1945, Rettungsaktionen in den wenigen besatzungsfreien Wochen beschränkten sich auf die Auslagerung von Schulmaterialien und Musikinstrumenten und kleinere Reparaturen an den Gebäuden. Vgl. StA 8.20.
45 Heimlich in das Gelände eingedrungene ehemalige Schüler stellten fest, dass Mitte der 1950er Jahre die Gebäude mit der Pergola noch vorhanden waren, 1967 fehlten sie, die übrigen waren mit russischem Einheitsgrau gestrichen und ihr Dachschiefer durch Wellplatten aus Asbestzement ersetzt. Boesch 1997, S. 78. Ein Schülerhaus war noch in den 1980er Jahren als Ruine erhalten.

Notes

1 The Landesschule Dresden was a boarding establishment which featured both a progressive grammar school and an upper secondary school.

2 Fischer 1927, p. 12.

3 Full name "Königlich-Sächsisches Kadettenkorps", English translation "Royal Saxon Cadet Corps".

4 This interpretation is a supposition; this issue is dealt with in great detail in Rother 2001.

5 See Rother 2001.

6 Conert 1929, p. 98.

7 Literally the „forest school at the fish house", the school was built on Dresden Heath in 1923.

8 Hübner-Grötzsch / Hübner 2009, p. 36–43.

9 Kramer 1927, p. 817.

10 For more precise details see Rother, 2001, p. 22 f.

11 With the estimate submitted by Dr. Kramer (acting on behalf of the Ministry of Popular Education) having totalled 3,115,000 marks, Dresden's Mayor Blüher, Saxon ministers Dr. Kaiser and Dr. Reinhold and department head Dr. Woelcker were hoping that the estimate submitted by Prof. Tessenow would reduce costs to 2,500,000 marks. See StA 2.3.1.

12 The bill of the 19. 5. 1925 was passed unanimously on the 29. 5. 1925 further to the reduction of the full-service hospital to an infirmary in the management building, a decrease in the number of boarding houses from 8 to 6 and corresponding increase in the pupil:teacher ratio from 15 to 20 pupils per teacher, cutbacks in the number of official staff and the enlargement of the gymnasium. See SHD 1306.

13 Both Herbert Conert, head of the Municipal Planning and Building Control Authority, and government planning department surveyor Thomas (the head of the new construction board), wrote that the basic principles behind the plans drawn up by the board of construction under the leadership of Undersecretary Dr. Kramer remained "definitive" as far as the joint plans drawn up by Kramer and Tessenow were concerned. See Conert, 1929, p. 98 and Fischer, 1927, p. 30.

14 Tessenow attached greater importance to the cohesion and symmetry of the overall complex. Kramer tended to emphasise individual buildings in implementation plans, introduced more detail into the classroom building, reduced its pergolas and added an additional wing to the southeast. "Tessenow's responsibility for the 'artistic leadership' of the project and the skilful contribution of Oskar Kramer are demonstrated in the completed school complex and the structures which are recognised as the work of the Undersecretary." Boesch 1997, p. 76 f.

15 Conert 1929, p. 103.

16 Kramer, 1927, p. 817–828 and Tessenow, 1986, (1st ed. 1916). This partially unrealised plan was also published in Schmidt, 1928, p. 21 and Behrendt, 1927, p. 668. The copy from the Saxon State Library included in the latter features a marginal note from Kramer stating that the plan was not to be implemented.

17 Kramer 1927, p. 824.

18 Hübner/Grötzsch/Klatte 2005, p. 15.

19 Kramer 1914.

20 Hübner-Grötzsch / Hübner 2008, p. 135 f.

21 For examples see Rother, 2001, p. 14.

22 Wolfgang Rother discusses the ornamentation of the building in great detail. See Rother 2001, p. 3–24.

23 Hofer 2005, p. 54.

24 Wangerin/Weiss 1976, p. 37.

25 De Michelis 1991, p. 107.

26 Konrad Wachsmann in: Grüning 1986, p. 123.

27 Wangerin/Weiss, 1976, p. 17. The students' designs were closely orientated on Tessenow's architectural language, and featured facilities which echoed the future Landesschule due to their axial symmetry, uniformity and incorporation of their surroundings.

28 Wangerin/Weiss 1976, p. 40.

29 Wangerin/Weiss 1976, p. 36 and p. 38.

30 Conert 1929, p. 104.

31 Conert 1929, p. 104.

32 Boesch 1997, p. 77.

33 See Lampugnani 1998, p. 305.

34 See Conert 1929, p. 104.

35 The confirmation of the construction resources required for the year 1941 (dated the 26. 6. 1941) recommended the removal of the pergolas in order to prevent accidents and reduce structural maintenance costs. This recommendation was made on the grounds that the "overabundant wooden pergolas have regularly generated significant maintenance costs due to their susceptibility to weathering and their contribution to the penetration of dampness into buildings". SHD 496.

36 Fischer 1929, p. 9 f.

37 Amlung 2000.

38 Conert 1929, p. 104; Fischer 1929, p. 10.

39 DN 332, p. 7.

40 Conert 1929, p. 98.

41 See Rother 2001, p. 6.

42 Scheffler 1928, p. 44–46.

43 Karl Scheffler, quoted in De Michelis, 1991, p. 100.

44 Lampugnani 1991, p. 19–21.

45 The "Nationalpolitische Erziehungsanstalten" were a type of educational establishment set up under National Socialism, and were also known by the abbreviations "NPEA" or, more colloquially, "NAPOLA". In this case the school also bore the name of the "Rudolf-Schröter-Schule".

46 For details on the relocation of the infirmary, see Sächsisches Hauptstaatsarchiv Dresden, Oberfinanzpräsident Dresden, Bestand 11177, SHD 496; for extensive correspondence regarding underground air-raid shelters and cover trenches see SHD 640.

47 Plans for this expansion were included in a submission made by institute director Dr. Barth on the 3. 9. 1937, confirmation of their rejection was received in the spring of 1938, see SHD 21352; for information on roof conversions see SHD 640.

48 The Landesschule was administered in trust by the Mayor of Klotzsche from 3. 7. 1945 onwards. Emergency measures carried out during the few weeks in which the school was not occupied were restricted to the removal of school equipment and musical instruments and the carrying out of minor repairs to buildings. See StA 8.20.

49 Former pupils who had secretly gained access to the site noted that the buildings and their pergolas were still standing during the mid-1950s; by 1967 they were no longer there. The other buildings had been painted in Russian uniform grey and had their roof slates replaced with corrugated asbestos cement sheeting. Boesch 1997, p. 78. One boarding house survived as ruins into the 1980s.

links / left
Rekonstruktion der Tessenowschen Pergolen nach historischem Vorbild (Südfassade).
Tessenow pergolas reconstructed according to the model of their historic predecessors (south façade).

rechts / right
Blick über die Schieferdächer der südlichen Bauten.
View across the slate roofs of the southern buildings.

oben / top
Kontrast von historischen
und modernen Materialien.
Contrast between historic
and modern materials.

rechts / right
Aufgang zum aufwendig sanierten
ehemaligen Lehrgebäude.
Steps up to the lavishly restored former
classroom building.

5

links / left
Wiederhergestellte zweigeschossige Pergola
von Tessenow an der Südfassade von Haus 5.
Reconstructed, Tessenow-designed two-storey
pergola on the south façade of building 5.

rechts / right
Fassadengliederung durch Schieferbänder
an Haus 4.
Façade design on building 4 featuring slate strips.

Terrassenmauern aus behauenem Sandstein fangen
im Süden des Geländes das Gefälle ab.
Terrace walls of hewn sandstone construction divide up
and support the slope of the southern section of the site.

oben / top
Relief mit antikisierender Szene
über dem südlichen Hofeingang von Haus 1.
Relief featuring an antique-style scene
above the southern entrance to the courtyard
from building 1.

rechts / right
Blick vom Campus auf die Ostfassade
von Haus 1.
View from the campus towards the east
façade of building 1.

Rudolf-Schröter-Schule – Die Staatliche Nationalpolitische Erziehungsanstalt (1934 – 1945)

The Rudolf-Schröter-Schule – a State National Political Educational Institution (1934 – 1945)

HANKA BLESSE

Trotz anders propagierter Verlautbarungen seitens nationalsozialistischer (Schul-)Politiker gab es nach der »Machtübernahme« 1933 kein schlüssiges Konzept nationalsozialistischer Pädagogik, das es nur umzusetzen galt. Stattdessen kennzeichneten Bildungs- und Schulpolitik Planlosigkeit und Willkür, Führungs- und Kompetenzchaos. Galten diese Unzulänglichkeiten aber auch für die gesellschaftspolitisch wichtige Frage der Elitenbildung im »Dritten Reich«? Wie entwickelte sich in diesem Zusammenhang die sächsische Nationalpolitische Erziehungsanstalt (NPEA),[1] eine der sogenannten »Musterschule[n] des Nationalsozialismus«? Kann überhaupt von einer Eliteschule gesprochen werden? Welches Ausleseverfahren, welche besonderen intellektuellen Leistungen, welche politische Moral sollte Schüler und Lehrer gleichermaßen auszeichnen? Welche generellen Intentionen verknüpften Schulpolitiker mit der Gründung der sächsischen Erziehungsanstalt? Und wie sehen im Rückblick ehemalige Schüler ihre Schulzeit?

Entwicklungslinien der Rudolf-Schröter-Schule

Unter dem Zeichen der Hitlerjugend – Die Anfangsjahre

Am 1. April 1934 wurde die ehemalige Landesschule Dresden in Klotzsche in eine Nationalpolitische Erziehungsanstalt umgewandelt. Absolventen dieser Schule sollten später exponierte Positionen innerhalb des neuen Staatsgefüges einnehmen, wobei eine ausschließliche Karriere innerhalb der Nationalsozialistischen Deutschen Arbeiterpartei (NSDAP) nicht vorgesehen war. Nach dem Dresdner Hitlerjungen Rudolf Schröter benannt, der in den Straßenkämpfen zwischen der nationalsozialistischen Sturmabteilung (SA) und Kommunisten 1931 in Leipzig ums Leben kam, trug sie den

Fahnenappell der NPEA Dresden-Klotzsche, Rudolf-Schröter-Schule.
Flag ceremony at the NPEA Dresden-Klotzsche, Rudolf-Schröter-Schule.

Siegel der Schule. Ab 1937 verwendet.
School stamp, used from 1937 onwards.

Despite the propagation of reports to the contrary by National Socialist (educational) politicians, a coherent National Socialist educational theory which simply needed to be put into practice did not exist further to the "assumption of power" in 1933. It was instead haphazardness and arbitrariness, chaotic leadership and a lack of competence which characterised educational and schools policy. Did these inadequacies also exist in the socio-politically important issue of elite education in the "Third Reich"? How did the Saxon Nationalpolitische Erziehungsanstalt (NPEA)[1], one of the so-called "beacon school[s] for National Socialism", develop in this regard? Can it even be talked about as an "elite school"? What were the selection procedures, special intellectual abilities and political ethics that were deemed to set both its pupils and teachers apart? Which general intentions led educational politicians to the foundation of the Saxon NPEA? And how do former pupils remember their time there?

offiziellen Namen »Staatliche Nationalpolitische Erziehungsanstalt Rudolf Schröter – Unterbann Rudolf Schröter im Obergebiet 4 Mitte der HJ«.[2]

Über die Motive zur Schulgründung gibt nur die Gedenkschrift Walter Kleints, des ersten Anstaltsleiters, Auskunft. Dessen Aufzeichnungen aus dem Jahre 1943 sind als Fotokopie erhalten geblieben. In dieser Gedenkschrift schildert er die Anfänge der Anstalt und seine persönlichen Erziehungs- und Bildungsvorstellungen. Zwar bemüht sich Kleint um Objektivität seiner Schilderung, tendenziell stilisiert er aber die Ereignisse an der Schule und ihren Geist.[3]

In jedem Fall gab es schon früh Überlegungen zur Gründung einer Schule unter nationalsozialistischem Vorzeichen – konkret im Zeichen ihrer Jugendorganisation, der Hitlerjugend (HJ). Während zunächst noch offen geblieben war, welcher Schultyp dafür infrage kommen sollte, schienen diese Pläne nach der »Machtergreifung« 1933 nunmehr realisierbar. Kleint war seit 1933 kommissarisch als Ministerialrat im sächsischen Volksbildungsministerium tätig und für die höheren Schulen in Sachsen zuständig. Aufgrund der prekären Finanzlage Sachsens und der geringen Einflussmöglichkeiten der nationalsozialistischen Parteiinstanzen zu diesem Zeitpunkt konnten sich seine Bemühungen aber nur auf die höheren Schulen mit Internatsbetrieb beschränken. Dort schien eine Einflussnahme und Formung der Schüler im nationalsozialistischen Sinne am ehesten Erfolg versprechend. Schon bald stellte sich jedoch heraus, dass zum einen die meisten Internate zu klein waren, »den neuen Geist, [...] in ihren ganzen Schulen durchzusetzen«, zum anderen geeignete Schulen, wie die beiden Fürstenschulen in Meißen und Grimma sowie die Landesschule Dresden, nicht ohne größere personelle Veränderungen in der Lehrerschaft umgewandelt werden konnten, denn ihre »andersartige Tradition [war] so stark«.

Anlass zur Umsetzung der Pläne brachte schließlich die Anfrage einer »außerschulische[n] Dienststelle des Reiches«[4] bezüglich der Übernahme des Geländes der Landesschule Dresden. In Sorge um den Verlust der Grundstücke entschlossen sich das sächsische Volksbildungsministerium, das Finanzministerium und die zuständigen Stellen der HJ

The developmental aims of the Rudolf-Schröter-Schule

Under the flag of the Hitler Youth – the early years

The 1st of April 1934 witnessed the conversion of the former Landesschule Dresden[2] in Klotzsche, a state school, into an NPEA. Though graduates from the nascent establishment were certainly to be groomed to take up high-ranking positions within the new state system, a career within the National Socialist German Worker's Party (NSDAP) alone was not foreseen. Named after Rudolf Schröter, a native of Dresden and local Hitler Youth member who had died in street fighting between National Socialist storm troopers (the SA) and Communists in Leipzig in 1931, the school was now officially the "Staatliche Nationalpolitische Erziehungsanstalt Rudolf Schröter – Unterbann Rudolf Schröter im Obergebiet 4 Mitte der HJ"[3].

Only the memoirs of Walter Kleint, the school's first headmaster, provide information on the motives behind its foundation. The notes he drew up in 1943 have survived as a photocopy, and deal with both the beginnings of the school and his personal views on upbringing and education. Though Kleint endeavours to remain objective in his reflections, he tends to stylize both the events which took place at the school and its spirit.[4]

In any case, the foundation of a school under the auspices of National Socialism – or, to be more precise, its junior organisation the Hitler Youth – began to be considered at an early stage. Though there was initially uncertainty as to which type of school would be suitable, the "assumption of power" in 1933 appeared to present the opportunity to implement existing plans. Walter Kleint had become a temporary employee of the Saxon Ministry of Popular Education that year, and was responsible for secondary schools

Besuch des Erziehungsministers Rust 1934.
Von links nach rechts: Hartnacke (Sächsischer Volksbildungsminister), Rust, Kleint (Anstaltsleiter).
Visit by Education Minister Rust, 1934. Left to right: Hartnacke (Saxon Minister of Popular Education), Rust, Kleint (headmaster).

für den Aufbau einer Nationalpolitischen Erziehungsanstalt, »freilich unter Verzicht auf die Auflösung der alten Landesschule und den Neuaufbau der Anstalt aus frischer Wurzel«.

Frühzeitig offenbarten sich Kompetenzstreitigkeiten innerhalb der zuständigen Stellen auf staatlicher und Parteiebene. Schließlich einigte man sich in den ersten Verhandlungen, dass die Rudolf-Schröter-Schule zwar als selbstständiger »Unterbann der HJ« geführt und der obersten Gliederung, dem »Obergebiet 4, Mitte der HJ«, direkt unterstellt werden sollte, »daß [jedoch] Eingriffe von außen im Interesse einer geordneten Entwicklung der Anstalt und ihrer Jungen unmöglich [sein], daß innen tatsächlich nur eine Erziehungsmacht [wirken sollte]«, nämlich die der Schule unter staatlicher Schulaufsicht.

Schon in der Namensgebung zeigte sich die starke Bindung an die HJ. Organisatorisch war die NPEA nach den Gliederungen der HJ hierarchisch strukturiert: Die Schule bildete den Unterbann, der wiederum in drei Gefolgschaften gegliedert war. Zu jeder Gefolgschaft zählten vier Schare, insgesamt zwölf Schare. Die Gesamtheit von 24 Kameradschaften ergab sich aus der Aufgliederung der Schare in jeweils zwei Kameradschaften. Zu jeder Kameradschaft gehörten zehn bzw. elf Schüler. Diese Struktur bot sich aufgrund der Gesamtanlage der Schule an: Außer den Gemeinschaftseinrichtungen, wie Turnhalle, Lehrgebäude etc., gab es auf dem Anstaltsgelände sechs Doppelhäuser, in denen je zwei Schare mit den für sie jeweils zuständigen Erziehern lebten.[5] Jede Schar sollte alle Altersstufen von der Untertertia zur Oberprima führen.

Auch das Anstaltsleben sollte im Geiste der Hitlerjugend geführt werden: Neben den täglichen Morgen- und Abendappellen wurden regelmäßig Feste und Feiern im Zeichen der nationalsozialistischen Jugendorganisation durchgeführt: »Das Leben sollte in Geist und Formen der idealen HJ ablaufen, hart, straff und zuchtvoll, aber mit viel Raum für die Erprobung wachsender Kräfte, jugendlicher Begeisterung und jungenhafter Fröhlichkeit.«[6]

Schon früh wurden zudem den Schülern eine Reihe von Aufgaben im Schulbetrieb als sogenannte Gefolgschaftsführer, als Unterbann-Adjutant, als Kassenwart oder als Pressereferent übergeben. Zwölf Schüler wurden als stellvertretende Scharführer eingesetzt.

Um die neuen Bildungs- und Erziehungsziele durchzusetzen, wurden Erzieher, junge, ledige Studienassessoren im Dienste eines Scharführers eingestellt; neun Studienräte wurden versetzt.[7] Kleint hatte eigenen Aussagen zufolge für diese Auswahl etwa hundert Studienassessoren »durchgeprüft« und aus ihnen zwölf »auserlesen«. Sie sollten, bündisch geprägt, »zwar umfassende Fachkenntnisse [besitzen], in erster Linie aber fähig [sein], in unserem [nationalsozialistischen] Sinne Jungenführer zu sein«.

»Wir haben keinen Vorzug vor ihnen«, so einer dieser neuen Erzieher »wir tragen den gleichen Dienstanzug mit kurzen Hosen wie sie; wir laufen und üben unter ihnen jeden Morgen; wir stehen unter der kalten Dusche wie sie und im Wetteifer mit ihnen bauen wir unsere Betten, putzen unsere Schuhe; wir essen aus der gleichen Schüssel [sic!]; wir nehmen an jedem Dienst unter den gleichen Bedingungen teil wie die Jungen [...]. Und wenn wir so stets unter ihnen stehen als Kameraden, so stehen wir doch immer auch als Führer vor ihnen. Wir ordnen an, wir zeigen und erklären, vor allem aber leben wir ihnen im großen wie im kleinen als Vorbild vor, in Ehre, Treue und Wahrhaftigkeit, in Leistung und Einsatzbereitschaft, in äußerer wie innerer aufrechter mannhafter Zucht.«[8]

Hier wird die vermeintlich fehlende bzw. flache Hierarchie zwischen Erzieher und Schüler idealisiert, Führer- und Gefolgschaftsprinzip bleiben jedoch erhalten. Nicht nur von den Jungen, sondern vor allem von den Erziehern wird eine bedingungslose Hingabe für die »Idee« unter dem Deckmantel erhabener Werte gefordert. Dabei wird der Begriff von Kameradschaft immer wieder heraufbeschworen, der sich mit einem Männlichkeitsideal von martialischer Stärke und Machtbewusstsein paart.

Große Veränderungen ergaben sich aber auch innerhalb der Schülerschaft: Allein bis Ostern 1935 verließen 75 ehemalige Landesschüler, ausgenommen die Abiturabgänger des gleichen Jahres, freiwillig oder gezwungenermaßen die Schule. Große ideologische Spannungen zwischen ehema-

Pimpfe bei einer Übung auf dem Gelände der NPEA.
Pimpfs carrying out an exercise on the grounds of the NPEA.

in Saxony. As a result of the state's precarious financial situation and the limited influence National Socialist party functionaries were able to exert at the time, his efforts were nevertheless restricted to measures related to secondary schools with boarders. It was here that the influencing and shaping of pupils for National Socialist purposes appeared to be most likely to succeed. This notwithstanding, two issues soon became apparent. On the one hand, the majority of boarding establishments were too small to "assert the new spirit [...] throughout their schools". On the other, suitable schools such as the two Fürstenschulen[5] in Meißen and Grimma and the Landesschule Dresden could not be converted without significant staffing upheaval on account of the strength of their "differing tradition".

Fahnenappell der NPEA Dresden-Klotzsche,
Rudolf-Schröter-Schule.
Flag ceremony at the NPEA Dresden-Klotzsche,
Rudolf-Schröter-Schule.

The implementation of plans for the school was finally put in motion by an enquiry from a "non-educational department of the state"[6] regarding the takeover of the Landesschule Dresden site. Concerned about the loss of the land concerned, the Saxon Ministry of Popular Education, the Ministry of Finance and the relevant authorities within the Hitler Youth movement took the decision to set up an NPEA. In doing so, they "naturally avoided the closure of the old Landesschule and the redevelopment of the school from scratch".

Power struggles on both a state and party level quickly arose within the various bodies involved. Initial negotiations eventually saw the parties agree that, although the Rudolf-Schröter-Schule was to be operated as an independent "Unterbann" unit of the Hitler Youth under the direct control of the Hitler Youth's "Obergebiet 4, Mitte" section[7] "outside intervention in the interest of the orderly development of the school and its boys would [nevertheless] be impossible, [and] only one internal educational authority [should be active]". That authority was to be the school acting under the supervision of the schools administration board.

Even the school's name showed the strong link between it and the Hitler Youth, and in hierarchical terms the NPEA was organised in the same way as the youth movement.[8] The school was the "Unterbann" group, which in turn was divided into three "Gefolgschaft" groups. Each "Gefolgschaft" comprised four "Schar" groups, of which the school had twelve. The "Schar" groups were further broken down into two "Kameradschaft" groups, each of which numbered ten or eleven pupils. This structure lent itself to the facilities available at the school, as in addition to shared areas such as the gymnasium, classroom building, etc., the site also featured six semi-detached houses, each of which could accommodate two "Schar" groups and their respective tutors.[9]

Schar 10, 1934.
Schar 10, 1934.

ligen Landesschülern und der neuen Schulleitung wurden dabei offenkundig, wie die Bewertung Kleints zeigt: »Die Rudolf-Schröter-Schule übernahm bei der Gründung den gesamten Schülerbestand der früheren Landesschule Dresden, der weder nach besonderen nationalsozialistischen noch nationalpolitischen Grundsätzen ausgewählt war. Auf die reine schulische Leistung der Jungen wurde ein bei weitem größerer Wert gelegt als auf ihre charakterliche und körperliche Eignung für künftige Führerstellen. So war es möglich, daß u. a. eine ganze Anzahl von Jungen hier mit heranwachsen konnte, die einen ausgesprochen intellektuellen und kritischen Typus darstellen, denen das Moment freudiger und rückhaltloser Begeisterung fehlt. Diese stark literarischen, grüblerischen, zum Teil snobistischen, zum Teil ehrgeizig-streberischen Naturen haben sich vom großen Schwung der nationalsozialistischen Revolution schwerer erfassen lassen als andere und standen der Umwandlung der Landesschule in eine Nationalpolitische Erziehungsanstalt und zugleich einen Unterbann der HJ außerordentlich skeptisch gegenüber. Die Formen ihrer Abwehr gingen von passiver Resistenz im Gemeinschaftsleben des Unterbanns bis zur offenen Wühlerei und Miesmacherei.«[9]

Neben der Ausgrenzung ehemaliger Landesschüler durch die Schulleitung trug das neue Ausleseverfahren ebenfalls zur Versetzung einer Reihe von Schülern bei. Für die Aufnahme in die Anstalt war jetzt eine fünftägige Aufnahmeprüfung für alle Bewerber zwingend. Zudem mussten Nachweise über arische Herkunft, ein Gesundheitszeugnis und Zeugnisse über die besondere körperliche und geistige Leistungsfähigkeit der Jungen erbracht werden. Damit nicht genug: »Die Auslese wird während der ganzen Schulzeit fortgesetzt; wer den strengen Anforderungen, die die ›Nationalpolitische Erziehungsanstalt‹ an sittliche, körper-

Each "Schar" group was to include all age groups from years 8 to 13, and therefore dispensed with classical age-group divisions.

School life was to adopt the spirit of the Hitler Youth. In addition to daily morning and evening roll calls, regular receptions and celebrations which echoed the National Socialist youth organisation also took place. "Life was to play out according to the spirit and conventions of the Hitler Youth in its purest form – tough, rigorous and disciplined, but with plenty of room to test out blossoming strengths, youthful enthusiasm and boyish gaiety."[10]

From an early stage pupils were given a range of roles such as "Gefolgschaft leader", "Unterbann aide-de-camp", "treasurer" and "press officer". Twelve pupils were appointed as acting "Schar leaders".

Probationary secondary school teachers – young, single tutors – were employed to work under the Schar leaders in order to ensure the achievement of the school's new educational and upbringing goals. This also saw the transferral of nine graduate secondary school teachers away from the NPEA.[11] In his own words, Kleint "scrutinised" around one hundred probationary secondary school teachers before "selecting" twelve of them. They were to be in the mould of the Bündische Jugend,[12] and though they were to "[have] comprehensive specialist knowledge", the most important selection criteria was their "ability to act as leaders of boys in the [National Socialist] way we deem suitable".

As one of these new tutors put it: "We have no priority over them. We wear the same uniform and shorts as they do; we run and train with them every morning; we stand under the [same] cold showers; alongside and in competition with them we make our beds and clean our shoes; we eat from the same bowl [sic]; we carry out all duties under the same conditions as the boys. [...] And even though this sees us stand amongst them as constant comrades, we always stand before them as leaders. We give orders, we show and explain, and above all we are a living example to them in all aspects: in honour, loyalty and truthfulness, in performance and readiness for duty, in honest, masculine discipline on both the outside and the inside."[13]

liche und geistige Tüchtigkeit stellen muß, nicht entspricht, muß abgehen. Das Wiederholen einer Klasse ist nur in besonders gelagerten Fällen möglich.«[10]

Schon hier zeichnen sich Akzentverschiebungen bei der zukünftigen Auswahl der Schüler ab: Nicht Wissen und Können werden jetzt vorrangige Auslesekriterien, sondern körperliche Fitness und vor allem Führungsqualitäten bzw. Führungswillen, die unter dem Begriff von »Charakterstärke« subsumiert werden.

Eindeutige »Zielvorgaben« die Schülerauslese betreffend gab es auch in anderer Hinsicht: Laut Gründungserlass aus dem Jahre 1934 sollte »[J]ede Klasse [...] Jungen aus allen Kreisen enthalten und als Abbild des Volkes sie zu wahrer Volksgemeinschaft über alle Standesunterschiede hinweg erziehen«[11], denn es galt, den schon in der Weimarer Republik oft kritisierten selektiven Mechanismus von Bildung und sozialer Herkunft zu durchbrechen. Es blieb aber bei propagandistischen Bekundungen, denn für den Schulbesuch meldeten sich zu wenige Arbeiterkinder. Zudem war der Anteil an Jungen, deren Väter höchste Staats- und Wirtschaftsämter einschließlich Ämter beim Militär bekleideten, außer in den Anfangsjahren der Schule, unterrepräsentiert. Gleichbleibend unbefriedigend blieb, dass »(I)m Gegensatz zu den übrigen Nationalpolitischen Erziehungsanstalten und den übrigen höheren Schulen [...] an der Nationalpolitischen Erziehungsanstalt Klotzsche fast ganz die Söhne von Eltern mit gehobener Lebenshaltung [fehlten].«[12] Stattdessen stammte das Gros der Schüler aus der unteren Mittelschicht, dem Kleinbürgertum. Das bürdete der Anstalt zusätzlich finanzielle Belastungen auf, denn ein Teil der Finanzen der Schule wurde über Schulgeld (20 RM monatlich), Kost- und Wohngeld (19,20 bzw. 12,50 RM monatlich) refinanziert, wie für die Höheren Schulen üblich. Da zudem Freistellen für einen Teil der Plätze vergeben wurden, war für die Auswahlinstanzen, wie die vorherige Schule, die Gemeinde oder Parteistellen, oftmals der Versorgungsaspekt Anlass, Schüler an die Rudolf-Schröter-Schule zu melden.

Vorerst wenig veränderte sich indes am eigentlichen Unterrichtsgeschehen. Weiterhin galten die Lehrpläne der Weimarer Republik und die für den Unterricht prägende

Despite this being an idealisation of the supposedly absent or flat hierarchies which were to structure relationships between tutors and pupils, the notion of leaders and followers still shines through. Unconditional devotion to an "idea" cloaked in the guise of grand values was not only required of the boys, but also – and in particular – of the tutors. The notion of comradeship and the masculine ideals of martial strength and consciousness of power were regularly evoked.

Substantial changes also took place amongst the pupils, with 75 of those who had attended the school during its time as the Landesschule leaving on either a voluntary or forced basis by the Easter of 1935 alone (this excludes pupils who gained their Abitur school leaving certificate that year). Kleint commented on the significant ideological tensions which manifested themselves between Landesschule-era pupils and the new school management: "The newly-founded Rudolf-Schröter-Schule took on all the pupils who had attended the Landesschule Dresden – pupils who had been selected according to neither specific National Socialist nor national political criteria. Far greater importance had been attached to these boys' scholastic ability than to the suitability of their character and physical attributes to future leadership positions. This created a situation in which, amongst other things, quite some number of boys grew into distinctly intellectual, critical types who lacked the spark to the flame of joyful and unrestrained enthusiasm. These highly literary, introspective types – some of them snobbish, some of them ambitious swots – were less easily swept along by the great impetus of the National Socialist revolution than some others, and regarded the conversion of the Landesschule into both an NPEA and an Unterbann of the Hitler Youth with a high degree of scepticism. Their methods of resistance ranged from passive recalcitrance in communal Unterbann life to barefaced agitation and troublemaking."[14]

The new selection process not only saw the school's management marginalise pupils who had attended it during its time as the Landesschule, but also contributed to the transfer of a number of pupils. Applicants now had to take

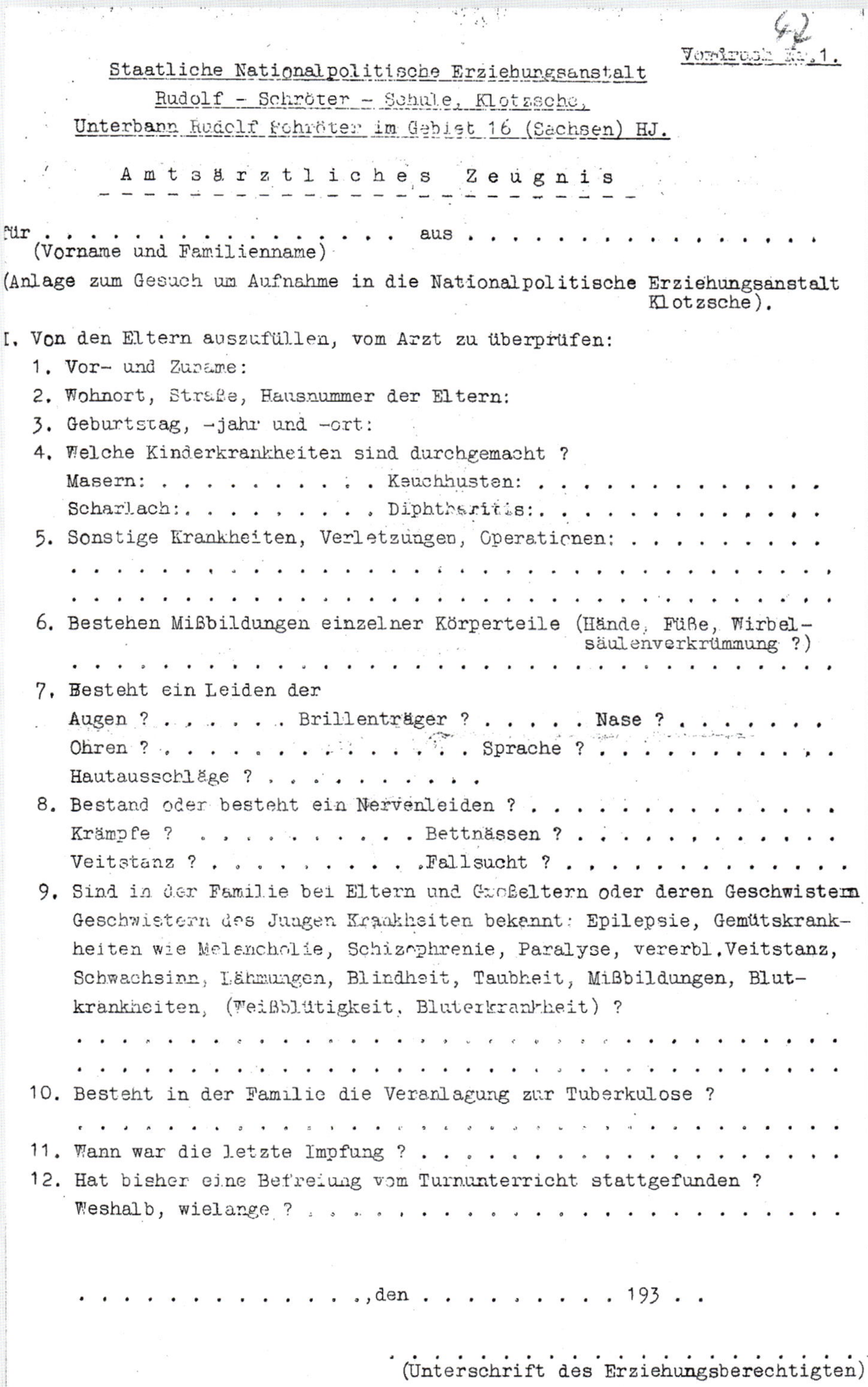

Vormerk. Nr. 1.

Staatliche Nationalpolitische Erziehungsanstalt
Rudolf - Schröter - Schule, Klotzsche,
Unterbann Rudolf Schröter im Gebiet 16 (Sachsen) HJ.

A m t s ä r z t l i c h e s   Z e u g n i s

für . . . . aus . . . .
(Vorname und Familienname)
(Anlage zum Gesuch um Aufnahme in die Nationalpolitische Erziehungsanstalt Klotzsche).

I. Von den Eltern auszufüllen, vom Arzt zu überprüfen:
1. Vor- und Zuname:
2. Wohnort, Straße, Hausnummer der Eltern:
3. Geburtstag, -jahr und -ort:
4. Welche Kinderkrankheiten sind durchgemacht ?
Masern: . . . . Keuchhusten: . . . .
Scharlach:. . . . . Diphtheritis:. . . . .
5. Sonstige Krankheiten, Verletzungen, Operationen: . . . .
. . . .
. . . .
6. Bestehen Mißbildungen einzelner Körperteile (Hände, Füße, Wirbelsäulenverkrümmung ?)
. . . .
7. Besteht ein Leiden der
Augen ? . . . . . . Brillenträger ? . . . . . Nase ? . . . .
Ohren ? . . . . Sprache ? . . . .
Hautausschläge ? . . . .
8. Bestand oder besteht ein Nervenleiden ? . . . .
Krämpfe ? . . . . Bettnässen ? . . . .
Veitstanz ? . . . . Fallsucht ? . . . .
9. Sind in der Familie bei Eltern und Großeltern oder deren Geschwistern Geschwistern des Jungen Krankheiten bekannt: Epilepsie, Gemütskrankheiten wie Melancholie, Schizophrenie, Paralyse, vererbl. Veitstanz, Schwachsinn, Lähmungen, Blindheit, Taubheit, Mißbildungen, Blutkrankheiten, (Weißblütigkeit, Bluterkrankheit) ?
. . . .
. . . .
10. Besteht in der Familie die Veranlagung zur Tuberkulose ?
. . . .
11. Wann war die letzte Impfung ? . . . .
12. Hat bisher eine Befreiung vom Turnunterricht stattgefunden ?
Weshalb, wielange ? . . . .

. . . ., den . . . . 193 . .

. . . .
(Unterschrift des Erziehungsberechtigten)

Aufgliederung nach Alter und Klasse bestand fort. Auch das Curriculum der Schule blieb erhalten: in der Betonung der naturwissenschaftlichen Fächer und der neuen Sprachen der Reformrealgymnasialzug (Untertertia bis Oberprima) sowie der Oberrealschulzug (Untertertia bis Oberprima) als Aufbauklasse, der in seine Untertertia Volksschüler aufnahm. Veränderungen gab es indes in den für die Nationalsozialisten wichtigen Fächern Deutsch, Geschichte, Geografie, Biologie einschließlich Rassenkunde, Sport und Wehrerziehung.[13]

Gravierende Einschnitte in das Schulleben brachten die Ereignisse im Zuge der Röhm-Affäre 1934. Die »Säuberungsaktionen« gegen die höhere SA-Führung nutzte Martin Mutschmann, Reichsstatthalter und Gauleiter in Sachsen, um seinen Konkurrenten Manfred von Killinger, SA-Führer und Ministerpräsident Sachsens, samt Kabinett politisch auszuschalten. Daraufhin wurden hohe Beamte wie Minister selbst ihrer Posten enthoben. So bekam ebenfalls Walter Kleint, in seiner Doppelfunktion als Ministerialrat im Volksbildungsministerium und als Anstaltleiter der Rudolf-Schröter-Schule, am 17. März 1935 seine Entlassungspapiere. Er trat wieder seine Stelle als Stadtschulrat in Dresden an. Zugleich wurde die gesamte oberste HJ-Führung des »Obergebietes 4, Mitte« abgesetzt und das »Obergebiet« selbst aufgelöst. Damit entfiel die unmittelbare Anbindung an die HJ: »Der für die SA so tragische 30. Juni, der Röhm-Putsch, geht, ohne irgendeinen tieferen Eindruck zu machen, an dem Leben der Rudolf-Schröter-Schule vorüber, obwohl er doch gerade für die sächsische HJ eine ernste Krise bringt […].«[14] Noch blieb die Schule dem Gebietsführer der HJ unterstellt, aber die Kontakte und der Einfluss der HJ auf den Schulalltag nahmen in der Folgezeit merklich ab.

Ärztliches Zeugnis. Formular von den Eltern vor dem Eintritt in die Schule auszufüllen.
Official medical certificate. Form to be filled out by parents prior to admission to the school.

part in a mandatory five-day entrance test in order to gain admission to the school, and were required to provide evidence of an Aryan background, a health certificate and testimonies to special physical and mental ability. The requirements did not stop there: “The selection process continues throughout a pupil’s time at the school; anyone who does not meet up to the strict requirements which the ‘NPEA’ is obliged to enforce in terms of moral, physical and mental competence is required to leave. The opportunity to repeat a year is only granted in special cases.”[15]

Even here, the changes in emphasis which were to influence pupil selection in the future are already apparent. Knowledge and ability were succeeded as primary selection criteria by physical fitness and, in particular, leadership qualities and a willingness to lead. These last two criteria were grouped under the term “strength of character”.

Further, clear targets were also set for the pupil selection process in another aspect. According to its founding edict of 1934, every class was to “[...] include boys from all walks of life and bring them up as an image of the people in order to form a true national community which transcends all class distinction.”[16] The motivation behind this was the desire to dismantle selective mechanisms of education and social standing which had already been subject to frequent criticism during the Weimar Republic. This notwithstanding, the insufficient number of applications received from working-class children meant that such mission statements were never raised above the level of propaganda. Moreover, and with the exception of the first few years of the school, the proportion of boys whose fathers held high-ranking roles in offices of the state (including the military) was low. It also remained unsatisfactory that “In contrast with the other NPEA schools and other secondary schools [...] the NPEA Klotzsche was almost completely

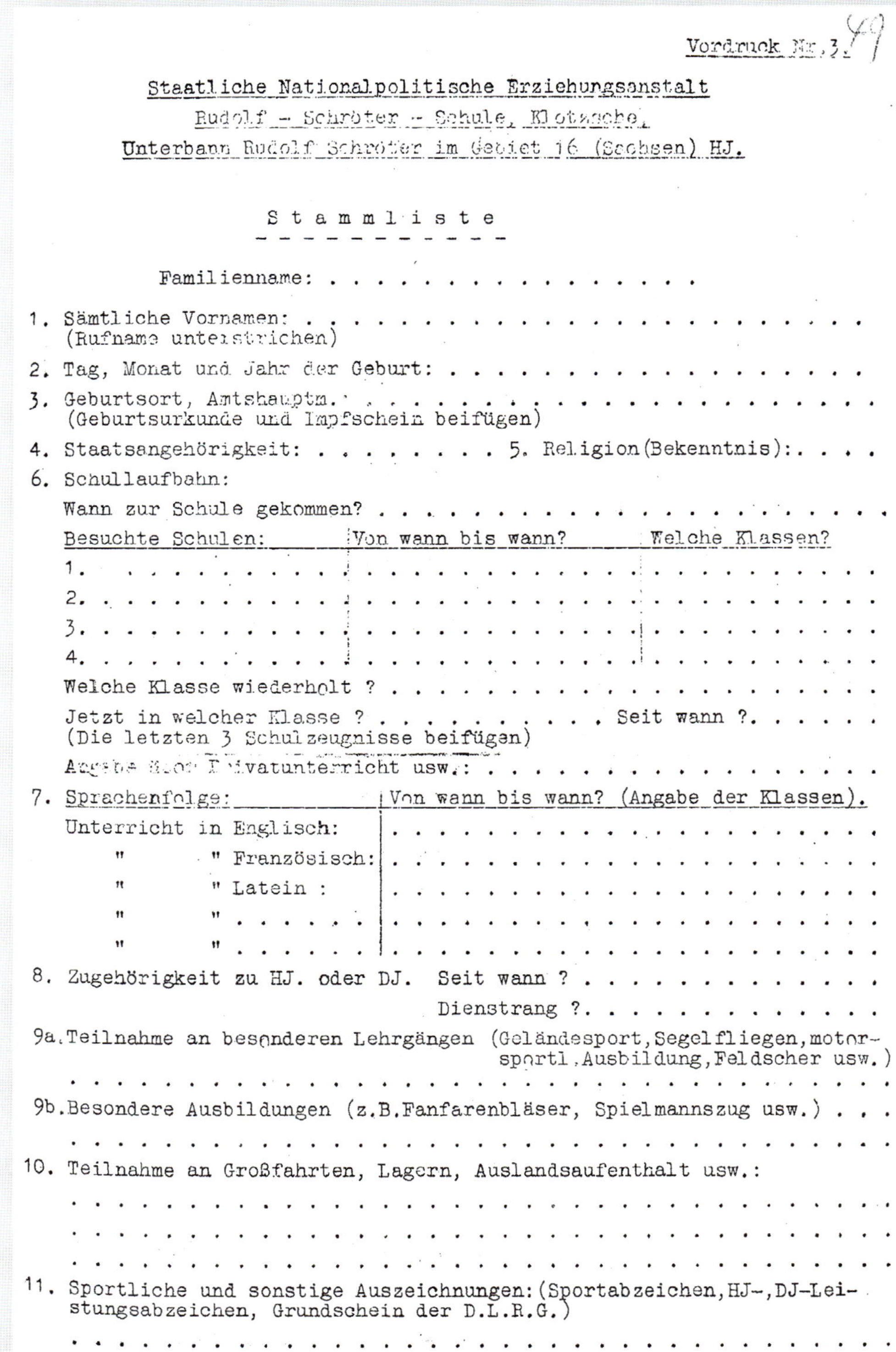

Vordruck Nr. 3. 49

Staatliche Nationalpolitische Erziehungsanstalt
Rudolf - Schröter - Schule, Klotzsche,
Unterbann Rudolf Schröter im Gebiet 16 (Sachsen) HJ.

S t a m m l i s t e

Familienname: . . . .

1. Sämtliche Vornamen: . . . .
(Rufname unterstreichen)

2. Tag, Monat und Jahr der Geburt: . . . .

3. Geburtsort, Amtshauptm.: . . . .
(Geburtsurkunde und Impfschein beifügen)

4. Staatsangehörigkeit: . . . . 5. Religion (Bekenntnis): . . . .

6. Schullaufbahn:
Wann zur Schule gekommen? . . . .

Besuchte Schulen:	Von wann bis wann?	Welche Klassen?
1.	. . . .	. . . .
2.	. . . .	. . . .
3.	. . . .	. . . .
4.	. . . .	. . . .

Welche Klasse wiederholt ? . . . .
Jetzt in welcher Klasse ? . . . . Seit wann ?. . . . . .
(Die letzten 3 Schulzeugnisse beifügen)
Angabe über Privatunterricht usw.: . . . .

7. Sprachenfolge:	Von wann bis wann? (Angabe der Klassen).
Unterricht in Englisch:	. . . .
" " Französisch:	. . . .
" " Latein :	. . . .
" "	. . . .
" "	. . . .

8. Zugehörigkeit zu HJ. oder DJ. Seit wann ? . . . .
Dienstrang ?. . . . .

9a. Teilnahme an besonderen Lehrgängen (Geländesport, Segelfliegen, motorsportl. Ausbildung, Feldscher usw.)
. . . .

9b. Besondere Ausbildungen (z.B. Fanfarenbläser, Spielmannszug usw.) . . .
. . . .

10. Teilnahme an Großfahrten, Lagern, Auslandsaufenthalt usw.:
. . . .
. . . .
. . . .

11. Sportliche und sonstige Auszeichnungen: (Sportabzeichen, HJ-, DJ-Leistungsabzeichen, Grundschein der D.L.R.G.)
. . . .

Stammliste. Formular von den Eltern vor dem Eintritt in die Schule auszufüllen.

List for the detailing of family heritage. Form to be filled out by parents prior to admission to the school.

Die weitreichenden Auswirkungen der Röhm-Affäre sind ein Spezifikum der sächsischen NPEA. Die starke Bindung der Schule an die HJ zog eine starke Bindung an die SA nach sich, die sich der nationalsozialistischen Jugendorganisation besondern verpflichtet fühlte. Zudem spiegelt die Absetzung des ersten Anstaltsleiters Kleint das Machtgefälle zwischen der sächsischen Parteiführung mit Gauleiter Mutschmann an der Spitze und der Regierung unter SA-Führer von Killinger wider. Die örtliche Parteiführung griff jetzt immer stärker in die Belange staatlicher Stellen, in diesem Fall in die Personalpolitik staatlicher Schulen, ein.

Versuche der Etablierung der Schule – Die Arbeit des zweiten Anstaltsleiters

Mit dem Weggang Kleints veränderte sich das schulische Klima. Dr. Herbert Barth, der neue Anstaltsleiter, im März 1935 zunächst kommissarisch eingesetzt, 1936 in diesem Amt bestätigt, war nicht wie Kleint der Bündischen Jugend verpflichtet. Weit mehr als dieser bemühte er sich um eine Angleichung an die preußischen NPEA, auch um den Preis des Verlusts eines spezifisch sächsischen Profils. In der Folge herrschte ein eher soldatischer Geist an der Schule, denn Barth war Soldat und Offizier im Ersten Weltkrieg und Mitglied des Freikorps. Der Wandel im Schulalltag wird nicht nur in der Gedenkschrift Kleints, sondern auch in verschiedenen Äußerungen in den »Rundklötzen«, den Rundschreiben ehemaliger Lehrer und Schüler der NPEA Dresden-Klotzsche, beschrieben: »Leider war Barth [...] zu wenig bündisch [...]. Ihm imponierte zu sehr der preußische Schnitt [...]. Barth übernahm schrittweise das Äußere der preußischen Anstalten, schwenkte nach und nach, fast servil, auf die Heißmeyersche Linie ein, was seitens des HJ-Gebiets eine laufend stärkere Zurückschaltung zur Folge hatte. Die HJ-Zugehörigkeit wurde, wie bei den preußischen Anstalten, eine stille Mitgliedschaft [...]. Nachdem die HJ-Großlager 1937 noch von uns besucht wurden, kühlte die Beziehung zur HJ merklich ab.«[15]

Dr. Herbert Barth, 2. Anstaltsleiter seit Ostern 1935.
Dr. Herbert Barth, second headmaster of the school (Easter 1935 onwards).

Besonders bei der Rekrutierung neuer Lehrer wurde Barths Linientreue offenkundig. In seinen Anfangsjahren zwischen 1935 und 1937 forcierte er den systematischen Wechsel des Lehrerkollegiums, indem er die Neueinstellung »nationalsozialistischer Vorkämpfer für die Blut- und Rassenlehren« maßgeblich voran trieb und nicht systemtreue Lehrer entließ: In der 31 Seiten starken Denkschrift vom September 1937 an das Volksbildungsministerium in Dresden gab er u. a. zu zehn Lehrern detaillierte Beurteilungen ab, die zu deren Versetzung zwingend beitragen sollten. Exemplarisch sei hier eine Beurteilung vorgestellt, die zeigt, wie vehement Barth von einem militärisch bestimmten Männlichkeitsbild durchdrungen war:

»Studienrat E. F. T., geb. 23. 5. 1885 (Zeichnen, Kunstgeschichte, Werkunterricht nach Prüfungsordnung von 1914) Beurteilung: unsoldatisch, unheroisch, weich, empfindsam, fachlich tüchtig. Er war 1919 bis April 1933 Mitglied der Loge Zum Goldenen Apfel in Dresden, zuletzt Meister vom Stuhl (III. Grad). [...] Er ist im Sinne der nationalpolitischen Erziehungsanstalten nicht mehr wandlungsfähig. Ehemaligen Freimaurern dürfen die Studienreferendare zur Ausbildung nicht zugewiesen werden. Studienrat T. als einziger für Zeichnen in Frage kommender Fachvertreter behindert also die Auswahl der Scharführer und Scharführeranwärter, soweit sie Studienreferendare sind. Sinngemäß muß weiter gelten, daß ehemaligen Freimaurern erst recht nicht Jungen für die Ausbildung zu besten Nationalsozialisten zugewiesen werden können.«[16]

War aber die hohe Einsatzbereitschaft der Erzieher- und Schülerschaft ausreichend, einer nationalsozialistischen Eliteschule gerecht zu werden? Zweifel sind angebracht, denn die finanzielle Ausstattung entsprach bei weitem nicht dem Budget preußischer Anstalten. Barth vermerkte sieben Millionen Reichsmark für die zehn preußischen Schulen jährlich. Sein eigenes Budget nahm sich dagegen weitaus bescheidener aus.[17] Erst 1938 konnte im sächsischen Staatshaushalt eine größere Geldsumme für die Anstalt bereitgestellt werden.[18] Noch 1937 musste Barth in einem Schrei-

lacking in sons whose fathers enjoyed a high standard of living."[17] The majority of pupils instead heralded from the lower-middle class, the petty bourgeoisie. This saddled the school with additional financial burdens, as it was part-financed – as was typical to secondary schools – by school fees (20.00 Reichsmarks per month) and charges for bed and board (12.50 and 19.20 Reichsmarks per month respectively). The fact that a certain number of free places were also awarded often led selecting authorities (such as the previous school, the parish or sections of the NSDAP) to enrol pupils at the Rudolf-Schröter-Schule on the basis of the care they received there.

Despite all this there was little initial change to classroom life. Syllabi drawn up during the Weimar Republic continued to be used, as did the divisions according to age group and school year which characterised lessons. The school curriculum was also retained, with emphasis placed on natural sciences and modern languages in the progressive grammar school (years eight to thirteen) and upper secondary (years eight to thirteen) sections of the school. The upper secondary section was set up as an accelerated learning route which took on elementary school pupils in their eighth year of school. Changes occurred in the subjects of German, history, geography, biology (including racial anthropology), sport and military training, all of which were of importance to the National Socialists.[18]

The events of the Night of the Long Knives in 1934 had a significant effect on school life. Martin Mutschmann, Saxony's Reich Governor and Gauleiter,[19] used the "purge" of top-ranking SA officials to bring about the political exit of not only his rival Manfred von Killinger, Saxony's prime minister and most high-ranking SA functionary, but also his entire cabinet. Senior civil servants all the way up to ministerial level were removed from their posts. On the 17th of March 1936 this wave of action also saw Walter Kleint – until that point both an undersecretary at the Ministry of Popular Education and the headmaster of the Rudolf-Schröter-Schule – relieved of his duties. He subsequently returned to his position as a city school inspector in Dresden. Simultaneous to this, the senior leadership of the

ben an August Heißmeyer[19], in dem er um Geldmittel für eine zweite sächsische NPEA bat, kritisch feststellen: »Bevor aber an die Errichtung einer zweiten Nationalpolitischen Erziehungsanstalt gedacht werden kann, ist zunächst die Rudolf-Schröter-Schule auf das Niveau der preussischen Nationalpolitischen Erziehungsanstalten zu bringen, um die drohende Gefahr zu bannen, daß die Rudolf-Schröter-Schule, die bereits im Reich nicht voll angesehen wird, nicht noch mehr ins Hintertreffen gerät und nicht mehr als Nationalpolitische Erziehungsanstalt anerkannt wird.«[20]

Nur schrittweise konnte die Ausstattung der Schule verbessert werden. Es fehlte praktisch an allem, nicht nur an der für die Nationalpolitischen Erziehungsanstalten vorgesehenen materiellen Ausrüstung für Exklusivsportarten wie Reiten, Segeln, Segelfliegen, Motorsport, Skilaufen, Fechten und Boxen. Auch die für Schüler aller NPEA vorgesehenen außerschulischen Aktivitäten, wie beispielsweise der Einsatz im Bergwerk, der sogenannte Landdienst oder Auslandsfahrten, konnten aufgrund der finanziellen Engpässe erst ab 1938 durchgeführt werden. Immer wieder verglich Barth seine Anstalt mit den preußischen Schulen und kam zu vernichtenden Ergebnissen.

Den Makel, keiner vollwertigen nationalsozialistischen Eliteschule zu entsprechen, wollte Barth aber nicht nur durch größeren Ehrgeiz wettmachen, ihm schwebte eine besondere rassische Profilierung vor, die die Anstalt wieder in günstiges Licht rücken sollte. So ließ er schon 1938 ein schärferes Ausleseverfahren für die betreffenden Neuzugänge einführen. Dass diesen Auslesekriterien weitestgehend entsprochen wurde, zeigen die Akteneintragungen des Volksbildungsministeriums: Allein Ostern 1938 wurden von 240 einberufenen Jungen 113 vom Rassereferenten des Oberabschnittes Elbe der Schutzstaffel der NSDAP (SS) als rassisch untauglich befunden und konnten der Schule nicht beitreten.[21] Barth zeigte sich zudem besonders dienstbeflissen in der Zusammenarbeit mit den hiesigen HJ-Verbänden und mit der städtischen Ortsgruppe der NSDAP, woraufhin die Schule »als eine Art Muster für die übrigen Nationalpolitischen Erziehungsanstalten« von der zuständigen Behörde für die NPEA gelobt wurde.

"Obergebiet 4, Mitte" section of the Hitler Youth was deposed and the "Obergebiet" itself disbanded. The school's direct link to the Hitler Youth had therefore been broken: "That most tragic of days for the SA, the 30th of June, the Röhm putsch, has passed by the Rudolf-Schröter-Schule without leaving any great mark. It has nevertheless created a serious crisis for the Hitler Youth in Saxony [...]."[20] Though the school continued to be answerable to the area head of the local Hitler Youth, contact between the two organisations and the influence of the Hitler Youth on day-to-day school life dropped off markedly in the ensuing period.

The far-reaching consequences of the Night of the Long Knives are a specific feature of the Saxon NPEA. Its strong bond with the Hitler Youth brought a strong bond with the SA with it, as the latter felt a particular responsibility towards the National Socialist youth movement. In addition, the dismissal of Kleint from his post as the first headmaster of the school reflected the difference in power between the administrations which served under SA-leader von Killinger and Saxon party head and Gauleiter Mutschmann. The local party leadership became more and more involved in the affairs of state departments, and this included the staffing policies for state schools.

Attempts to establish the school: the work of the school's second headmaster

Kleint's departure was accompanied by a change in atmosphere at the school. Its new headmaster, Dr. Herbert Barth, was employed on a provisional basis from March 1935 onwards before having his position made permanent in 1936. Unlike Kleint, he was not beholden to the Bündische Jugend. He made far greater efforts than his predecessor to assimilate the characteristics of the Prussian NPEA, and was even prepared to do so at the expense of a specific Saxon profile. Barth had been both a soldier and officer in the First World War and a member of the volunteer corps, and a somewhat soldierly spirit took hold at the school. This change in day-to-day school life was not only commented

Die Kriegsjahre

Ostern 1941 wurde Barth an die Deutsche Oberschule für Jungen in Kamenz versetzt, fast zeitgleich mit der Übernahme der sächsischen NPEA in den Kompetenzbereich des Reiches am 1. April des gleichen Jahres.[22] Mit der Neustrukturierung der Nationalpolitischen Erziehungsanstalten endeten generell aber nicht die Schwierigkeiten der sächsischen Anstalt: Der im September 1939 begonnene Krieg brachte erneut Engpässe in der Finanzierung und Unterhaltung der Schule. Da viele Lehrer und Erzieher zum Kriegsdienst einberufen wurden, war ein systematischer Unterricht kaum mehr möglich. Einer Statistik aus dem Jahre 1942 zufolge wurden allein in Klotzsche von 39 angestellten Erziehern 20 zur Wehrmacht einberufen.[23] Zusätzliche Probleme traten auf, weil viele Lehrer und Erzieher an andere NPEA oder Heimschulen wechseln mussten. Der akute Lehrermangel an der Anstalt konnte zwar gemildert werden, indem Lehrer aus anderen höheren Schulen als Aushilfen eingestellt und nunmehr sogar Frauen an der Schule beschäftigt wurden, dennoch litt der Unterrichtsbetrieb unter dem Mangel und dem ständigen Wechsel der Lehrerschaft. Einschnitte gab es auch in der Organisation der Schule. Mit Wirkung Ostern 1940 wurde der Schulzug »Oberschule für Jungen in Aufbauform«, in der Volksschüler ab der 8. Klasse in die Schule aufgenommen werden konnten, abgebaut. Stattdessen wurde eine sogenannte 2. Klasse, ab 1941 eine 1. Klasse eingerichtet.[24] Bis zum Kriegsende im Mai 1945 gab es somit offiziell die Klassenstufen eins bis acht an der NPEA, auch wenn die oberen Jahrgänge nicht mehr an der Schule weilten: »Die Anstalts-›Mannschaft‹ ist [...] zum Kindergarten geworden. Einen 8. oder

Hochrangige Offiziere zu Besuch, im Hintergrund Schülerheim F, heute Haus 4.
High-ranking officers pay the school a visit. Rear of shot: boarding house F, now building 4.

upon in Kleint's memoirs, but also in the "Rundklotz" circulars sent by former teachers and pupils of the NPEA in Dresden-Klotzsche: "Barth was unfortunately [...] not bündisch enough [...]. He was too impressed by the Prussian style [...]. Barth gradually adopted the outward appearance of the Prussian schools and followed the example of Heißmeyer ever more closely, almost to the point of servility. The Hitler Youth therefore slipped further and further into the background. As had already been witnessed in the Prussian schools, Hitler Youth affiliation became a passive membership. The relationship with the Hitler Youth became noticeably cooler after our visit to the Hitler Youth Jamboree in 1937."[21]

Barth's loyalty to the party line was made particularly apparent by the new teachers he recruited. From taking up his position in 1935 to 1937 he forced through the systematic replacement of the teaching staff by pushing for the employment of "National Socialist pioneers in blood lines and scientific racism" and dismissing non-conformist teachers. The 31-page memorandum he sent to the Ministry of Popular Education in Dresden in September 1937 included detailed assessments of ten teachers he wished to have transferred as a matter of urgency. One of those assessments was typical of the strength of the militarily-influenced notion of masculinity he was permeated by: "Graduate secondary school teacher E.F.T., born on the 23.5.1885 (art, art history, handicrafts according to the examination regulations of 1914).

Assessment: unsoldierly, unheroic, soft, sensitive, competent in his field. From 1919 to April 1933 he was a member of the "Zum Goldenen Apfel" lodge in Dresden, finishing as a Worshipful Master (third level of office). [...] He can no longer be converted to the principles of the NPEA. Student teachers may not be assigned to former freemasons for training. Being the only suitable specialist representative of the art department, Teacher T. therefore restricts the selection of Schar leaders and Schar leader candidates to non-student teachers. It is logical to continue to adhere to the convention that former freemasons are particularly unsuitable for the training of boys as top-notch National Socialists."[22]

7. Zug gibt es ja längst nicht mehr, einzelne Jungen dieser Jahrgänge sind eigentlich nur noch aus Versehen hier, weil sie entweder zu jung für den grauen Rock oder infolge einer Erkrankung noch nicht wieder soldatentauglich waren. Der 6. Zug ist [...] mit einem Teil des 7. Zuges als Flak-Helfer eingesetzt [...]. Der 5. Zug ist vor einigen Tagen ins Generalgouvernement abgereist, um dort Dienst als Lagerführer in der Kinderlandverschickung zu tun.«[25]

Schleichend veränderte sich das Schulklima auch in anderer Hinsicht: Der Einfluss der SS nahm zu, denn August Heißmeyer, als Inspekteur aller NPEA und Behördenchef, war trotz formal staatlicher Aufsicht der Schulen nicht Bernhard Rust, dem Reichsminister für Wissenschaft, Erziehung und Volksbildung, sondern im Rang des Obergruppenführers der SS unterstellt. Die Zusammenarbeit erstreckte sich von der Teilnahme an Aufmärschen der SS über Vorträge bis zur Organisation von Fahrten für die »Jungmannen«. Regelmäßig besuchte Heißmeyer mit seinen Mitarbeitern die Anstalt. Daneben erschienen zu Feiern und Festakten hohe Funktionsträger der SS. Nicht zuletzt trug der Sportverein der Schule den Namen der SS (SS Sportgemeinschaft Dresden). Bestätigung finden diese Angaben auch durch Eugen Wittmann, den ehemaligen Unterrichtsleiter und ab Ende Februar 1944 bis Kriegsende Schulleiter der Rudolf-Schröter-Schule[26], der die daraus resultierenden Spannungen innerhalb der Lehrerschaft beschrieb: Viele Nicht-Mitglieder fühlten sich demnach als »Erzieher zweiten Grades« und hatten zudem die Befürchtung, sie kämen durch eine SS-Mitgliedschaft »unter eine viel stärkere Aufsicht als bisher...«[27]

In den letzten Kriegstagen gab es für alle NPEA »klare Befehle«: Für jede Anstalt war eine Aufnahmeanstalt von der Inspektion der NPEA bestimmt worden, die Belegschaft und »Jungmannen« im Zweifelsfall aufnehmen sollte. Alle in der Nähe wohnenden Schüler wiederum sollten beurlaubt werden. Für Klotzsche gab es keine Ausweichanstalt mehr. Stattdessen wurde die Schule von der Ankunft der Schülerschaft der NPEA Loben (Lublinitz) und Annaberg aus Oberschlesien überrascht. Wer beim Eintreffen der russischen Armee letztendlich noch in Klotzsche anwesend

Was the high level of initiative in evidence amongst tutors and pupils nevertheless sufficient to meet the standards of an elite National Socialist school? Doubts are justified, as the school's financial resources did not come close to the budgets available to the Prussian NPEA. Whereas Barth mentioned an annual sum of seven million Reichsmarks for the ten Prussian schools, his own budget made a far more modest impression.[23] It was 1938 before the Saxon state budget made a sizeable sum available to the school.[24] As late as 1937, Barth was compelled to pass critical comment to August Heißmeyer in a letter in which he requested funds for a second Saxon NPEA[25]: "Before the creation of a second NPEA can be considered, it is vital that the Rudolf-Schröter-Schule be brought up to the level of the Prussian NPEA. This is necessary in order to avert the imminent threat of the Rudolf-Schröter-Schule lagging even further behind and losing its status as an NPEA, especially as it already suffers from a lack of respect within the Reich."[26]

School equipment could only be improved or replaced on a step-by-step basis. Inadequacies were felt in almost every area, and were not restricted to the equipment required for the exclusive sports an NPEA was to offer its charges – riding, sailing, gliding, motor sports, skiing, fencing and boxing. Financial restrictions also dictated that the extra-curricular activities NPEA pupils were to engage in could only be offered from 1938 onwards. These activities included working in a mine, so-called "Landdienst" (unpaid work on a farm) and trips abroad. Time and again Barth compared his school with its Prussian peers, always to arrive at damning conclusions.

Barth's attempts to overcome the stigma attached to the school's failure to live up to the standards of a fully-fledged elite National Socialist school were not restricted to the effort which accompanied his burning ambition. He also had a special racial profile in mind – one he believed would return the school to favour. As early as 1938 this saw him introduce an even stricter selection process for prospective pupils. The fact that these new selection criteria were kept to in the majority of cases is reflected in the files of the Ministry of Popular Education, which show that, in the Easter

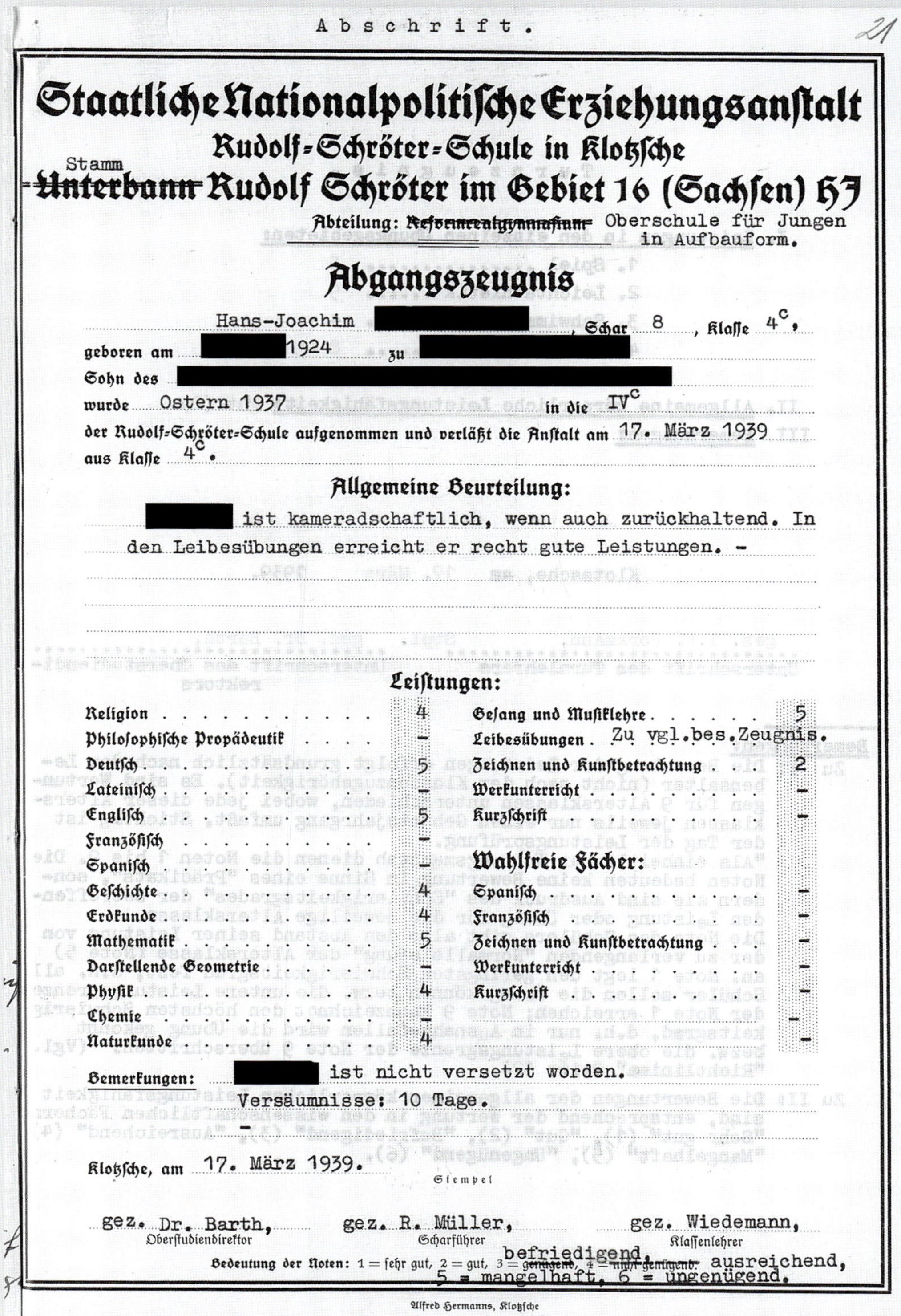

Abschrift.

21

Staatliche Nationalpolitische Erziehungsanstalt

Rudolf-Schröter-Schule in Klotzsche

~~Unterbann~~ Stamm Rudolf Schröter im Gebiet 16 (Sachsen) HJ

Abteilung: ~~Reformrealgymnasium~~ Oberschule für Jungen in Aufbauform.

Abgangszeugnis

Hans-Joachim [redacted], Schar 8, Klasse 4c,

geboren am [redacted] 1924 zu [redacted]

Sohn des [redacted]

wurde Ostern 1937 in die IVc

der Rudolf-Schröter-Schule aufgenommen und verläßt die Anstalt am 17. März 1939

aus Klasse 4c.

Allgemeine Beurteilung:

[redacted] ist kameradschaftlich, wenn auch zurückhaltend. In den Leibesübungen erreicht er recht gute Leistungen. –

Leistungen:

Religion	4	Gesang und Musiklehre	5
Philosophische Propädeutik	–	Leibesübungen	Zu vgl. bes. Zeugnis.
Deutsch	5	Zeichnen und Kunstbetrachtung	2
Lateinisch	–	Werkunterricht	–
Englisch	5	Kurzschrift	–
Französisch	–		
Spanisch	–	**Wahlfreie Fächer:**	
Geschichte	4	Spanisch	–
Erdkunde	4	Französisch	–
Mathematik	5	Zeichnen und Kunstbetrachtung	–
Darstellende Geometrie	–	Werkunterricht	–
Physik	4	Kurzschrift	–
Chemie	–		–
Naturkunde	4		–

Bemerkungen: [redacted] ist nicht versetzt worden.

Versäumnisse: 10 Tage.

–

Klotzsche, am 17. März 1939.

Stempel

gez. Dr. Barth, Oberstudiendirektor   gez. R. Müller, Scharführer   gez. Wiedemann, Klassenlehrer

Bedeutung der Noten: 1 = sehr gut, 2 = gut, 3 = ~~genügend~~ befriedigend, 4 = ~~nicht genügend~~ ausreichend, 5 = mangelhaft, 6 = ungenügend.

Alfred Hermanns, Klotzsche

Abschrift eines Zeugnisses der Rudolf-Schröter-Schule.

Copy of a report issued by the Rudolf-Schröter-Schule.

war, ist noch unsicher. Vieles deutet darauf hin, dass die Klotzscher Schüler schon vorher in ihre Heimatorte entlassen wurden.

Nach der Kapitulation der Deutschen Wehrmacht am 7./8. Mai 1945 wurden sowohl die Nationalpolitischen Erziehungsanstalten als auch die Adolf-Hitler-Schulen durch die alliierten Militärregierungen verboten. Absolventen aller Schulen, nicht nur der Nationalsozialistischen Ausleseschulen, die mit einem »Reifevermerk« in die Wehrmacht eingezogen worden waren, hatten die Reifeprüfung nachzuholen. Fast ausnahmslos wurden indes die an den NPEA beschäftigten Lehrer und Erzieher in den Schuldienst des bundesdeutschen Staates übernommen.[28] Für sie war nur der Nachweis einer regulären pädagogischen Ausbildung notwendig. Welchen Werdegang Lehrer und Erzieher der NPEA Dresden-Klotzsche nach Kriegsende konkret nahmen, müssen weitere Forschungen zeigen.

Eliteauswahl oder Elitepropaganda?

Die »Auslese« der Schüler und Lehrer sollte alleinige Zugangsberechtigung zur Aufnahme an die Rudolf-Schröter-Schule sein. Wie sind aber die Auswahlkriterien selbst – »arische Herkunft, Gesundheit, Charaktertüchtigkeit, besondere körperliche und geistige Leistungsfähigkeit«[29] – zu bewerten? Basierten sie auf transparenten, mess- und überprüfbaren Indikatoren?

Nur auf sportlichem Gebiet kann mit Sicherheit von hohem bzw. höchstem Niveau an der Schule und damit von Elitecharakter gesprochen werden.[30] Dies unterstreichen auch die Äußerungen Eugen Wittmanns, des letzten Schulleiters, der aber hinsichtlich der Diskrepanz zwischen intendierter und tatsächlicher Außenwirkung der Schule nicht ohne Enttäuschung bekennen musste:

of 1938 alone, the senior racial adviser of the Elbe section of the elite corps of the NSDAP (the SS) deemed 113 of 240 applicants racially unsuitable and therefore unfit to attend the school.[27] In addition, the zeal exhibited by Barth in his work with local Hitler Youth groups and the local city branch of the NSDAP led to the school being praised as "a sort of example to the other NPEA" by the board responsible for the NPEA.

The war years

Barth was transferred to the Deutsche Oberschule für Jungen[28] in Kamenz in the Easter of 1941, a move which came almost simultaneous to the Saxon NPEA being brought under the authority of the Reich on the 1st of April that same year.29 The restructuring of the NPEA network nevertheless failed to completely solve the difficulties at its Saxon branch, which had struggled under the weight of additional restrictions on its finances and maintenance since the outbreak of war in the September of 1939. Another issue was the calling up of a large number of teachers and tutors for military service, which rendered structured teaching practically impossible. According to statistics published in 1942, in Klotzsche alone 20 of 39 full-time tutors were conscripted to the Wehrmacht.[30] The mandatory transfer of many teachers and tutors to other NPEA or boarding schools led to further problems. Though it was possible to alleviate the resultant acute lack of teaching staff at the school by employing teachers from other secondary schools on a temporary basis (or even by allowing women to work at the school), lessons suffered as a result of a shortage of and constant changes in teaching staff. The school structure also experienced cutbacks, and the "Oberschule für Jungen in Aufbauform"[31] section of the school, which until that point had taken on state pupils from eighth-year age upwards, was disbanded in the Easter of 1940. A so-called "second year" was created in its place, with a "first year" added in 1941.[32] By the end of the war in May 1945 the NPEA therefore officially covered eight school years – this despite

»Wir wollten den Dresdnern […] beibringen, daß wir nicht nur eine Schule sind wie alle anderen, noch eine Sportschule, sondern daß sich in unseren Anstalten der Nationalsozialismus in der jungen Generation eine Form schafft, die pädagogisch weiterwirkt auf die anderen Schulen, daß man uns nicht mehr einseitig betrachtet als Sportanstalt, sondern als eine politische Einrichtung […].«[31]

Welcher politische wie persönliche Beurteilungsspielraum den Verantwortlichen indes gerade bei den pseudowissenschaftlichen Merkmalen wie »Erbgesundheit« und »Rassereinheit« eingeräumt wurde, zeigen Selbstzeugnisse ehemaliger Schüler: »Es gehört nämlich auch dazu, daß er [Dr. Barth] der militärischen Besichtigung entsprechend, […] auf einen möglichst günstigen Eindruck bedacht war. Dabei war er Brillenträgern und solchen, die rassisch nicht ganz dem Muster entsprachen, gegenüber rücksichtslos (›Ins 2. oder gar 3. Glied!‹).«[32] Barths persönliche Profilierung beeinflusste die rassenbiologischen Kriterien je nach Bewerberlage und Führerbedarf.

Auf intellektuellem Gebiet gab es im Allgemeinen keine überdurchschnittlichen Leistungen, wie erhalten gebliebene Reifezeugnisse bestätigen.[33] Im Übrigen korrespondierte dies durchaus mit den Prioritäten nationalsozialistischer Erziehungsideologie, in deren Mittelpunkt nicht Wissensbildung, sondern »Bildung des Charakters« und »Förderung der Willens- und Entschlusskraft« standen. Letztere wiederum zielte auf den Führungseinsatz insofern, als dass die Absolventen aller NPEA bedingungslos »für Volk und Führer« und damit für den »Kampfeinsatz« vorbereitet werden sollten. Darauf war der Bildungsgang letztlich ausgerichtet.

Der Unterricht selbst unterschied sich nicht grundlegend von dem anderer höherer Schulen des Landes. Ein geschlossenes Konzept für die Nationalpolitischen Erziehungsanstalten hat es für die Gesamtzeit ihres Bestehens nicht gegeben. Zwar traf man sich regelmäßig zu Anstaltsleitertagungen, bei denen auch über schulpädagogische Fragen diskutiert wurde, das eigentliche Unterrichtsgeschehen lag indes immer in der Verantwortung der Schulleitung und Lehrerschaft.[34]

the fact that its upper-year pupils were no longer present: "The school 'team' has […] become a kindergarten. An eight or seventh year has been lacking for some time, and the few boys in those years who have been left behind are only here as a result of oversight, because they are too young to wear the grey coat or because they are unfit for service further to illness. The sixth year and some of the seventh year have been […] put into action as anti-aircraft auxiliaries […]. A few days ago the fifth year left for the General Government to serve as camp leaders within the children's evacuation programme."[33]

The atmosphere at the school experienced an additional, insidious shift. Though the NPEA were technically under state control, their inspector and administrative head, August Heißmeyer, answered to the SS in his capacity as an Obergruppenführer[34] rather than to Bernhard Rust, the Reich Minister of Science, Education and National Culture. The influence of the SS at the school therefore increased, with cooperation ranging from participation in SS rallies to lectures and the organisation of trips for the "young men". In addition to regular visits to the Saxon school by Heißmeyer and his colleagues, its celebrations and ceremonies were also attended by high-ranking SS functionaries. The school sports club even bore the name of the SS ("SS Sportgemeinschaft Dresden"). These details are verified by Eugen Wittmann, a teacher at the Rudolf-Schröter-Schule and holder of the position of headmaster from the end of February 1944 until the end of the war.[35] He describes the tensions which arose amongst the teaching staff, which left many non-SS-members feeling like "second-class teachers" and fearful that SS membership would see them placed "under even closer supervision than before…"[36]

The last days of the war saw "clear orders" issued to all NPEA. On the one hand, the NPEA inspectorate assigned each school with a backup school which was to take in its staff and "young men" if required. On the other, all pupils who lived in the local area were granted leave to go home. Though Klotzsche itself did not have a backup school, it was surprised by the arrival of pupils from the NPEA in Loben (Lublinitz) and the Upper Silesian town of Annaberg.

Studierzimmer. Study room.

It remains uncertain who was still in Klotzsche when the Russian army arrived. Many clues indicate that the pupils of the Klotzsche NPEA had already been sent back to their home towns.

The capitulation of the German Wehrmacht on the $7^{th}/8^{th}$ of May 1945 was followed by the imposition of a ban on both NPEA and "Adolf Hitler" schools by the military governments set up by the Allies. On the one hand, all school leavers – and not just those from selective National Socialist

Für die Rudolf-Schröter-Schule sind zwar keine Unterrichtsaufzeichnungen, Hospitationsprotokolle oder ähnliches erhalten geblieben, Einblick können aber die zahlreichen Veröffentlichungen der Fachlehrer in der Zeitschrift »Die höhere Schule« (Monatsschrift des Nationalsozialistischen Lehrerbundes Sachsen) geben. Schon die Überschriften wie beispielsweise »Die Reden Hitlers als Grundlage einer politischen Schulung«, »Zur Judenfrage. Eine Unterrichtsskizze«, »Geländespiele mit selbstgezeichneten Kartenskizzen« verweisen auf den Inhalt der Publikationen. Was nicht weiter verwunderlich erscheint, wähnte man sich doch, als Lehrer einer Eliteschule Richtlinien für einzelne Unterrichtsfächer zu entwerfen, die als Vorbild für andere höhere Schulen gelten sollten.

Wenn aber wenig verifizierbare Größen, wie rassebiologische Aspekte und die »Bildung des Charakters« zu Auslesemaßstäben wurden, weder überdurchschnittliche Schulleistungen, der Sport ausgenommen, noch die Ausstattung der Schule ein Elitekonzept rechtfertigen, worauf stützte sich dann die Bezeichnung »Elite«?

»Und die Begeisterung ist echt und wird anhalten. [...] Sie sind stolz darauf, der Rudolf-Schröter-Schule anzugehören, einer harten Gemeinschaft gewiß, aber einer Elite durch freiwillige, frohe Pflichterfüllung. Und sie fühlen, viele wohl schon bewußt, daß sie, jeder zu seinem Teile, mit Träger des Ganzen sind, mit aller Verantwortung, die sich daraus dem Ganzen gegenüber, gegen die Führer und die Kameraden und für ihre eigene Haltung ergibt.«[35]

Das Eliteversprechen und das sich ausbildende Elitebewusstsein beflügelten vor allem die Schüler und trugen den alles entscheidenden Einsatzwillen, für »Führer und Volk« kämpfen zu wollen. Besondere Faszination übten dabei das militärische Auftreten sowie die nächtlichen Fest- und Feierrituale auf die Jungen aus. Hier wurde Elite-Bewusstsein inszeniert, ein Kollektiv-Bewusstsein beschworen, das sich im unbedingten Kampfeswillen im Krieg bewähren sollte, denn erst dort würde man zum Manne reifen.

Um aber allen diesen Erwartungen gerecht werden zu können, unterzogen sich Schüler wie Lehrer gleichermaßen besonderen Härten im Alltag. Ob militärischer Drill und

schools – who had been given a "leaver's note" and conscripted into the Wehrmacht were obliged to retake their school leaving exams. On the other, and almost without exception, teachers and tutors who had been employed at NPEA schools were adopted into the federal German teaching system.[37] All that was required of them was certification that they had completed a legitimate course of teacher training. The post-war paths taken by the teachers and tutors of the NPEA in Klotzsche are a matter for separate research.

Elite selection or elite propaganda?

Success in the "selection process" was designed to be the only way for pupils and teachers to gain admission to the Rudolf-Schröter-Schule. But how are the selection criteria involved – "Aryan heritage, health, strength of character, special physical and mental ability"[38] – to be assessed? Were they based on transparent, measurable and checkable indicators?

It is only on a sporting level that the school can be said to have undoubtedly been on a high or the highest – and therefore elite – level.[39] This is underlined by the comments of Eugen Wittmann, the school's last headmaster, who was forced – not without disappointment – to make the following admission regarding the discrepancy between its intended and actual outward impression: "We wanted to show the people of Dresden that we were not only different to other schools – and besides that a sports school – but also that our National Socialist schools were creating a model amongst the younger generation which had a knock-on educational effect on other schools. That we should no longer be one-sidedly regarded as a sports school, but as a political institution."[40]

The extent to which those responsible for the selection process were given personal and political room to manoeuvre in their assessment of such pseudo-scientific aspects as "soundness of heritage" and "racial purity" is indicated in the testimonies of former pupils: "The fact that he [Dr. Barth] was intent on making the best impression possible in the military inspection was also part and parcel of it. His approach saw him treat spectacle wearers and the like – those who did not fit the racial profile – with particular ruthlessness ('Stick them in the second or third rank!)."[41] The extent to which Barth's personal notion of an ideal profile influenced the consideration of racial-biological criteria was dependent on the candidates available and the current need for leaders.

The fact that intellectual performance did not tend to venture above the average is confirmed by contemporary school leaving certificates.[42] This actually corresponds with the priorities set out by National Socialist educational ideology, which demoted the fostering of knowledge in favour of "character building" and the "promotion of willpower and determination". These latter priorities were aimed at the promotion of leadership skills, in so far as all NPEA graduates were to be prepared to unquestioningly serve their "nation and leader" and be "sent into battle". That, in the end, was the aim of the education provided at the school.

Lessons themselves were not fundamentally different to those taught at other secondary schools around the country, and indeed the NPEA lacked a cohesive overall concept throughout their existence. Though pedagogical issues and other matters were discussed at regular meetings between headmasters[43], what actually went on during lessons remained the responsibility of the respective headmasters and teaching staff.

Although no lesson notes, hospital protocols or similar documents pertaining to the Rudolf-Schröter-Schule have survived, the numerous publications by its specialist subject teachers which appeared in "Die höhere Schule" (the monthly journal of the Saxon section of the National Socialist Teachers' Association) offer an insight into school life. Their content is clear from their titles alone (for example "Hitler's speeches as a foundation for a political education", "On the Jewish question. A draft lesson.", "Orienteering using self-drawn sketch maps."). Somewhat unsurprisingly, they presumed that their position as teachers at an elite

»Vormittagsplan Winterhalbjahr 1936/37

Montag – Sonnabend

6 Uhr	Wecken
bis 6.10 Uhr	Morgenturnen
bis 6.35 Uhr	Duschen, Fertigmachen
bis 6.45 Uhr	Anzug- und Stubendurchsicht
6.50 Uhr	Flaggenhissung
7 Uhr	Frühstück
7.20 – 12.45 Uhr	Unterricht
13 Uhr	Mittagessen
13.25 – 14.25 Uhr	Bettruhe

Sonnabend

von 12.45 Uhr an Nachturlaub bis Sonntag 22 Uhr

Nachmittag
siehe besonderen Plan

21.10 Uhr	Zapfenstreich für U III und O III
22 Uhr	Zapfenstreich für U II – O I

Nachmittagsplan Winterhalbjahr 1936/37

Montag

14.40 – 15.20 Uhr	O I a, b und U I a Spiel
	O II c Spiel
15.25 – 16.05 Uhr	O II c und U III a Spiel
16.10 – 16.50 Uhr	O II a und O II b Spiel
	O I c und U I c Spiel
Außerdem	
14.40 – 16.05 Uhr	wahlfrei Latein
17.05 Uhr	Kaffee
17.25 – 19.25 Uhr	Arbeitsstunde
19.35 Uhr	Dienstausgabe und Essen
20.10 – 21.10 Uhr	Fanfarenzug
	Spielmannszug
	Laienspiel (Zoche)
	Instrumentalkreis (Stöckel)
20.10 – 21.30 Uhr	Fechten
	Werkunterricht (Pappe)

[...]

Sonntag

1mal im Monat vormittags Dienst.«[39]

Disziplin von jedem Schüler geschätzt wurden, wie der Unterrichtsleiter bei der Zehnjahresfeier der NPEA im April 1944 vorgab, ist fraglich. Selbstzeugnisse ehemaliger Schüler beklagen gerade »das ganze soldatische Gepräge« als »maßlos übertrieben«[36]: »Gemeinschaftsleben [...] durch ›schwerer Pflichten tägliche Bewahrung‹, durch den soldatischen Dienst in seiner vielgescholtenen und doch so notwendigen Gleichförmigkeit, Pünktlichkeit und Unabdingbarkeit, in seiner Rücksichtslosigkeit gegen persönliche individuelle Wünsche, ein Leben, geregelt durch gute Gewohnheiten und Sitten, ist der Acker, auf dem die Früchte wachsen. [...] Vom Wecken bis zum Zapfenstreich kennt jeder seine Pflichten. Die Jüngsten gewöhnen sich daran, die Älteren finden es recht; wer über die sachliche Härte erst klagt, der lobt sie am Ende.«[37]

Die Woche war – wie Auszüge aus dem Organisationsplan für das Winterhalbjahr 1936/37 zeigen – straff organisiert. Den Jungen blieb dabei nur wenig Zeit zur Muße; sie waren rund um die Uhr in das Schul- und Internatsleben eingebunden.[38]

Gleichzeitig jedoch bot die Schule ihren Schülern große Chancen und Gelegenheiten zur Entfaltung ihrer Talente. Welcher Junge durfte schon am Reitunterricht teilnehmen oder eine Segelfliegerausbildung absolvieren? Ganz zu schweigen von der Möglichkeit, die Fahrerlaubnis für PKW und Motorrad zu erwerben. Dass diese Privilegien aber um den Preis eines bedingungslosen Kampfes für »Führer und Volk« im Krieg erkauft wurden, zeigt die hohe Zahl an Kriegstoten und Verwundeten unter der Lehrer- und Schülerschaft. Die Selbstzeugnisse ehemaliger Schüler bilanzieren ernüchtert:

links: Auszüge aus dem Organisationsplan für das Winterhalbjahr 1936/37.
right: Extracts from the schedule for the winter and spring terms of 1936/37.

school gave them the authority to draw up subject guidelines which were to serve as examples to other secondary schools.

If, however, few verifiable dimensions such as racial-biological characteristics or "character traits" were used as selection benchmarks, and neither above-average scholastic performance – with the exception of sport – nor school facilities justified an elite concept, what was the designation "elite" based on?

"And the enthusiasm is real and is set to last. [...] They are proud to belong to the Rudolf-Schröter-Schule – a tough community, certainly, but one rendered elite by duties carried out voluntarily and with good cheer. They also already sense, many of them perhaps consciously, that they are all, in their own way, upholders of the whole. This includes all the related responsibility they have to the whole, their leaders and comrades and their own standing."[44]

The promise of elite status and a growing elite consciousness were a particular source of inspiration to pupils, who demonstrated the all-important willingness to fight for their "leader and nation". They were particularly fascinated by military style and the celebrations and ceremonial rituals which took place in the evenings. The elite, collective consciousness these events were used to invoke was supposed to prove its worth in the form of an unconditional willingness to fight on the field of battle, which was built up in pupils' minds as the only situation in which they could become men.

Daily life nevertheless saw both pupils and teachers undergo exceptional hardships in order to satisfy all of these expectations. It is debatable whether or not military drill and discipline was valued by every pupil to the extent claimed by the teacher at the tenth anniversary celebrations of the NPEA in April 1944. Indeed, the testimonies of former pupils complain about "the whole military bent" as being "completely over the top"[45]:

"A communal life [...] formed by the 'weighty duties of daily preservation', by military service in all its chastising and yet so necessary uniformity, punctuality and indispensability, its ruthless treatment of personal, individual wishes, a life controlled by habits and customs, is the soil from which

"Morning timetable, winter and spring terms 1936/37

Monday – Saturday

6:00	Wake-up call
Up to 6:10	Morning gymnastics
Up to 6:35	Shower, dress
Up to 6:45	Uniform and room inspection
6:50	Raising of the flag
7:00	Breakfast
7:20 – 12:45	Lessons
13:00	Lunch
13:25 – 14:25	Bed rest

Saturday

From 12:45: leave until 22:00 on Sunday.

Afternoon – see separate plan.

21:10	Sounding of the last post (years 8 and 9)
22:00	Sounding of the last post (years 10 to 13)

Afternoon timetable, winter and spring terms 1936/37

Monday

14:40 – 15:20	Years 13a, 13b and 12a: game
	Year 11c: game
15:25 – 16:05	Years 11c and 8a: game
16:10 – 16:50	Years 11a and 11b: game
	Years 13c and 12c: game
Also	
14:40 – 16:05	Latin (optional)
17:05	Coffee
17:25 – 19:25	Chores
19:35	Allocation of duties, dinner
20:10 – 21:10	Bugle practice
	Marching band practice
	Amateur dramatics (Zoche)
	Music group (Stöckel)
20:10 – 21:30	Fencing
	Handicrafts (cardboard)

[...]

Sunday

Morning duty once a month."[40]

the fruit will grow. [...] Each and every one of them knows their duties from the wake-up call to the last post. The youngest of the boys grow used to it, the elder amongst them see it as right and proper; he who complains about the clinical harshness in the beginning will praise it in the end."[46]

The school week was tightly organised, as is illustrated by extracts from the schedule for the winter and spring terms of 1936/37. The boys were incorporated into school and boarding life around the clock, and only had a small amount of leisure time[47]:

At the same time, however, the school offered its pupils excellent opportunities to develop their talents. Which other boys were able to take riding lessons or train as a glider pilot, not to mention gain a driving license for cars and motorcycles? The fact that these privileges were granted in exchange for the recipients' willingness to fight unconditionally for their "leader and nation" in the war is reflected in the high number of war casualties and wounded amongst both pupils and teachers. The testimonies of former pupils paint a sobering picture: "The fact that we were able to do arms drill earlier and were tougher than others is not enough to justify the view that Klotzsche offered an elite upbringing in the sense of the 'selection of the best' (= the definition of elite in a dictionary). The only reason for us to be seen as performing at a high level was our ability to operate as fighting machines, deliver meaningless phrases in a commanding voice in order to keep people under control and the example we set to others in our willingness to sacrifice our lives for our 'leader, people and fatherland'"[48]

In spite of their significant disillusionment, the testimonies of pupils and teachers show that they also idealised their time at the school. This notwithstanding, there is cause for hope that, based as it is on knowledge and powers of judgment, an elite consciousness can provide a social counterweight to ignorant and irrational politics.

»Nur daß wir früher Gewehrklopfen konnten als andere und daß wir härter waren als andere, berechtigt noch nicht zur Feststellung, daß in Klotzsche eine elitäre Erziehung im Sinne einer ›Auslese der Besten‹ (= Elitedefinition in einem Lexikon) erfolgte. Unser einziger hoher Leistungsstandard war darin zu erblicken, daß wir als Kampfmaschinen zu agieren in der Lage waren, Leerfloskeln, welche zur Führung von Menschen notwendig waren, lautstark repetieren konnten und ansonsten imstande waren, Vorbild zu sein in der Bereitschaft, unser Leben für ›Führer, Volk und Vaterland‹ hinzugeben.«[40]

Neben der starken Desillusionierung verklärten Lehrer und Schüler gleichermaßen ihre Zeit an der Schule, wie die Selbstzeugnisse dokumentieren. Nichtsdestotrotz nährt es aber auch die Hoffnung, dass Elitebewusstsein, das im Gegensatz dazu auf Wissen und Urteilskraft beruht, ein gesellschaftliches Gegengewicht zu ignoranter und irrationaler Politik sein kann.

Anmerkungen

1 Nachfolgend wird der Lesbarkeit halber für Nationalpolitische Erziehungsanstalt die Abkürzung NPEA, umgangssprachlich NAPOLA, verwendet.
2 Nach der Röhm-Affäre Sommer 1934 trug sie den Namen »Staatliche Nationalpolitische Erziehungsanstalt. Rudolf-Schröter-Schule. Unterbann Rudolf-Schröter im Gebiet 16 (Sachsen) HJ«, später an Stelle des Unterbannes die Bezeichnung »Stamm«.
3 Vgl. Kleint 1943. Alle nachfolgenden Zitate sind dieser Publikation entnommen.
4 Welche Dienststelle gemeint ist, konnte bis zum jetzigen Zeitpunkt nicht ermittelt werden.
5 Vgl. zu den baulichen Ausführungen u.a. Kramer/Tessenow 1929, S. 99.
6 Kleint 1943, S. 17.
7 Die Versetzungen gestalteten sich als äußerst schwierig, denn aufgrund der schwierigen Finanzlage Sachsens und zurückgehender Schülerzahlen gab es kaum freiwerdende Planstellen.
8 Kleint 1943, S. 20.
9 SHD 21361, S. 244.
10 Verordnungsblatt 1934, H. 8, S. 36.
11 Ebd.
12 SHD 21350, S. 233 (Schreiben des Leiters der NPEA in Klotzsche an das sächsische Volksbildungsministerium vom 3. 1. 1939).
13 Laut Scholz traten zu den üblichen 5 Sportstunden pro Woche 25 Wehrsportstunden und 5 Schwimmstunden hinzu. Vgl. Scholtz 1973, S. 70.
14 Kleint 1943, S. 42 f.
15 Rundbrief 1976, S. 2 f.
16 SDH 21352, Bl. 12.
17 Genaue Zahlenangaben für die sächsische NPEA können hier nicht genannt werden, denn für die Rudolf-Schröter-Schule gab es bis 1938 keine eigene im sächsischen Staatshaushalt ausgewiesene Kostenstelle.
18 Vgl. u. a. Sächsisches Gesetzblatt 1938, S. 80 f. Gesetz über den Staatshaushaltsplan, Einzelplan V (Ministerium für Volksbildung), Kapitel 70a (Rudolf-Schröter-Schule).
19 Zu diesem Zeitpunkt Inspekteur der Landesverwaltung der NPEA in Preußen, später aller NPEA.
20 SHD 21352, S. 1 (Bericht über eine Besprechung zwischen Anstaltsleiter Dr. Barth und Vertretern des sächsischen Volksbildungsministeriums vom 24. 7. 1937).
21 SHD 21356, S. 122.
22 Ob dieser Versetzung Querelen mit seinem neuen Vorgesetzten August Heißmeyer, Inspekteur der Nationalpolitischen Erziehungsanstalten, vorangingen, kann nicht abschließend geklärt werden. Die Zeitgleichheit beider Ereignisse aber ist augenfällig!
23 Vgl. Potsdamer Kameradschaft 1943, H. 1, S. 42 f.
24 6. Klasse bzw. 5. Klasse nach heutiger Zählung.
25 Aussage eines Lehrers der NPEA in: Blätter der Nationalpolitischen Erziehungsanstalt Klotzsche in Sachsen 1943, H. 14/15, S. 36.
26 Nachdem Barth Ostern 1941 versetzt wurde, blieb die Schule das Jahr über ohne Anstaltsleiter. Erst am 1. Dezember 1941 wurde Dr. Hartmut Nestler, zunächst kommissarisch, mit der Leitung der Anstalt beauftragt. Er arbeitete bis zu seiner Einberufung in die Wehrmacht Ende Februar 1944 als Schulleiter.
27 Ueberhorst 1969, S. 429 (Auszug aus einem Tonbandinterview des Herausgebers vom 11. 3. 1968 mit Eugen Wittmann, letztem Anstaltsleiter der NPEA in Klotzsche).
28 Ob Lehrer in den Schuldienst der DDR übernommen worden sind, ist nicht bekannt.
29 Verordnungsblatt 1934, H. 8, S. 36.
30 Beispielsweise in Wettkämpfen wie dem »Lauf rund um den Großen Garten« in Dresden, »Elbstaffeln«, Reichsjugendwettkämpfen und Skiwettkämpfen der Höheren Schulen Sachsens, die in verschiedenen zeitgenössischen Zeitungen und Zeitschriften dokumentiert sind.
31 Ueberhorst 1969, S. 429.
32 Rundbrief 1976, S. 3.

33 Kritisch anzumerken sei, dass auch diese nicht in jedem Fall ein objektives Bild des Unterrichtsniveaus widerspiegeln können.
34 Die Fachgemeinschaft für Geschichte der NPEA Naumburg erarbeitete sogar ein Geschichtslehrbuch, das ausschließlich für alle NPEA galt.
35 Kleint 1943, S. 30.
36 Stellungnahme des ehemaligen Schülers R. S. seine Schulzeit an der Rudolf-Schröter-Schule betreffend (April 1994).
37 Blätter der Nationalpolitischen Erziehungsanstalt Klotzsche in Sachsen 1944, H. 18, S. 40.
38 Von 1935 bis 1942 besuchten 2116 Schüler die Rudolf-Schröter-Schule. Die Gesamtsschülerzahl pro Schuljahr betrug zwischen 213 (1942) und 321 (1937) Schülern. Die Anzahl der Lehrer bzw. Erzieher schwankte in den gleichen Jahrgängen zwischen 27 und 36. Im Vergleich zu den höheren Schulen lag das Lehrer-Schüler-Verhältnis mit ca. 7 bis 11 Schülern pro Lehrer bzw. Erzieher unter dem Durchschnitt.
39 SHD 21351, Blatt 53 ff.
40 Stellungnahme des ehemaligen Schülers H. J. zum Weihnachtsrundbrief 1976, S. 17.

Notes

1 For ease of reading, the term "Nationalpolitische Erziehungsanstalt" (State National Political Educational Institution) has been shortened to "NPEA" (referred to colloquially as "NAPOLA") in the following sections.
2 The Landesschule Dresden was a boarding establishment which featured both a progressive grammar school and an upper secondary school.
3 After the Night of the Long Knives in the summer of 1934, the school bore the name of "Staatliche Nationalpolitische Erziehungsanstalt. Rudolf-Schröter-Schule. Unterbann Rudolf-Schröter im Gebiet 16 (Sachsen) HJ". The term "Unterbann" was later replaced by "Stamm".
4 See Kleint 1943. All of the following quotes are taken from the aforementioned publication.
5 A "Fürstenschule" was a state boarding school for the fostering of upper-level civil servants and clergy.
6 The identity of the department in question remains unknown.
7 An "Unterbann" was the lower section of the "Bann" classification, the second-largest sub-division of the Hitler Youth. An "Obergebiet" was the upper section of the "Gebiet" classification, the largest sub-division of the Hitler Youth. "Mitte" further specifies the section as being the central area of Obergebiet 4.
8 The following section uses the terms "Gefolgschaft","Schar" and "Kameradschaft". These were the words used for the third-smallest, second-smallest and smallest sub-divisions of the Hitler Youth respectively.
9 See related constructional specifications, including Kramer/Tessenow 1929, p. 99.
10 Kleint 1943, p. 17.
11 The transfers were extremely difficult to bring about, as Saxony's troubled financial situation and declining pupil numbers meant that hardly any posts were becoming available.
12 "Bündische Jugend" was the name given to the German Youth Movement in its second phase after the First World War.
13 Ibid, p. 20.
14 SHD 21361, p. 244.
15 Regulations set out in 1934, edition 8, p. 36.
16 Ibid.
17 SHD 21350, p. 233 (memorandum from the head of the NPEA in Klotzsche to the Saxon Ministry of Popular Education, dated the 3rd of January 1939).
18 According to Scholtz (1973), the standard 5 hours of sport per week were supplemented by 25 hours of military training and 5 hours of swimming. See Scholtz 1973, p. 70.
19 A Gauleiter was the leader of one of the "Gau" administrative regions set up by the NSDAP.
20 Kleint 1943, p. 42 f.
21 25th circular (1976), p. 2 f. (comments made by E. S. on the specifics of the NPEA in Klotzsche).
22 SHD 21352, Sheet 12.
23 As there was no cost item for the Rudolf-Schröter-Schule in the Saxon state budget until 1938 it is not possible to give precise figures on the Saxon NPEA here.
24 See (amongst others) Saxon law gazette 1938, p. 80 f. Gesetz über den Staatshaushaltsplan, Einzelplan V (Ministerium für Volksbildung), Chapter 70a (Rudolf-Schröter-Schule).
25 At that time Heißmeyer was the Prussian NPEA authority's inspector, a position he later held for all NPEA.
26 SHD 21352, p. 1 (report on a meeting between headmaster Dr. Barth and representatives of the Saxon Ministry of Popular Education on the 24th of July 1937).
27 Ibid., SHD 21356, p. 122.
28 English translation: German Grammar School for Boys.
29 It is not possible to make a definitive statement on whether or not this transfer was the result of quarrels between Barth and his new superior and NPEA inspector, August Heißmeyer. The simultaneity of the two events is striking all the same!
30 See Potsdamer Kameradschaft 1943, edition 1, p. 42 f.
31 6th year and 5th year respectively in modern terms.
32 English translation: Progressive Grammar School for Boys.
33 Statement made by an NPEA teacher in the 1943 gazette of the Nationalpolitischen Erziehungsanstalt Klotzsche in Sachsen, edition 14/15, p. 36. The years mentioned in this quote relate to the number of years spent at the NPEA, and therefore do not correspond with the 13-year system otherwise used.
34 Obergruppenführer was a paramilitary rank in the NSDAP. First created as a rank of the SA, it went on to be the highest SS rank behind that of Reichsführer-SS (held by Heinrich Himmler) until 1942.
35 The school was without a headmaster for the majority of 1941 after the transferral of Barth in the Easter of that year. It was only on the 1st of December 1941 that Dr. Hartmut Nestler was appointed as the new headmaster of the school, initially on a temporary basis. He was the headmaster of the school until being conscripted into the Wehrmacht at the end of February 1944.
36 Ueberhorst 1969, p. 429 (Extract from a taped interview with Eugen Wittmann, the last headmaster of the NPEA in Klotzsche, recorded by the publisher on the 11th of March 1968).
37 It is unknown whether or not teachers were adopted into the teaching system of the GDR.
38 Regulations set out by the Saxon Ministry of Popular Education in 1934, edition 8, p. 36.
39 Examples come in the form of competitions such as "the run around the Großer Garten" in Dresden; "Elbe relays"; Reich-wide youth competitions; and skiing competitions against other Saxon secondary schools, which are documented in various contemporary newspapers and magazines.
40 Ueberhorst 1969, p. 429.
41 Rundbrief 1976, p. 3.
42 It is nevertheless to be noted that these documents do not necessarily provide an objective portrait of lesson quality.
43 The history department at the NPEA in Naumburg even drew up a history textbook which was only to be used in NPEA schools.
44 Kleint 1943, p. 30.
45 Statement made by former pupil R. S. on his schooldays at the Rudolf-Schröter-Schule (April 1994).
46 The 1944 gazette of the Nationalpolitischen Erziehungsanstalt Klotzsche in Sachsen, issue. 18, p. 40.
47 From 1935–1942 a total of 2116 pupils attended the Rudolf-Schröter-Schule. The total number of pupils per year ranged between 213 (1942) and 321 (1937). The number of teachers and tutors varied between 27 and 36 during those years. The school's average ratio of between seven and eleven pupils per teacher was below average when compared with other secondary schools.
48 SHD 21351, Sheet 53 ff.
49 Statement made by former pupil H. J. in the Christmas circular of 1976, p. 17.

links / left
Architektonisches Detail
an der Nordostecke von Haus 1 .
Architectural detail on the
north-east corner of building 1.

rechts / right
Südfassade von Haus 4.
The south façade of building 4.

links / left
Lernraum in der Dresdner Heide.
Learning space in Dresden Heath.

rechts / right
Freiraum für Kunst – Ergebnisse
eines Steinmetz-Workshops in der Akademie.
Space for art: the results of a stonemasonry
workshop at the Academy.

Aufgang zu Haus 3, dem ehemaligen Rektorat.
Steps up to building 3
(the former headmaster's building).

rechts / right
Akademiehotel mit Aula von Südosten.
South-east view of the Academy Hotel and auditorium.

links / left
Akademiehotel mit Haupteingang.
Academy Hotel featuring main entrance.

rechts / right
Begrünte Flachdächer.
Vegetated flat roofs.

Alltag und Kaserne – Stationierungsort des sowjetischen Militärs (1945 – 1992)

Daily routine and barracks life – the site as a Soviet military base (1945 – 1992)

GÖTZ KRÜGER

In den 1980er Jahren war die ehemalige Landesschule Dresden nur noch ein Mythos: Die gesamte Anlage war nun sowjetisches Militärgelände. Als Passant konnte man sie noch am besten sehen, wenn man mit der Straßenbahn am alten Eingang der Schule vorbeifuhr. Hinter den vielen Bäumen war das Lehrgebäude jedoch fast nur zu erahnen.

Die ersten Einheiten der Roten Armee kamen am Morgen des 8. Mai 1945 nach Klotzsche. Sie verfolgten die in Richtung Prag ziehenden deutschen Truppen. In der darauffolgenden Nacht wurde in Berlin die bedingungslose deutsche Kapitulation unterzeichnet.

Im Juni 1945 wurden vom sowjetischen Oberkommando die nötigen Anweisungen erlassen, um zu einem geordneten, auf längere Zeit ausgerichteten Besatzungsregime überzugehen. Damit begann die zielgerichtete Auswahl und Zuordnung von Kasernen und anderen geeigneten Objekten für die einzelnen Einheiten. Das betraf auch das Gelände der ehemaligen Landesschule bzw. NPEA.[1] Ein wesentlicher Grund für die dauerhafte militärische Nutzung bestand in den unmittelbar südlich gelegenen ausgedehnten Kasernenanlagen, die in den 1930er Jahren für Görings Luftwaffe gebaut worden waren.

In Klotzsche beschlagnahmte die Rote Armee außerhalb der Kasernen und der Landesschule eine größere Zahl von Wohnungen und ganze Häuser zur Unterbringung von Offizieren. Einige davon wurden bis zum Abzug von ihnen bewohnt.

Im Juni 1945 wandte sich Oskar Kramer mit Vorschlägen für einen zügigen Wiederaufbau der zerstörten Stadtgebiete an den sowjetischen Stadtkommandanten von Dresden.[2] Briefwechsel zum Areal der Landesschule aus dieser Zeit gibt es im Familienarchiv Oskar Kramers nicht. Das lässt den Schluss zu, dass der in Langebrück wohnende Architekt zu dieser Zeit keine Gefahren für sein Werk erkennen konnte.

Jury bei Wettkampf für Kinder an einem 9. Mai, im Hintergrund das ehemalige Schülerheim C, heute Haus 5. Jury judging a 9th of May children's competition, former boarding house C (now building 5) to the rear of shot.

Angehörige des Stabes im Herbst 1989. Unmittelbar links vom Birkenstamm Oberst Schlakunow, Stabschef der 11. Gardepanzerdivision. Staff officers in the autumn of 1989, incl. Colonel Shlakunov, head of the 11th Guards Tank Division (directly to the left of the birch trunk).

By the 1980s the former Landesschule Dresden[1] site was little more than a myth. The entire complex had become a Soviet military base, and was still best visible from the tram as it passed the old school entrance. The classroom building was only just discernible through the dense trees which separated it from the road.

The first Red Army units arrived in Klotzsche on the morning of the 8th of May 1945. They were in pursuit of German troops retreating towards Prague, and indeed an unconditional German surrender was signed in Berlin that evening.

June 1945 saw the Soviet High Command issue instructions for the installation of a structured, long-term occupying regime. This move included the target-orientated location and classification of barracks and other suitable properties for each individual army unit.

Im Februar 1946 wurde die Rote Armee in Sowjetarmee umbenannt und bald danach begann der Kalte Krieg. Mehr als vier Jahrzehnte standen sich auf deutschem Boden zwei hochgerüstete Militärblöcke gegenüber, die davon ausgingen, dass die Gegenseite jeden Moment angreifen könnte. Deshalb gab es auch nach dem Aufbau der beiden neuen deutschen Armeen noch Hunderttausende ausländische Soldaten in dem geteilten Land. Die sowjetischen Truppen unterstanden einem Oberkommando in Wünsdorf und nannten sich »Gruppe der Sowjetischen Streitkräfte in Deutschland«.

The site of the former Landesschule and NPEA was one of those to be chosen.[2] One fundamental motive behind its selection for long-term military usage was the existence of extensive barracks directly to its south. These quarters had been built for Göring's Luftwaffe during the 1930s.

In Klotzsche itself, the Red Army set about accommodating its officers by seizing a large number of apartments and entire houses outside of the boundaries of their barracks and the Landesschule site. Some of these residences went on to be used for this purpose right up until the troops eventually withdrew.

June 1945 saw Oskar Kramer contact the Soviet City Commander responsible for Dresden with proposals as to how destroyed sections of the city could be rebuilt quickly.[3] As his family's archives do not include any correspondence from that period which pertains to the Landesschule site, it can be concluded that Kramer – who had moved to Langebrück in the meantime – did not foresee any danger to his work.

The Cold War began soon after the Red Army was renamed the Soviet Army in the February of 1946. For over four decades two highly armed military blocks were to face each other down on German soil, each expecting the other to attack at any time. This saw the soldiers of the two newly formed armies on either side of the inner-German border supplemented by hundreds of thousands of foreign forces. Soviet troops were answerable to a High Command post in Wünsdorf, and were collectively known as the "Group of Soviet Forces in Germany"

The structures and duties of the new occupants

The movements and activity of Soviet troops in Dresden during the initial post-war years have not yet been the subject of definitive research. It is nevertheless known that a number of relocations took place during that period, with increasing mechanisation during the 1950s also leading to a variety of restructurings and renamings. It was at that time that the Soviet 11th Guards Tank Division made the

Strukturen und Aufgaben der neuen Nutzer

Für die ersten Jahre nach dem Krieg ist die Geschichte der sowjetischen Truppen in Dresden noch nicht aufgearbeitet. In diesem Zeitraum gab es verschiedene Verlegungen und in den 1950er Jahren folgten mit der wachsenden Motorisierung Umbildungen und Umbenennungen. Seit damals befand sich im Gelände der Landesschule der Stab der sowjetischen 11. Gardepanzerdivision. Die offiziellen Namen einzelner Formationen der Sowjetarmee waren lang und umständlich. Sie enthielten Hinweise auf den Zweiten Weltkrieg und Auszeichnungen. Bei der 11. Gardepanzerdivision wurden im Namen die Karpaten und Berlin sowie der Rotbannerorden und der Suworow-Orden angeführt. Der Gardetitel war ebenfalls eine Auszeichnung für erfolgreiche Kämpfe.

In den 1980er Jahren bestand die Division aus drei Panzerregimentern, einem motorisierten Schützenregiment, einem Artillerieregiment und einem Flugabwehr-Raketenregiment. Außerdem gehörten zu ihr noch weitere Einheiten, von denen hier nur ein Nachrichten- (Fernmelde-) Bataillon, ein Aufklärungsbataillon, ein Pionierbataillon, ein Sanitätsbataillon und ein Instandsetzungsbataillon genannt sein sollen. Die Einheiten befanden sich in Dresden, Meißen und im Raum Königsbrück. Lediglich die Artillerie lag in Karl-Marx-Stadt, dem heutigen Chemnitz. Die Vermutung, dass auch eine Staffel Kampfhubschrauber auf dem Heller im Dresdner Norden zur Division gehörte, wurde von damaligen sowjetischen Zeitzeugen bis heute nicht bestätigt. Drei Bataillone waren in den Kasernen direkt südlich vom Stab stationiert.

Die 11. Gardepanzerdivision war ein modern ausgerüsteter, schlagkräftiger Verband der höchsten Bereitschaftsstufe. Sie gehörte zur 1. Gardepanzerarmee, deren Stab sich ebenfalls in Dresden befand. Nominell hatte die Division über 320 Kampfpanzer, mehr als 300 weitere gepanzerte Kampffahrzeuge und über hundert Geschütze mit einem Kaliber größer als 120 Millimeter. Zur Stärke gibt es nur unscharfe Angaben, man kann von über 13 000 Mann ausgehen.

Landesschule site its headquarters. The official names of individual Soviet Army units were long and complicated, and featured references to action in the Second World War and decorations. In the case of the 11th Guards Tank Division, mention was made of the Carpathians, Berlin, the Order of the Red Banner and the Order of Suvorov. Its "Guards" title had been granted in honour of success on the battlefield.

During the 1980s the Division consisted of three tank regiments, a motorised rifleman's regiment, an artillery regiment and a surface-to-air missile regiment. Of the other units which belonged to it, only the signals, reconnaissance, engineering, medical and maintenance battalions are worthy of note here.

The Division's units were stationed in Dresden, Meißen and the Königsbrück area. Artillery troops were its only forces to be based in Karl-Marx-Stadt (now Chemnitz). The supposed existence of a squadron of attack helicopters attached to the Division and based on the raised Heller area to the north of Dresden has never been confirmed by contemporary Soviet witnesses. Three battalions were stationed in the barracks directly south of Division headquarters.

The 11th Guards Tank Division was a modernly equipped, powerful unit on the highest level of alert. It belonged to the 1st Guards Tank Army, which was also headquartered in Dresden. The Division nominally had over 320 battle tanks, more than 300 other armoured vehicles and over 100 guns with a calibre of more than 120 millimetres. Though available details on troop numbers are vague, a force of over 13,000 can be presumed.

In the event of war, the Division's officers were to guarantee that its Commander was in a position to lead the Division effectively and successfully. The Chief of Staff and his specialists were to draw up detailed plans for the achievement of this goal. Other officers were to ensure that all headquarters work ran smoothly, for example by keeping all lines of communication open. The medical and financial sections each had their own superiors. Headquarters also appointed a supervisor to every special unit within the Division. One unit which should not be forgotten is the polit

Der Divisionsstab hatte im Kriegsfall dafür zu sorgen, dass der Kommandeur die Division erfolgreich führen konnte. Dazu gab es den Stabschef und seine Spezialisten, die die entsprechenden Operationen im Detail planen sollten. Andere Offiziere hatten die Arbeit des Stabes sicherzustellen, so zum Beispiel das Funktionieren aller Nachrichtenverbindungen. Es gab einen Chef des medizinischen Dienstes und einen Finanzchef. Für alles, wofür spezielle Einheiten in der Division existierten, hatte der Stab einen Verantwortlichen. Nicht vergessen werden darf die für sozialistische Armeen wichtige Polit-Abteilung. Sie hatte mindestens zehn Mitarbeiter, die sich um die richtige Einstellung der Armeeangehörigen kümmern sollten. Dabei leiteten sie lediglich die Politarbeiter in den unterstellten Einheiten an. Äußeres Zeichen ihrer Aktivitäten waren die überall sichtbaren Propaganda-Tafeln.

Glücklicherweise gab es in den Jahrzehnten der sowjetischen Präsenz in Deutschland keinen Krieg, doch auch in Friedenszeiten hatte der Stab viel zu tun. Für das ordentliche Funktionieren der gesamten Division mussten seine Angehörigen sorgen. Mehrmals im Jahr waren große Übungen unterstellter Einheiten zu organisieren, in größeren Abständen Übungen der ganzen Division. Zweimal im Jahr wurde je ein Viertel der Wehrpflichtigen ausgetauscht, die neuen Soldaten mussten eingegliedert und ausgebildet werden.

Nach dem Ende offizieller Feierlichkeiten an einem Festtag stehen Stabsmitarbeiter entspannt auf dem Sportplatz.
Division employees stand at ease on the sports field after the end of the official part of a celebratory day.

Leben in der Sowjetarmee

Die einfachen Soldaten dienten zwei Jahre in der Sowjetarmee. Wenn sie in die DDR kamen, bedeutete das für sie nichts Gutes. Unterbringung und Verpflegung waren aus deutscher Sicht miserabel, das war beim Dienst in ihrer Heimat nicht anders. Hier aber durften sie die Kaserne nur in Gruppen unter Leitung eines Vorgesetzten verlassen. Es gab kaum Urlaub. Sie waren in einem fremden Land, dessen Sprache sie nicht kannten. In der DDR herrschten andere Regeln und Gepflogenheiten als in der Sowjetunion, an die man sich beispielsweise als Kraftfahrer erst gewöhnen musste.

Anders war es für die Berufssoldaten. Sie gliederten sich in Offiziere und Fähnriche. Letztere bildeten eine besondere Dienstgradgruppe, die ähnliche Aufgaben wie Berufsunteroffiziere in westlichen Armeen erfüllte. Die Berufssoldaten kamen meist für fünf Jahre in die DDR und konnten dabei ihre Familien mitbringen. Sie wurden gut bezahlt. Im letzten Jahrzehnt der DDR hatten sie hier oft wesentlich bessere Wohnbedingungen als zu Hause. In speziellen Militärläden, aber auch außerhalb der Kasernen, fanden sie ein Warenangebot vor, das sie von zu Hause nicht kannten. Dresden mit seinen kulturellen Möglichkeiten und vielen sonstigen Ausflugszielen war bei Sowjetischen Militärs besonders beliebt.

Außerdem arbeiteten sowjetische Zivilbeschäftigte für die Armee. Sie hatten Posten inne, die man im Kriegsfall nicht brauchte.

Blick vom Schänkhübel auf das eingezäunte Gelände, links das ehemalige Pförtnerhaus.
View from the Schänkhübel onto the site, former porter's lodge to the left of shot.

section, which was an important feature of Socialist armies. It comprised at least ten employees charged with ensuring that army members behaved correctly. In reality, however, these employees effectively only gave instructions to polit workers in subordinate units. One obvious sign of their activities were the propaganda boards on display throughout their jurisdiction.

Though there was thankfully no war in Germany during these decades of Soviet presence, peacetime also gave Division headquarters plenty to do. Its staff were to ensure that it ran smoothly, and were responsible for the organisation of numerous large manoeuvres for its subordinate units each year. Division manoeuvres were organised at longer intervals. As a quarter of all conscripts were replaced twice a year there was a constant need to integrate and train new soldiers.

Life in the Soviet Army

Ordinary soldiers served two years in the Soviet Army, and being sent to the GDR was not necessarily good news for them. Though their accommodation and rations were poor by German standards, this was by no means different to the conditions they experienced back in their homeland. After arrival they were only permitted to leave barracks in groups and under the supervision of a superior. There was hardly any holiday, and they were stationed in a foreign country with a language they were unversed in. The rules and customs of the GDR, for example motoring etiquette, were different to those which prevailed in the Soviet Union and required a certain degree of getting used to.

It was a different story for regular soldiers. They were divided into officers and officer cadets, the latter being a special rank group which had similar duties to those fulfilled by non-commissioned officers in western armies. Regular soldiers sent to the GDR tended to serve there for five years and were permitted to bring their families with them. They were well paid, and the last decade of the GDR era often saw them experience better living conditions in

Gebäudesubstanz: Verfall, Instandhaltung, Neubau und Nutzung

Die Sowjetische Armee hat die Instandhaltung und Instandsetzung der von ihr in der DDR genutzten Gebäude nie im ausreichenden Maß durchgeführt. Das lag nicht an den Verantwortlichen vor Ort, sondern war Politik des Oberkommandos. Eine Durchführung der notwendigen Leistungen wäre andererseits zu Lasten der DDR gegangen, da man die benötigten Kapazitäten und Materialien von ihr bezogen hätte. Der sozialistische deutsche Staat war jedoch nicht einmal in der Lage, die überkommene zivile Bausubstanz zu erhalten. Diese Tatsache führte zu einem sich ständig verschlechternden Zustand insbesondere der Gebäudehüllen. Reparaturen wurden teilweise mit primitiven Mitteln vorgenommen. Die Fassaden erhielten eine graue Farbgebung, die ohne Gerüste, zum Teil durch Anspritzen aus Schläuchen, aufgetragen wurde. Die Dächer im Bereich der Landesschule waren mit Wellasbestplatten eingedeckt worden – eigentlich nur eine provisorische Lösung.

In sowjetischen Kasernen kam es immer wieder zu Bränden, deren Schäden selten komplett beseitigt wurden. Manchmal waren danach ganze Gebäudeteile nicht mehr nutzbar und blieben bis zum Abzug in diesem Zustand. In der Landesschule gingen während der militärischen Nutzung mehrere Gebäude verloren. Das betraf die Schülerheime B und D (heute Haus 7 und 8) sowie die Aula und den nördlichen Teil der zu ihr gehörenden Wirtschaftsgebäude. Hier zeigten sich nach dem Abzug Trümmerhaufen, aus denen stattliche Bäume wuchsen. Die Untergeschosse waren noch weitgehend erhalten. Deutsche und ehemals sowjetische Zeitzeugen beschreiben diese Situation schon für die 1970er Jahre. Bereits im Jahrzehnt zuvor sollen die Gebäude zerstört gewesen sein.[3] Der genaue Zeitpunkt und Hergang sind bis jetzt nicht bekannt. Im Untergeschoss unter der Aula war 1995 geschwärztes Mauerwerk zu erkennen.

Das Schülerheim C (heute Haus 5) war in den 1980er Jahren eine Ruine. Noch vor dem Ende des Jahrzehnts wurde diese abgetragen. Luftaufnahmen von 1991 zeigen das mit Gras bedeckte Untergeschoss.

Der sogenannte »alte Fünfgeschosser«, errichtet von DDR-Baubetrieben, 1994.
The so-called "old five-floorer" erected by GDR construction workers, 1994.

their German outpost than they would have done at home. Special military stores and shops outside of the confines of their barracks offered soldiers a range of products the likes of which they had never seen at home. Dresden's cultural riches and wide variety of excursion options made it a particularly popular posting with Soviet military personnel.

The Soviet civilians who worked for the army carried out duties which would have been non-critical in the event of war.

Im Inneren der verbliebenen Gebäude wurde jedoch alles weitgehend instand gehalten. Fenster und Türen waren ordentlich gestrichen, ebenso die Wände. Bei letzteren fand der in der Sowjetunion beliebte Ölsockel in auffälligen Farben breite Anwendung. Verschiedene Räume wurden tapeziert. Im Lehrgebäude waren die in Nischen befindlichen Wandschränke mit Glastüren intakt. An anderer Stelle war man nicht so sorgsam: Um die allgemeine Elektroinstallation hat sich niemand gekümmert, denn in Sicherungskästen fand sich nach dem Abzug immer noch die alte deutsche Beschriftung der Stromkreise.

Die sowjetische Seite setzte andere Schwerpunkte und hatte eigene Vorstellungen von Ordnung. So war es in sowjetischen Kasernen üblich, die Bordsteinkanten an den Stra-

Building fabric: dilapidation, maintenance, construction and usage

The maintenance and repairs carried out by the Soviet Army to the buildings they used in the GDR were always inadequate. This was the policy of the High Command, and not the fault of those responsible at a local level. Necessary measures would in any case have been implemented at the expense of the GDR, which was obliged to provide any capacities or materials required. This was despite the fact that the Socialist German state was not even in a position to maintain its own antiquated civilian building stock.

This situation led to constant deterioration in the condition of the Klotzsche complex, and in particular building shells. Some repairs were carried out using primitive methods, the painting of façades being one example. Not only was the grey paint applied entirely without the use of scaffolding, but hoses were also used to spray the paint on in some areas. Roofs in the area of the Landesschule were covered in using corrugated asbestos sheeting – technically only a temporary solution.

Fires were a regular occurrence in Soviet barracks, with related damage rarely completely repaired. In some cases this rendered entire building sections unusable right up until the forces withdrew. Numerous buildings were lost at the Landesschule during its period of Soviet military usage, including boarding houses B and D (now buildings 7 and 8), the assembly hall building and the northern section of its

Das von der Sowjetarmee 1979 selbst erbaute Wohnhaus, August 1994.
The residence built by the Soviet Army itself in 1979, August 1994.

ßen und auch Rasenkantensteine entlang der Wege weiß anzustreichen. Bei der Landesschule ist das durch Luftaufnahmen gut dokumentiert. Die alten Fußwege mit ihrer Befestigung aus Natursteinplatten waren bis zuletzt erhalten geblieben. Für die Nutzung des Geländes durch Fahrzeuge waren weitere Wege aus Betonplatten dazu gekommen.

Die ordentliche Unterbringung von sowjetischen Familien war bis zuletzt ein mehr oder weniger großes Problem. Schrittweise wurde dies durch unterschiedliche Neubauten verbessert, auch im Bereich der Landesschule. Mitte der 1970er Jahre errichteten Baubetriebe der DDR einen Wohnblock vom Typ IW 74 mit fünf Etagen. Dieser Plattenbau befand sich zwischen Königsbrücker Landstraße und Lehrgebäude, etwas nach Norden versetzt. In jedem der drei

adjoining management building. Though all that remained of them after the army had left were piles of rubble pierced by stately trees, the majority of basement levels remained intact. Contemporary German and Soviet witnesses confirm that this situation existed from as early as the 1970s onwards. Though the buildings are even said to have been destroyed as early as the preceding decade[4], exact times and sequences of events remain unclarified. In 1995 blackened masonry was still discernible on the basement level beneath the assembly hall.

Boarding house C (now building 5) stood as ruins during the 1980s, and had been pulled down completely and disposed of by the end of decade. Aerial photos taken in 1991 show a covering of grass on top of its basement level.

Eingänge waren drei Wohnungen auf einer Etage vorhanden, darunter eine Einraum-Wohnung. In diesen Einraum-Wohnungen wurden auch Familien einquartiert.

1979 begann die Sowjetarmee mit eigenen Mitteln den Bau eines Wohnhauses. Es entstand dicht an der Königsbrücker Landstraße, neben dem Lehrerwohnhaus N. Das Gebäude hatte zwei Etagen und drei Eingänge. Gebaut wurde es aus hellen Ziegeln, die unverputzt blieben.

Wenige Jahre später wurden noch zwei Plattenbaublöcke in der gleichen Art wie der erste errichtet. Sie standen rechtwinklig zur Straße, nicht weit von dieser entfernt, etwa auf der Höhe Nordseite des Sportplatzes. An einem war ein Heizhaus angebaut. Die Bewohner des »Städtchens« unterschieden jetzt zwischen dem »alten Fünfgeschosser« und den »neuen Fünfgeschossern«. Unmittelbar südlich von letzteren gab es weitere Wohngebäude. Sie lagen nicht mehr auf dem ursprünglichen Gelände der Landesschule, wurden aber allgemein als zum Stabsgelände gehörig betrachtet. Es handelte sich um sechs eingeschossige Doppelhäuser, die wenige Jahre vor dem Zweiten Weltkrieg mit den Kasernen entstanden waren. Hier wohnten meist höhere Offiziere mit ihren Familien.

Auf dem Gebiet der Landeschule lag damit Mitte der 1980er Jahre ein größeres Wohngebiet. Man lebte hier ähnlich wie in der Sowjetunion. Nachbarn trafen sich zwischen den Häusern auf selbstgebauten Bänken, Wäsche flatterte im Wind und Kinder bevölkerten einen Spielplatz mit verschiedenen Geräten. Im Frühjahr wurden in der Umgebung

19

links / left
Eines der sechs Doppelhäuser am Rande des Schulgeländes. In den 1930er Jahren mit den Kasernen für die Luftwaffe errichtet. One of the six semi-detached houses on the periphery of the school site. Originally erected for the Luftwaffe along with its barracks during the 1930s.

rechts / right
Diese Kinder wurden 1986 in der Grundschule Nr. 15 eingeschult. Hier mit ihrer Lehrerin B. Borisowna vor dem Eingang der Schule. These children started at Primary School No. 15 in 1986. They are shown here in front of the entrance to the school with teacher B. Borisovna.

der Wohngebäude freiwillige Arbeitseinsätze, sogenannte Subbotniks, durchgeführt. Die sowjetischen Bewohner brachten die Außenanlagen in Ordnung, wie nicht weit entfernt zur gleichen Zeit deutsche Mieter in ähnlichen Wohnanlagen.

Die größeren Kinder suchten Abenteuer und streiften im gesamten Gelände herum. Bei ihnen erfreuten sich die Trümmerhaufen im Nordosten des Schulgeländes großer Beliebtheit. Oft drangen sie dort in die noch bestehenden Untergeschosse ein.

Viele Kinder der Berufssoldaten und Zivilbeschäftigten waren im schulpflichtigen Alter. Für sie gab es in der DDR eigene sowjetische Schulen. In Dresden befand sich die sowjetische Schule Nr. 15. Ihr Hauptteil war im Bereich des Armeestabes auf der Dr.-Kurt-Fischer-Allee (heute Stauffenbergallee) untergebracht. Die ersten drei Klassen aber wurden in der Grundschule im Gelände des Stabes der 11. Gardepanzerdivision unterrichtet. Die Grundschule befand sich im östlichen Flügel des Lehrgebäudes der Landesschule. Die vom Campus aus gesehen rechte Tür war der Eingang zu den Klassenräumen.

In der Sowjetunion herrschten strengere Moralvorstellungen. Vielleicht wurde deshalb das Relief mit den nackten Körpern von Lehrer und Schülern über der Tür mit einem Transparent verdeckt. Anfang der 1980er Jahre stand darauf die Bezeichnung »Sowjetische Grundschule Nr. 15«.

The interiors of the surviving buildings had nevertheless been maintained a large extent. Windows and doors were decently painted, as were walls. The latter featured the widespread usage of the oil-painted, brightly coloured skirting which enjoyed popularity in the Soviet Union. A number of rooms were wallpapered. Though the glass-doored wall cabinets fitted in niches in the classroom building remained intact, the same degree of care was not necessarily taken in other areas. General electrical installations were not looked after at all, as was confirmed by the old German circuit labelling still in place in fuse boxes after the troops had withdrawn.

Einige Jahre später gab es neben der Tür ein offizielles rotes Schild mit der goldenen Aufschrift »Grundschule Nr. 15« und über dem Relief hing ein Propagandaplakat. 1990 war es verschwunden. Die Klassenzimmer wurden in einem ordentlichen Zustand gehalten und mit modernen Schulmöbeln aus DDR-Produktion ausgestattet. In einem Raum waren die Wände liebevoll mit lustigen Figuren bemalt, darunter die damals sehr bekannten sowjetischen Trickfilmhelden Hase und Wolf. Vor dem schulisch genutzten Teil des Lehrgebäudes standen Geräte für den Sportunterricht: Sprossenwände, Barren, Recks in unterschiedlichen Höhen und Basketballkörbe.

Der kleine Sportplatz östlich des Lehrgebäudes, unmittelbar vor den Klassenräumen der Grundschule. Im Hintergrund Gebäude F (heute Haus 9), August 1994. The small sports field to the east of the classroom building and directly in front of the primary school classrooms. Rear of shot: building F (now building 9). August 1994.

Occupying Soviet forces not only set themselves different priorities, but also had their own ideas when it came to orderliness. It was standard practice in Soviet barracks to have street curbs and grass edging stones along paths painted white. In the case of the Landesschule this is well-documented by aerial photos. The old footpaths and their natural stone paving were preserved until the very end of the Soviet presence, with further routes paved with concrete slabs also added in order to facilitate vehicular usage of the site. Though the proper accommodation of Soviet families remained a relatively troublesome issue right until the forces withdrew, the situation was gradually alleviated by the addition of various new buildings, some of which were located within the vicinity of the Landesschule.

The mid-1970s saw GDR construction workers erect a five-storey IW 74-type residential block set slightly to the north between the Königsbrücker Landstraße and the classroom building. Each of its three entrances provided access to three apartments per floor, one of which was a one-room apartment. Even the one-room apartments were used to accommodate families.

In 1979 the Soviet Army began the construction of a residential building using its own resources. It was erected adjacent to teacher residence N, and was situated right on the Königsbrücker Landstraße. Built using bright bricks which were to remain unplastered, the building had two stories and three entrances.

A further two prefabricated blocks were built a few years later in the same style as the first Soviet-built residence. They stood square to and not far from the road, and were level with the northern edge of the playing field. A boiler house adjoined one of the buildings. The residents of the "little town" now began to distinguish between the "old five-floorer" and the "new five-floorers". Additional residential buildings existed directly to the south of the two new blocks. Though these six single-storey, semi-detached houses were not technically on the former Landesschule site, they tended to be seen as belonging to Division headquarters. Built together with the barracks a few years before the Second World War, they were primarily used for the accommodation of high-ranking officers and their families.

Verschiedene Tafeln mit sowjetischen Symbolen und Propaganda befanden sich daneben. Eine dieser Tafeln zeigte auf der einen Seite eine Friedenstaube und die Losung »Sport ist der Botschafter des Friedens«. Auf der Rückseite jedoch war eine Micky-Maus mit Tennisschläger dargestellt – in einer DDR-Kaserne undenkbar.

Der größte Teil des Lehrgebäudes wurde vom Stab der Division genutzt. Im Erdgeschoss war der Schulbereich durch eine Mauer im hofseitigen Gang abgetrennt. Die linke Tür auf der Seite des Campus war zur Hälfte zugemauert. Im Innenhof waren nur noch zwei Türen benutzbar.

Der verbliebene südliche Teil des Wirtschaftsgebäudes, August 1994. The surviving southern section of the management building, August 1994.

Die Eingangshalle am Haupteingang des Lehrgebäudes hatten die sowjetischen Nutzer völlig verändert. Hier war links eine Pförtnerloge aus Holzteilen und Kunststoffplatten eingebaut worden. Aus ihr heraus wurde der Zugang zum Stab kontrolliert. Neben der Halle befand sich das Dienstzimmer des operativen Diensthabenden. Er hatte zu jeder Zeit bei ungewöhnlichen Ereignissen oder Alarm dafür zu sorgen, dass die notwendigen Maßnahmen, auch in unterstellten Einheiten, eingeleitet wurden. Der Tresor für die dazu vorbereiteten Unterlagen blieb nach dem Abzug leer, aber beschriftet stehen. Enthalten waren sowohl versiegelte Dokumente für den Ernstfall, als auch für Übungsalarmierungen. Der Gebäudeflügel parallel zur Außentreppe vor dem Haupteingang enthielt die Nachrichtenzentrale, in der alle Drahtverbindungen ankamen. Daneben muss es auch noch die in einem solchen Bereich notwendige stationäre Funkstelle gegeben haben, da hinter dem Gebäude ein Antennenmast stand.

By the mid-1980s the Landesschule site had become the location of a sizeable residential area. Life there played out in a similar way to life in the Soviet Union: neighbours met on home-made benches between buildings, laundry fluttered in the wind and children swarmed over a playground with various pieces of play equipment. The springtime saw voluntary work, or "subbotniks", carried out around the residential buildings. This involved Soviet residents tidying the grounds adjacent to their residences – just as German tenants were doing on similar estates just a short distance away.

Von den noch erhaltenen Gebäuden wurde das Schülerheim A (heute Haus 6) durch die Stabskompanie genutzt, deren Soldaten hauptsächlich die Arbeit des Stabes sicherzustellen hatten. Unter ihnen waren viele Kraftfahrer. Sie hatten von hier aus einen kurzen Weg zu ihren Fahrzeugen. Der an das Schülerheim anschließende Rest des früheren Wirtschaftsgebäudes enthielt einen Speisesaal. Außerdem befanden sich dort Sporträume. Der größere war als Halle für Ballsportarten eingerichtet. Ein anderer, niedrigerer diente auch der Nahkampfausbildung. Dazu waren bebilderte Schautafeln an einer Wand angebracht. In der Sowjetarmee ein oft genutztes Mittel, da nicht alle Wehrpflichtigen die russische Sprache gut beherrschten.

Die beiden Gebäude E und F (heute Haus 4 und 9) dienten offensichtlich sowohl Stabszwecken, wie auch als Unterkunft. Hier saßen Verantwortliche für die rückwärtigen Dienste. Es gab auch eine Druckerei für die Divisionszeitung. Diese enthielt hauptsächlich Propaganda und durfte die Grenzen der Kasernen nicht verlassen. Im Gebäude E (heute Haus 4) befand sich der Militärladen mit einem guten Angebot, besonders an Industriewaren. Dieses Angebot lockte die Offiziersfrauen aus den anderen Einheiten des großen Kasernengeländes an. Das gefiel dem damaligen

links / left
Berufssoldat in Zivil. Im Gebäude F (heute Haus 9) befanden sich Teile des Stabes, die für die rückwärtigen Dienste zuständig waren.
Regular soldier in civilian clothes. Building F (now building 9) housed some of the staff officers responsible for support services.

rechts / right
Im Hintergrund Gebäude E, in dem sich unter anderem der beliebte Laden befand. Davor der kleine Pavillon der Buchverkaufsstelle, August 1994.
One of the facilities housed by building E (rear of shot) was the popular shop. The small pavilion from which books were sold stands in front of it. August 1994.

Older children roamed around the entire site looking for adventure, and particularly enjoyed the mounds of rubble on the north-eastern section of the school site – often managing to force their way into surviving basement levels.

Many children of regular soldiers and civilian employees were of school age. Soviet schools existed for them in the GDR, with Soviet School No. 15 located in Dresden. Whereas its main section was accommodated in the area of the army headquarters on the Dr.-Kurt-Fischer-Allee (now the

Divisionskommandeur nicht, sodass am Ende der 1970er Jahre ein Blechzaun das Gelände der Landesschule, einschließlich der sechs alten Doppelhäuser, von den anderen Kasernen abtrennte. In dem Verkaufsraum war ein Schild mit einer Selbstverpflichtung angebracht. »Das Kollektiv unseres Ladens arbeitet nach der Devise: Wir garantieren eine hohe Kultur der Bedienung, Effektivität und Rhythmik«. Für eine Buchverkaufsstelle hatte man einen einfachen kleinen Pavillon neben Gebäude E (heute Haus 4) errichtet. Wie ein

Stauffenbergallee), pupils in its first three years were taught at a primary school on the site of the headquarters of the 11th Guards Tank Division. The primary school was located in the east wing of the Landesschule's classroom building, and was accessible through the right-hand door (when viewed from the campus).

A stricter set of moral standards applied in the Soviet Union, and this was perhaps the reason why a banner was used to cover up the naked pupils and teachers of the relief above the door. At the start of the 1980s the banner read "Soviet Primary School No. 15". A few years later an official red sign with the golden inscription "Primary School No. 15" had been installed next to the door and a propaganda poster covered the relief. By 1990 the sign had disappeared.

Classrooms were kept in orderly condition and equipped with modern school furniture made in the GDR. The walls of one room were lovingly painted with amusing figures such as "the Hare and the Wolf", a pair of very well-known Soviet cartoon heroes.

Sports equipment in the form of wall bars, parallel bars, bars of various heights and basketball nets stood in front of the section of the classroom building used for academic purposes. Various notice boards displaying Soviet symbols and propaganda stood next to them. The front side of one of these boards showed a dove and the maxim "Sport is the ambassador of peace". Its rear side, on the other hand, showed Mickey Mouse with a tennis racquet in his hand – unthinkable in a GDR barracks.

Drei Stabsoffiziere nach dem Freizeitsport. Rechts der von einer Mauer umgebene »Park« mit einem Stabsfahrzeug. Im Hintergrund Gebäude A (heute Haus 6), Unterkunft der Stabskompanie.
Three of the Division's officers after sport during their leisure time. Right of shot: the "park" (surrounded by a wall) and a staff vehicle. Rear of shot: building A (now building 6), used to accommodate staff officers.

The largest section of the classroom building was used by the Division's staff officers, and was separated from the school area at ground-floor level by a wall in the courtyard-side corridor. Half of the left-hand door on the campus side was bricked up, and only two doors on the inner courtyard were still usable.

The foyer at the main entrance to the classroom building was changed completely by its Soviet occupants. A porter's lodge of wood and plastic construction was integrated into its left-hand side and used to control access to Division headquarters. The office of the operations officer on duty

ehemaliger Offizier berichtete, wurden in solchen Läden Bücher angeboten, die man in der Heimat nur schwer bekam. Im Bereich der alten Turnhalle war der »Park« angelegt worden. So bezeichnete man den abgegrenzten Bereich einer Kaserne, in dem sich die Fahrzeuge befanden. Diese standen bereit zum Ausrücken bei Alarm, aufgetankt und mit allem Notwendigen, auch Munition, beladen. Hier waren das einige Fahrzeuge, die als »fahrbare Büros« für die Sicherstellung der Arbeit des Stabes im Gelände, also auch bei Übungen, notwendig waren. Dafür gab es spezielle Aufbauten, die ausgeklappt werden konnten und so bequeme

was located adjacent to the foyer. In the instance of any unusual events or alarms he was to ensure that the necessary measures were implemented. This included measures to be carried out by subordinate units. Though the safe labelled as containing documents required in such circumstances was still in place after its owners' withdrawal, it had been emptied prior to their departure. It would have contained sealed documents pertaining to emergencies and practice alarms.

The wing parallel to the outside steps in front of the main entrance housed the Division's communications centre, which in turn provided a central gathering point for all communication lines. The presence of a radio mast behind the building indicates that a stationary radio station – which would have been required in this type of area – also existed.

Of the other surviving buildings, building A (now building 6) was used by the Headquarters Company, whose main duty was to ensure that the work of the Division headquarters ran smoothly. Many of them were drivers, and only had a short distance from the building to their vehicles.

The adjacent remains of the former management building included a dining hall and sports rooms, the largest of which was set up for ball games. One room with a lower ceiling was used for hand-to-hand combat training, and featured illustrated instruction posters on one of its walls. This method of training was used regularly in the Soviet Army due to the limited command of the Russian language exhibited by some of its conscripts.

Buildings E and F (now buildings 4 and 9) were apparently used by staff officers and as accommodation. Support services were also based there, and included a print shop

Der »Park« für die Fahrzeuge im Bereich der ehemaligen Spielplätze. Rechts im Bild die zur Garage verkommene frühere Turnhalle. August 1994.
The vehicle "park" in the area of the old sports pitches; right of shot: the former gymnasium, run-down and used as a garage. August 1994.

Arbeitsräume boten. Weitere LKW mit Anhänger sollten Vorräte und Ausrüstung transportieren. Die mit umfangreicher Nachrichtentechnik ausgestatteten Fahrzeuge zur Führung der Division im Gefecht gehörten zum Nachrichtenbataillon und waren in dessen Kaserne, nur wenige hundert Meter weiter südlich, untergebracht.

Die alte Turnhalle hatte ihr ursprüngliches Aussehen verloren und diente als Garage unter einem flachen Dach. Die großen Fenster waren erweitert und mit Blechtoren versehen worden. Daneben standen neu erbaute Garagen. Die Flächen der früheren Spielplätze vor und hinter der Turnhalle wurden betoniert und im hinteren Teil nach Süden erweitert. Dort schloss sich noch ein Pistolenschießstand an. Der Sportplatz wurde sowohl für dienstliche Zwecke, wie auch in der Freizeit genutzt. Gern spielte man Fußball. Auch für die Kinder wurden in diesem Bereich Wettkämpfe organisiert, die schon Elemente militärischer Körperertüchtigung enthielten.

Der alte Eingang zur Landesschule diente als Einfahrt und Zugang zum Gelände des Divisionsstabes. Dort war für die kontrollierenden Soldaten ein kleines Gebäude aus Ziegeln gebaut worden, das mit der üblichen grauen Farbe gestrichen war. Die Zufahrt wurde mit einem blechverkleideten Rolltor verschlossen, auf dem zwei fünfzackige goldene Sterne angebracht waren.

Schräg gegenüber von diesem Eingang lag der Komplex des Schänkhübels. Dieser wurde von der Sowjetarmee als »Haus der Offiziere« genutzt. Von den großen Veranstaltungen waren dabei offensichtlich die Neujahrsfeiern der Höhepunkt, da in der atheistischen Sowjetunion Weihnachten nicht gefeiert wurde. Viele Kulturangebote waren für die Familien bestimmt, wichtig für ihr Wohlbefinden in der fremden Umgebung. Der Chef des Klubhauses wohnte mit seiner Familie im Dachgeschoss.

for the printing of the Division gazette. This publication primarily consisted of propaganda, and copies were not to be taken outside of the confines of the barracks.

Building E (now building 4) housed the well-stocked military shop, which carried a particularly good range of mass-produced goods. This variety attracted the attention and custom of the wives of officers from other units on the larger barracks site. This did not wash well with the then Division Commander, and by the end of the 1970s a sheet metal fence had been erected around the Landesschule site and its six old semi-detached houses in order to separate them from

oben / top
Freizeitfußballer der Mannschaft »Rapid« Ende der 1980er Jahre auf dem Sportplatz der Landesschule vor einem soliden Fußballtor. Im Hintergrund die sogenannten »neuen Fünfgeschosser«.
Amateur footballers from the "Rapid" team in front of a sturdy football goal on the Landesschule sports pitch at the end of the 1980s. Rear of shot: the so-called "new five-floorers".

rechts / right
Musikgruppen aus Wehrpflichtigen gab es in sowjetischen Kasernen seit den 1970er Jahren. Die Gruppe »Pritschina« bei einer Neujahrsfeier im »Haus der Offiziere«.
Soviet barracks featured music groups made up of conscripts from the 1970s onwards. Here: the band "Pritschina" at New Year's celebrations in the "Officer's Club".

the other barracks. A sign put up in the salesroom proclaimed this self-commitment: "Our shop collective works according to the following motto: We guarantee a culture of the utmost in service, effectiveness and rhythm".

A small, simple pavilion was erected next to building E (now building 4) for the purpose of selling books. According to one former officer, the books available for purchase in such shops would have been difficult to come by back in the Soviet Union.

The Division "park" was set up in the area of the old gymnasium. "Park" was the name given to the sectioned-off area of a barracks where motor vehicles were stored. Vehicles were kept fully fuelled and loaded with all necessary equipment – including ammunition – in order to be ready to move out in the event of an alarm. The vehicles in question were the "portable offices" required for the continuation of Division operations whilst in the field, and featured special assemblies which could be folded out to form comfortable workspaces. Supplies and equipment were transported using other HGVs with trailers. The vehicles which carried the comprehensive telecommunications equipment required in order to command the Division when in battle were part of the signals battalion, and were therefore kept in the respective barracks just a few hundred metres south of the Landesschule site.

The appearance of the old gymnasium changed markedly. Converted to a garage, its roof was flattened and its large windows expanded and fitted with metal doors. New garage buildings were added alongside it. The former playgrounds in front of and behind the gymnasium were concreted over, and the section behind it was extended southwards towards the site of a new pistol shooting range.

The playing field was used for both formal purposes and leisure activities. Football was a popular pursuit. The com-

Причина
Новым Годом

Kontakte zu den Deutschen

Zur deutschen Umgebung gab es offizielle, halboffizielle und inoffizielle Kontakte. Die offiziellen Kontakte waren vorgeschrieben und erfolgten zu bestimmten, jährlich wiederkehrenden Anlässen. Dabei wurden gegenseitig Festveranstaltungen besucht und man nahm an Kranzniederlegungen teil. Da in Dresden auch der Stab der 1. Gardepanzerarmee präsent war, musste man sich oft mit der Prominenz des damaligen Stadtbezirkes Nord begnügen. Offizielle Kontakte gab es auch zu Einheiten der Nationalen Volksarmee (NVA). In Dresden lag der Stab der 7. Panzerdivision der NVA, sodass man hier einen gleichartigen Partner hatte.

Daraus ergaben sich auch die halboffiziellen Kontakte, die von vorgesetzten Dienststellen nicht vorgegeben waren. Das waren nicht nur Fußballspiele zwischen Soldaten: Die sowjetische Seite zeigte schon mal einem ausgewählten Kreis neue Waffen, die die Deutschen noch nicht hatten. Diese halfen bei der Ausbildung von Kraftfahrern im Großstadtverkehr oder stellten bei einer Havarie an der Hauptwasserleitung ihre Wasserwagen vor die sowjetischen Wohnblocks. Deutsche Offiziere halfen auch dabei, Kontakte zu Betrieben zu knüpfen.

Es klingt heute unwahrscheinlich, aber in der DDR herrschte Arbeitskräftemangel. Einige Betriebe waren interessiert, sowjetische Soldaten als Aushilfe zu bekommen. Deren Lohn wurde auf eigenen Konten gutgeschrieben. Mit diesem Geld konnten Material und Leistungen an offiziellen Zuteilungen vorbei eingekauft werden. Auf diese Weise erhielt das Dienstzimmer des Divisionskommandeurs eine in den Deutschen Werkstätten Hellerau angefertigte Wandverkleidung. Auch der gute Zustand der Innenräume in der Landesschule wird zum Teil so finanziert worden sein.

Der westliche Teil des Geländes 1991 mit den Wohngebäuden. Unten in der Bildmitte das ehemalige Lehrgebäude, damals Stab und Grundschule. The western section of the site and its residential buildings in 1991. Centre-of-shot at the bottom of the photo is the former classroom building, then used by the Division and the primary school.

petitions organised for children in this area included elements of military physical training.
The old entrance to the Landesschule served as the point of vehicular access to and from the site of the Division headquarters. A small brick building painted in ubiquitous grey was built there in order to provide shelter for soldiers on sentry duty. The vehicular entrance was controlled using a rolling metal-clad gate emblazoned with two five-point golden stars.

The Schänkhübel Inn was located diagonally opposite this entrance, and was used by the Soviet Army as its "Officer's Clubhouse". With Christmas not celebrated in the atheist Soviet Union, New Year's celebrations appear to have been the highlight of the large events held there. Many of the clubhouse's cultural offerings were aimed at families, and made an important contribution to their well-being in what were otherwise foreign surroundings. The head of the clubhouse lived with his family on the top level of the building.

Contact with the Germans

The foreign troops came into official, semi-official and unofficial contact with their German surroundings. Official contact was subject to a number of conditions and occurred on specific annual occasions. This involved reciprocal attendance at celebratory events and participation in wreath-laying ceremonies. As the headquarters of the 1st Guards Tank Division was also located in Dresden, the 11th Division often had to make do with entertaining leading officials from what was at that time the city's North district. Official contact also existed with units in the National People's Army (NVA), and in the Dresden-based 7th Tank Division of the NVA the 11th Guards Tank Division had a partner on its own level.

This led to semi-official contact which had not been arranged by superior departments. Such meetings were by no means restricted to football matches, and on occasion would see the Soviets show a selected group of Germans a range of new weapons the latter did not yet have at their disposal. For their part, the Germans helped train HGV drivers to drive

Die Wende und das Ende

Ende der 1980er Jahre wurde die 11. Gardepanzerdivision jäh aus ihren eingefahrenen Abläufen gerissen. Es gärte im ganzen Ostblock. Bei den Massenprotesten ab Oktober 1989 blieben die sowjetischen Truppen in den Kasernen. Das war eine neue Erfahrung für alle. Im Juni 1953 hatten sowjetische Panzer den Bestand der DDR gesichert und im August 1968 war die Division in Richtung Prag gerollt und ist im Herbst wieder zurück gekommen.

Nach der Maueröffnung entwickelte sich alles immer schneller auf die Deutsche Einheit zu. Die Sowjetunion unter Gorbatschow tat nichts dagegen. Mit der Wiedervereinigung am 3. Oktober 1990 befand sich der Divisionsstab über Nacht mitten in einem kurz vorher noch als feindlich betrachteten Staat. Zu dieser Zeit wurde der Stationierungsvertrag abgeschlossen, der der Sowjetarmee etwa vier Jahre Zeit gab, ihre Truppen aus Deutschland in die Heimat zu verlegen.

Seit der Währungsunion erhielt man den vorher in Mark der DDR gezahlten Sold in Deutscher Mark. Es gab Dinge zu kaufen, an die der normale Sowjetbürger niemals im Leben herangekommen wäre. Besonders begehrt waren Autos, erschwinglich waren sie nur gebraucht. Mancher Offizier schaffte sich einen gebrauchten Westwagen an. Andere kauften den Einheimischen PKW aus sowjetischer Produktion ab, in weiser Berücksichtigung der Ersatzteilprobleme. Eine Luftaufnahme vom 30. Oktober 1991 zeigt einen im Gelände neu entstandenen Parkplatz voller PKW.

Mitten in die Abzugsvorbereitung hinein platzte im Dezember 1991 das Ende der Sowjetunion. Plötzlich dienten in einer Einheit Bürger verschiedener Staaten. Diese schlossen sich zu einer »Gemeinschaft Unabhängiger Staaten« zusammen. Die einzelnen Divisionen wurden jetzt bei ihrem Abzug in unterschiedliche Staaten verlegt. Von deutscher Seite bezeichnete man die Gesamtheit der noch auf eigenem Gebiet befindlichen ehemaligen Sowjetsoldaten als »GUS-Truppen«.

Im Sommer 1992 war auf dem Gelände der Landesschule das große Einpacken angesagt. Jeder Familie stand ein relativ kleiner brauner Container zur Verfügung. Die Zukunft

in city traffic and parked their water tankers in front of Soviet residential blocks if mains water connections to the buildings became damaged. German officers also aided their counterparts in setting up links with businesses. Though it may sound improbable to today's ears, the GDR actually suffered from a shortage of manpower. Some companies were therefore keen to gain the services of Soviet soldiers as temporary workers. The wages they earned were paid to their own accounts, and enabled them to buy their way around the official allocation of materials and services. It was in this way that the office of the Division Commander came to be fitted with wall cladding manufactured at the Deutsche Werkstätten in Hellerau.[5] The good condition of interior areas at the Landesschule is also likely to have been financed in this way.

The fall of Communism – and the end

The late 1980s saw the 11th Guards Tank Division abruptly ripped out of its familiar routines: the entire Eastern Bloc was seething with unrest. Soviet troops nevertheless remained in their barracks despite the mass protests which took place from October 1989 onwards. This was an entirely new experience for all concerned. In June 1953 Soviet tanks had been used to preserve the existence of the GDR, whilst in August 1968 the Division had rumbled to Prague before returning to their barracks that autumn.

Though the momentum towards a unified Germany increased after the Fall of the Wall, the Soviet Union under Gorbachev did nothing to slow or stop it. Once reunification had formally taken place on the 3rd of October 1990, the Division suddenly found itself at the centre of a country it had only recently regarded as its enemy. The stationing contract signed at that time gave the Soviet Army four years to move its troops from Germany back to within its domestic borders.

The advent of a unified German currency meant that wages previously paid in GDR marks were now paid in German marks. Items became available for purchase which a normal Soviet citizen would never have had the remotest chance of buying. Cars were very much in demand, though only second-hand vehicles were affordable. Many an officer bought a Western model, however the more prudent amongst them bought a Soviet-produced car for which they would be able to source spare parts after returning home. An aerial photo of the site taken on the 30th of October 1991 shows a newly created parking area-already full of vehicles.

rechts / right
Der östliche Teil des Areals im Oktober 1991. Mehr als die Hälfte der Bausubstanz in diesem Bereich ist verloren.
The eastern section of the site during the October of 1991. More than half of the building fabric in this section has been lost.

am neuen Stationierungsort war ungewiss. Am 18. und 19. August fanden in Dresden die offiziellen Veranstaltungen zur Verabschiedung der in Dresden und Sachsen stationierten Streitkräfte der früheren Sowjetarmee statt. Die 11. Gardepanzerdivision wurde nach Weißrussland verlegt.

Das Gelände der Landesschule war durch die militärische Nutzung bis zur Unkenntlichkeit verändert worden. Dabei wirkten der Verlust wichtiger Bauten, der Zustand der verbliebenen Gebäude und die dazugekommenen Bauwerke in gleicher Weise negativ.

Von 1945 bis 1992 war dieses Gebiet für mehrere Tausend Menschen für eine Zeit ihr Zuhause. Insbesondere die damaligen Kinder haben noch intensive und positive Erinnerungen an diesen Lebensabschnitt. Ein Beispiel dafür ist Michail Alabugin aus Odessa, der seit mehreren Jahren Kontakt zu den jetzigen Eigentümern hält, um über die frühere Nutzung zu informieren. Er hat für dieses Buch Fotos aus der sowjetischen Zeit beschafft. Das Schicksal des Geländes wird auch in zahlreichen Internetforen verfolgt und diskutiert, die viele hilfreiche Informationen für diesen Beitrag beisteuern konnten.

Anmerkungen
1 Im Folgenden hier nur als Landesschule bezeichnet.
2 Kramer 1945.
3 Boesch 1997, S. 78.

Notes
1 The Landesschule Dresden was a boarding establishment which featured both a progressive grammar school and an upper secondary school.
2 Hereinafter simply referred to as "the Landesschule".
3 Kramer 1945.
4 Boesch 1997, p. 78.
5 Deutsche Werkstätten in Hellerau is a renowned designer and manufacturer of high-quality furniture and interior design elements.

The forces were only halfway through their withdrawal preparations when the Soviet Union collapsed in December 1991. With one fell swoop the serving members of a unit were representatives of a number of different states. The states in question responded by forming themselves into a "Commonwealth of Independent States" (or "CIS"), with each individual division to be transferred to a different state upon withdrawal. Germans now described all of former Soviet soldiers still on their territory as "CIS troops".

During the summer of 1992 the Landesschule site was the scene of a great deal of packing. Each family was provided with a relatively small brown container, and faced an uncertain future at a new base. The official farewell celebrations for the former Soviet Army forces which had been stationed in Dresden and Saxony took place in Dresden on the 18th and 19th of August. The 11th Guards Tank Division was transferred to Belarus.

The Landesschule site had been changed beyond recognition by over four decades of military usage. The loss of architecturally significant structures, the condition of surviving buildings and the type of constructions erected on the site by the Soviet military were all seen in a similarly negative light.

The area had been a temporary home for many thousands of people between the years of 1945 and 1992, and the children who spent time there still have particularly intense, positive memories of that part of their lives. Now a resident of Odessa, Michail Alabugin is one such example. He has not only been in contact with the current owners for a number of years in order to garner information about the previous usage of the site, but has also worked to obtain Soviet-era photos for the purposes of this book. The fate of the site is retraced and discussed in numerous internet forums, which have provided of a wealth of useful information during the writing of this contribution.

Kontrastierende Formen und Materialien.
Contrasting forms and materials.

Edelstahl und Sandstein.
Stainless steel and sandstone.

Campus mit Seminarhäusern,
vom Akademiehotel gesehen.
Campus featuring seminar buildings
(viewed from the Academy Hotel).

links / left
Akademiehotel von Nordosten.
North-east view of the Academy Hotel.

oben / top
Treppenturm und Fassadendetail am Akademiehotel.
Stairwell and façade detail on the Academy Hotel.

links / left
Atrium des Akademierestaurants.
The atrium of the academy restaurant.

rechts / right
Blick von Haus 6 zum Akademiehotel
mit verglasten Treppentürmen.
View from building 6 towards the
Academy Hotel and its glazed stairwells.

Rekonstruktion einer Ruine – Akademie für Arbeitsschutz (1992 bis heute)

The reconstruction of a ruin – the Academy for Occupational Safety and Health (1992 to the present day)

MICHAEL BARTSCH

Jahrzehntelang war man als Dresdner achtlos die Königsbrücker Straße hinaufgefahren. Nördlich der Bahnüberführung begann hinter dem grauen Zaun der »Russenkaserne« im Heidewald unbekanntes Gelände. Nur Eingeweihte und Ortskundige wussten noch etwas von der früheren Landesschule auf der Bergkuppe am Ortseingang Klotzsche. Als die GUS-Streitkräfte 1992 abzogen, harrte das Gelände seiner Wiedererweckung.

Denn es sah aus wie auf den meisten Hinterlassenschaften der GUS-Truppen. Ursprüngliche Gestalt und Verwendungszweck der abgenutzten Gebäude waren kaum noch erkennbar. Von den Internats- und Wirtschaftsgebäuden, die um den großen Gartenhof entlang der west-östlichen Hauptachse gruppiert waren, standen nur noch drei. Bei der früheren Turnhalle, heute durch den Hotelneubau ersetzt, befanden sich LKW-Parkplätze und eine Montagebühne für Panzer. Offenbar wurde dort Motorenöl kurzerhand ins Erdreich abgelassen. Bis zu sechs Meter Tiefe musste der kontaminierte Boden später ausgehoben werden.

Wer sollte ein solches ruinöses Brachfeld wieder beleben? Die ehemaligen GUS-Liegenschaften fielen nach Abzug der Streitkräfte zunächst an den Bund. Der wiederum versuchte, die Liegenschaften an die Länder abzugeben. Sachsen war am 11. August 1993 das erste Bundesland, mit dem er ein entsprechendes Verwaltungsabkommen unterzeichnete. Der damalige Finanzminister und spätere Ministerpräsident Georg Milbradt war von dem vermeintlichen Bundes-Geschenk nicht durchweg begeistert. Die Liegenschaften an der Stauffenbergallee und entlang der Königsbrücker Straße bezeichnete er zwar als »Filet-Grundstücke«, wies aber zugleich auf die mit ihnen verbundene Altlastenbeseitigung hin.

Der Polier beim Richtspruch zum Richtfest am 22. Oktober 1999.
The foreman delivers his address at the topping-out ceremony, 22nd of October 1999.

Beim Wiederaufbau 1998–2001 wurden erhaltene Gebäudeteile sorgfältig integriert.
Reconstruction work from 1998 to 2001 included the careful integration of surviving building sections.

For decades the residents of Dresden drove up the Königsbrücker Straße without giving it a second thought, yet from the northern side of the railway bridge onwards the grey fence of the "Russian barracks" obscured a largely unknown section of Dresden Heath from view. Though only insiders and locals still knew anything about the former Landesschule site on the hilltop at the entrance into Klotzsche, the withdrawal of CIS troops from it in 1992 fostered hope for a period of revival.

The state in which the site found itself was typical of the legacy left by CIS troops. The original structures and intended purposes of its dilapidated buildings were only just discernible, and only three of the boarding and management buildings which had been grouped along the west-east axis of the large, lawned courtyard were still standing.

Von der Landesschule zur Akademie der Deutschen Gesetzlichen Unfallversicherung

Nun lag die Aufgabe beim Freistaat, die Grundstücke möglichst gewinnbringend zu veräußern. Zu diesem Zeitpunkt war noch nicht abzusehen, dass der Hauptverband der gewerblichen Berufsgenossenschaften einmal mit dem Land Sachsen über die ehemalige Landesschule in Klotzsche verhandeln würde. Die Weichen wurden 1992 wiederum auf Bundesebene gestellt. Am 20. Juni 1991 hatte der Bundestag eine »Unabhängige Föderalismus-Kommission« eingesetzt, die paritätisch von Mitgliedern des Bundestages und des Bundesrates besetzt war. Gemeinsam sollten Bund und Länder Vorschläge erarbeiten, wie Bundesbehörden und bundesweit tätige Institutionen möglichst gerecht auf das gesamte Gebiet des vereinigten Deutschlands verteilt werden. Im Klartext meinte dies den teilweisen Umzug in das Beitrittsgebiet der ehemaligen DDR. Das galt auch für Körperschaften öffentlichen Rechts, also auch für die Träger der Sozialversicherung. Nach den am 26. Juni 1992 vom Bundestag gebilligten Empfehlungen sollte unter anderem eine der großen Berufsgenossenschaften mit bis zu 500 Mitarbeitern ihren Hauptsitz nach Ostdeutschland verlegen.

Diese Empfehlung stieß beim Hauptverband der gewerblichen Berufsgenossenschaften auf Skepsis. Zum einen hatten die Berufsgenossenschaften bereits begonnen, ihre Strukturen auf die neuen Bundesländer auszudehnen. Zum anderen hätten intakte Institutionen in Westdeutschland aufgelöst, Liegenschaften verkauft und die Mitarbeiter umgesiedelt werden müssen. Nur wenige große der 35 Berufsgenossenschaften hätten überhaupt die Dimensionen der vorgesehenen Ansiedlung im Osten erreicht. Ein solches Vorhaben musste deshalb als unwirtschaftlich gelten.

Veränderungen im Sozialgesetzbuch VII legten eine andere, sinnvollere Lösung nahe. Der Präventionsauftrag der gesetzlichen Unfallversicherung wurde zu dieser Zeit erweitert. Nicht nur gegen Unfälle oder Berufskrankheiten galt es, Vorsorge zu treffen, sondern auch weit vorgreifend gegen arbeitsbedingte Gesundheitsgefahren. Damit verbunden war bundesweit ein erhöhter Aufwand an Qualifi-

The area around the former gymnasium – which has now been replaced by a new hotel – had been turned into HGV parking spaces and a repair ramp for armoured vehicles. The fact that engine oil had obviously been allowed to simply drain off into the earth necessitated the later excavation and removal of contaminated soil down to a depth of six metres.

Whose responsibility was it to regenerate such a ruinous piece of wasteland? Real estate vacated by withdrawing CIS troops was initially transferred to the federal government, which in turn attempted to pass it on to the respective federal states. Though the 11th of August 1993 saw Saxony become the first federal state to sign a corresponding administrative agreement, its then Minister of Finance and future Prime Minister, Georg Milbradt, was not entirely enthusiastic about this supposed "gift". Despite describing the respective pieces of real estate on the Stauffenbergallee and the Königsbrücker Straße as "choice properties", he tempered this by referring to the decontamination measures they necessitated.

From the Landesschule to an academy operated by the Deutsche Gesetzliche Unfallversicherung

It was now the task of the Free State of Saxony to sell the properties in the most profitable way possible. It could not be foreseen at that stage that the Hauptverband der gewerblichen Berufsgenossenschaften (the German Federation of Institutions for Statutory Accident Insurance and Prevention, hereinafter "HVBG") would later enter into negotiations with the Saxon government over the development of the former Landesschule site in Klotzsche. The route towards these negotiations began at national government level in 1992. An "Independent Federalism Commission" comprising an equal number of upper and lower house members had been set up by the Bundestag on the 20th of June 1991, and was to ensure that the state government and federal states worked together to deliver proposals on how federal authorities and nationwide institutions could be distributed around reunified

Georg Milbradt, sächsischer Staatsminister der Finanzen, und Herbert Kleinherne, Vorstandsvorsitzender des HVBG, unterzeichneten am 14. Juni 1995 den Kaufvertrag für das Gelände.
Georg Milbradt, Saxon Minister of Finance, and Herbert Kleinherne, then chairman of the HVBG, signed the purchase contract for the site on the 14th of June 1995.

zierung, Beratung und Forschung. So wurde bereits ein Ausbau der Akademie in Hennef/Sieg bei Bonn nahe des Hauptverbandssitzes in Sankt Augustin erwogen. Diese Absicht ließ sich ohne schmerzhafte Einschnitte leicht in Richtung Sachsen umlenken. Im Sommer 1993 fanden dazu im Sächsischen Sozialministerium Vorgespräche statt. Am 26. November fasste die Mitgliederversammlung des Hauptverbandes in Köln den Beschluss, dem Gedanken der Föderalismuskommission dadurch Rechnung zu tragen, »dass eine Akademie für Arbeitssicherheit und Gesundheitsschutz der Berufsgenossenschaften in Sachsen gegründet werden soll«. Dieser Vorschlag wurde von der Kommission am 9. Dezember 1993 »einmütig begrüßt«, wie es in einem Schreiben an den damaligen Vorstandsvorsitzenden des Hauptverbandes Klaus Hinne heißt.

Germany in the fairest possible way. Put simply, a number of organisations including public corporations – and therefore social accident insurance institutions – were to be relocated to the former GDR. Recommendations approved by the Bundestag on the 26th of June 1992 featured the relocation of the headquarters of one of the large (here: up to 500 employees) Berufsgenossenschaften to Eastern Germany.

This recommendation was met with scepticism by the HVBG. On the one hand, the Berufsgenossenschaften had already begun to expand their structures to include the new federal states. On the other, such a measure would have necessitated the breakup of functioning institutions in western Germany, the selling of real estate and the resettlement of employees. In addition, only a few of the 35 Berufsgenossenschaften were of a size appropriate to the planned development in the east of the country. A project of this type was therefore seen as unviable.

Amendments included in German Social Code, Book VII (SGB VII) suggested an alternative, more sensible solution. They expanded the prevention brief to be fulfilled by statutory accident insurers from accidents and occupational diseases alone to include the prevention of work-related risks. This represented an increased amount of training, consultancy and research effort on a nationwide scale. With the option of expanding the academy in Hennef/Sieg near Bonn – a site close to the Sankt Augustin headquarters of the HVBG – already having been deliberated, it was not only a simple step to redirect this momentum towards Saxony, but also one which avoided painful cutbacks elsewhere.

Preliminary discussions on this issue took place at the Saxon Ministry of Social Security during the summer of 1993. On the 26th of November that year the general assembly of the HVBG in Cologne decided to act upon the ideas set out by the Federalism Commission, stating that "an academy specialising in occupational safety and health operated by the Berufs-

Architekturmodell der Akademie, 1998.
Architectural model of the academy, 1998.

Klaus Hinne, Vorstandsvorsitzender des HVBG, bei der Ansprache zum ersten Spatenstich am 23. September 1998.
Klaus Hinne, chairman of the HVBG, speaks at the cutting of the first sod on the 23rd of September 1998.

Auch der Freistaat Sachsen unterstützte das Vorhaben. Statt der aufwendigen Umsiedlung von 500 Mitarbeitern durften etwa 150 neue Arbeitsplätze für Sachsen erwartet werden.

Für die neue Gemeinschaftseinrichtung, die der Qualifizierung, der Arbeitsschutzforschung und der Beratung dienen sollte, konnten drei Hauptunterstützer gewonnen werden. Die Berufsgenossenschaft Energie Textil Elektro (damals Feinmechanik und Elektrotechnik), die Verwaltungs-Berufsgenossenschaft und die Berufsgenossenschaft für Gesundheitsdienst und Wohlfahrtspflege waren bereit, eigene Akademien und Beratungszentren einzurichten.

genossenschaften should be founded in Saxony". According to a letter to Klaus Hinne (the chairman of the HVBG at that time), this recommendation was "welcomed unanimously" by the Commission on the 9th of December 1993. The Free State of Saxony also supported the project, which was to involve the creation of around 150 new jobs in Saxony rather than the costly relocation of 500 employees.

The HVBG was able to gain three main backers for the new shared facility, which was to be used for the purposes of training, research into occupational safety and health and the provision of consultancy services. The organisations in question were the BG for the Energy, Textile and Electric Sectors (then the BG responsible for the Precision Engineering and Electrical Industries), the BG responsible for the Administrative Sector and the BG responsible for the Health and Welfare Services, which were all prepared to set up their own academies and advice centres.

The planning process and the selection of a suitable location within Saxony began in 1993. Of the two Dresden candidate sites which quickly asserted themselves against the "competition", the CIS demilitarisation site and former home of the Landesschule exhibited significant advantages over its rival (a piece of land located close to Leuben gravel pit). The proximity of the former to both Dresden airport and the motorway network were just as important to its case as its inviting surroundings on the fringes of Dresden Heath, the micro-climate in Klotzsche (a former climatic health resort) and the character lent to the site by its previous educational usages. These factors justified the higher costs of the planned retention of historic building fabric when compared with the construction of an entirely new complex.

In 1994 the Siemens group acquired the former barracks located directly adjacent to the Landesschule site for the purpose of constructing its huge SIMEC semi-conductor plant. The plant's role as memory chip manufacturer for the Qimonda subsidiary later saw it drawn into a vortex of declining sales. Once Siemens had abandoned its original plan to convert the former Landesschule into a training centre of its own, the path was clear for the Berufsgenossenschaften to take up residence there.

Symbolischer erster Spatenstich vor den Ruinen des Lehrgebäudes am 23. September 1998.
Von links nach rechts: Ludger Fortmeier, Dr. Harald Maurer, Klaus Hinne, Prof. Dr. Rolf Bialas.
Cutting of the symbolic first sod in front of the ruins of the classroom building, 23rd of September 1998.
From left to right: Ludger Fortmeier, Dr. Harald Maurer, Klaus Hinne, Prof. Dr. Rolf Bialas.

Unsubsidised construction

Despite its vested interest in the recycling of former CIS real estate, the Saxon government was less obliging to the prospective users of the former Landesschule site than to the developers of the politically important "beacon" project just a stone's throw away. In contrast to the support it provided to the neighbouring owners, it not only charged the 1995 market price of 79 marks per square metre for the ten-hectare Landesschule property, but also failed to subsidise either the purchase of the site or the sum of around 90 million EUR spent on the construction of the new complex. The

1993 begannen die Planungen und die Standortsuche in Sachsen. Zwei Dresdner Angebote setzten sich schnell gegenüber der »Konkurrenz« durch, wobei die ehemalige Landesschule auf der GUS-Konversionsfläche deutliche Vorzüge gegenüber einem anderen Grundstück nahe der Leubener Kiesgrube aufwies. Die Nähe des Flughafens und der Autobahn fielen ebenso ins Gewicht wie die einladende Umgebung der Dresdner Heide, das Mikroklima des ehemaligen Luftkurortes Klotzsche und der Charakter des Ortes als frühere Bildungsstätte. Diese Gründe rechtfertigten den absehbar höheren Aufwand unter Einbeziehung der historischen Bausubstanz als bei einem Neubau. 1994 hatte in unmittelbarer Nachbarschaft auf dem ehemaligen Kasernengelände der Siemens-Konzern ein Grundstück für sein großes SIMEC-Halbleiterwerk erworben, das als Speicherchiphersteller der Tochter Qimonda später in den Sog der Absatzkrise geriet. Als der Konzern auf seine ursprüngliche Absicht verzichtete, in der ehemaligen Landesschule ebenfalls ein Schulungszentrum einzurichten, war der Weg für die Berufsgenossenschaften frei.

Bauen ohne jede Subvention

Bei allem Interesse an der Verwertung ehemaliger GUS-Liegenschaften zeigte sich der Freistaat jedoch weniger entgegenkommend als beim »Leuchtturm« und politischen Prestigeobjekt nebenan. Für die rund zehn Hektar verlangte er im Jahr 1995 den Marktpreis von 79 DM je Quadratmeter. Anders als beim Nachbarn flossen weder in den Grundstücksverkauf noch in die Baukosten von insgesamt etwa 90 Millionen Euro irgendwelche Subventionen. Auch das Grünflächenamt der Stadt Dresden ging mit dem Akademiebau strenger um als mit dem imageträchtigen Nachbarn, wo Baumfällungen Proteste nicht nur der Naturschützer auslösten. Es achtete genau auf Ersatzbepflanzungen und Ausgleichsflächen. Am 13. Juni wurde der Verkauf vertraglich besiegelt und einen Tag später auf einer großen Pressekonferenz gefeiert. Finanzminister Milbradt bescheinigte damals der Investition »erhebliche wirtschaftsfördernde Auswirkungen«. Für den Hauptverband der Berufsgenossenschaften räumte der Vorstandsvorsitze der

Baustelle des Akademiegeländes 1999.
Building work on the academy site, 1999.

Dresden Green Space Authority was another body to treat the academy development more strictly than its prestigious neighbour. This was in spite of the fact that the outcry against the latter's tree-felling activities was not restricted to conservationist groups. One example of the Authority's strictness was its painstaking monitoring of both replacement plantings and adherence to compensatory areas.

The sale of the site was contractually concluded on the 13th of June before being heralded at a large press conference the next day. Minister of Finance Milbradt hailed the investment as one which would have a "significant stimulating effect on the economy". Speaking on behalf of the HVBG, chairman Herbert Kleinherne conceded that there had been difficulties during the clarification of a wide variety of property-related issues, but went on to thank all partners for their eventual cooperation.

One of these partners was the neighbouring SIMEC chip plant. The academy and the chip plant both stand on a large, natural granite slab which connects them on a subterranean level, and this geological feature effectively forces the two parties to ensure reciprocal consideration and agreement where practical issues are concerned. This is due to the fact that the excellent stability and freedom from vibration provided by the slab were not only major reasons behind Siemens' decision to move to Klotzsche, but are also prerequisites for the sensitive production of nanometre-level chip architectures. One of the conditions of the sale of the site to SIMEC therefore obliges the state of Saxony to refrain from selling any properties within a radius of one kilometre to third parties.

It was for this reason that the 13th of June 1995 also witnessed the signing of a neighbourhood agreement between the SIMEC plant and the HVBG. The agreement saw SIMEC

Herbert Kleinherne Schwierigkeiten bei der Klärung der zahlreichen Grundstücksfragen ein, dankte aber allen Partnern für das schließliche Entgegenkommen.
Einer dieser Partner war die nebenan entstehende SIMEC-Chipfabrik. Denn die geologischen Gegebenheiten erzwingen nachgerade gegenseitige Rücksichtnahme und Arrangements in praktischen Fragen. Akademie und Chipfabrik sind auf unterirdische Weise miteinander verbunden – durch eine große, natürliche Granitplatte. Die durch sie gewährleistete Ruhe und Erschütterungsfreiheit hatte wiederum die Standortwahl des Nachbarn beeinflusst, der für die sensible Produktion der Chiparchitekturen im Nanometerbereich einen hochstabilen Untergrund benötigt. Beim Verkauf des Geländes an die SIMEC hatte sich der Freistaat verpflichtet, im Umkreis von einem Kilometer keine Grundstücke an Dritte zu veräußern.

Ebenfalls am 13. Juni 1995 wurde deshalb ein Nachbarschaftsvertrag zwischen dem SIMEC-Werk und dem Hauptverband unterzeichnet. Darin akzeptiert der Nachbar die Einrichtung der Akademie und die damit verbundenen Bautätigkeiten unter bestimmten Auflagen. So durften ab 1. August 1995 keine vibrationsauslösenden Abbruchmaßnahmen auf dem Gebiet der ehemaligen Landesschule durchgeführt werden, wobei die Siemens-Fabrik aber stundenweise Ausnahmen zuließ. Mit der SIMEC-Produktionsaufnahme ab Juni 1998 sollten Grenzwerte bei der Bodenerregung eingehalten werden. Grundsätzlich erhob der Nachbar aber keine Einwände gegen den Betrieb der Akademie.

Für Verzögerungen und Störungen der teuren Produktion wäre der Verband der Berufsgenossenschaften haftbar gemacht worden. Strapaziert worden ist der Vertrag allerdings nie. Das Verhältnis zum Nachbarn funktionierte ebenso gut wie die Vibrationsdämmung in dessen Produktionsanlagen.

consent to the establishment of the academy and related construction measures providing a number of clauses were kept to. One such clause stipulated that no vibration-inducing demolition measures were to be carried out on the Landesschule site after the 1st of August 1995. Exceptions were permitted on an hour-by-hour basis further to coordination with the Siemens plant. Another clause set the threshold ground vibration values which were to be adhered to further to the commencement of production at the SIMEC facility in June 1998. Despite the inclusion of these clauses, SIMEC essentially had no objections to the activities carried out on the academy site.

The HVBG would have been made liable for any delays or interruptions which affected the expensive production process. Despite this, the contract has never put to the test, and the academy's relationship with its neighbour has worked just as well as the vibration absorbers in the latter's production facilities.

Compromises reached with monument preservation authorities

Though realised under time pressure, the construction project was certainly not carried out in an inconsiderate, cavalier fashion. If anything the opposite was true. The ensemble was listed by the Monument Preservation Authority in 1993, and the Society for the Preservation of the Landesschule set up by its former pupils in the same year also exhibited a keen interest in the restoration of what had been their own miniature "school town". The state the complex had been left in was nevertheless disheartening to all concerned. In relative terms, the best-preserved structure was the classroom building originally designed by Oskar Kramer. The adjoining headmaster's and deputy headmaster's houses were also still standing, as was the small porter's lodge directly adjacent to the Königsbrücker Landstraße. Only three of the six Heinrich Tessenow-designed boarding houses had survived. The assembly hall building existed as ruins.

Kompromiss mit dem Denkmalschutz

Bauen unter Zeitdruck bedeutete nun gerade nicht rücksichtsloses Bauen – ganz im Gegenteil. 1993 war das Ensemble unter Denkmalschutz gestellt worden. Auch ehemalige Landesschüler, die 1993 einen Förderverein gegründet hatten, zeigten reges Interesse an der Wiederherstellung ihrer ehemaligen kleinen »Schulstadt«. Doch deren jetziger Zustand musste eher entmutigen. Am relativ besten erhalten präsentierte sich das von Oskar Kramer entworfene eigentliche Lehrgebäude. Auch die angrenzenden Wohnhäuser von Rektor und Konrektor standen noch, ebenso das kleine Pförtnerhaus unmittelbar an der Königsbrücker Landstraße. Von den sechs ehemaligen Lehrer- und Schülerwohnheimen Heinrich Tessenows hingegen waren drei gar nicht mehr, die Aula nur noch in Resten vorhanden.

Am 23. September 1998 erfolgte auf dem Gelände der erste Spatenstich. Es soll nicht verschwiegen werden, dass die Interessen der Denkmalpflege mit den Zielen und Möglichkeiten des Bauherrn kollidierten. Das beauftragte Braunschweiger Architekturbüro Manfred Stautmeister bezeichnete die Tessenow-Gebäude jenseits des Kramerschen Schulbaus als »nicht restaurierbar« und plante einen Neubau im Geist und im Grundriss der ursprünglichen Anlage. Demgegenüber verlangte das Landesamt für Denkmalpflege den Erhalt aller noch vorhandenen Gebäude und die Wiedererrichtung der Pergolen. Auch die Tessenow-Gesellschaft lehnte jeden Eingriff in die historische Bausubstanz ab.

Solche Maximalforderungen aber waren mit einem modernen, barrierefreien Schulungszentrum unvereinbar. Zumindest die innere Gliederung der verbliebenen ehemaligen Schülerwohnheime stand der künftigen Nutzung völlig entgegen. Schritt für Schritt näherte man sich seit 1995 einem Kompromiss mit der Denkmalpflege. Es ging um eine deutlichere Integration der denkmalgeschützten Restsubstanz. Der Hauptverband der gewerblichen Berufsgenossenschaften unterbreitete den Vorschlag, statt der von der Denkmalpflege favorisierten heutigen Gebäude vier und neun die komplette Südseite mit den Gebäuden vier bis

The first sod of the new development was cut at the site on the 23rd of September 1998. It is nevertheless to be noted that the interests of monument preservation clashed with the aims of the developer and the options open to them. Having been commissioned to provide designs for the project, the Braunschweig-based Manfred Stautmeister firm of architects deemed the Tessenow buildings across from the Kramer classroom building "unrestorable", and drew up plans for a new ensemble which echoed the original complex in terms of its spirit and layout. The State Monument Preservation Authority had other ideas, and demanded that all buildings still standing be retained and the pergolas which had been a feature of the original design rebuilt. The Tessenow Society also disapproved of any interference with surviving sections of historic building fabric.

Exacting demands of this type were nevertheless incompatible with the creation of a modern, barrier-free academy. If nothing else, the inner layout of the former boarding houses was completely at odds with their intended usage. From 1995 onwards, plans gradually edged closer to a suitable compromise with the demands of the Monument Preservation Authority. In particular, listed building fabric was more clearly integrated into the new complex. The HVBG submitted a proposal to rebuild the entire south side as a homogenous ensemble comprising what are now buildings 4 to 6. The proposal included the integration of original façades and retaining walls, and went against the Monument Protection Authority's preference for the reconstruction of what are now buildings 4 and 9. Whereas the outer walls of buildings 4 and 6 had been preserved, building 5 no longer existed and needed to be rebuilt from scratch. The Monument Preservation Authority agreed to these plans and permitted the demolition of courtyard-side

Richtfest am 22. Oktober 1999 in der heutigen Lobby des Akademiehotels.
Topping-out ceremony in what is now the lobby of the Academy Hotel, 22nd of October 1999.

sechs als einheitliches Ensemble wiederherzustellen, Originalfassaden und Stützmauern inbegriffen. Die Häuser vier und sechs waren zumindest mit den Außenmauern erhalten, das mittlere Gebäude fünf fehlte und musste komplett neu aufgebaut werden. Dem stimmte die Denkmalpflege zu und erlaubte den Abbruch der hofseitigen funktionsstörenden Anbauten. Aufwendig wurden die Außenmauern bei der Entkernung abgestützt. Den vorspringenden Gebäudeteilen der Südseite sind jetzt schmale traufhohe Pergolen vorgeblendet, die an die Originale erinnern. Natursteinmauern aus behauenem Elbsandstein bilden die Gebäudesockel Richtung Gästeparkplatz. Ebenfalls aus Naturstein bestehen die Mauern der Terrassen, die das Gefälle des Geländes abfangen und einladende Terrassenhöfe abschließen.

Die nördlichen drei Gebäude wurden hingegen komplett neu errichtet. Die Symmetrie der Anlage blieb dabei erhalten. Bis zuletzt wurde über die dekorativen zweigeschossigen Pergolen mit ihren Holzlamellen gestritten, die einst die Internatsgebäude miteinander verbunden hatten. Sie erschienen dem Bauherrn in der Ursprungsform nicht mehr zumutbar. Traufhohe Stahlkonstruktionen erinnern nunmehr an die Originalform, tragen aber in drei Metern Höhe ein Glasdach, das einen geschützten Durchgang bis zum Kopfbau des Hotels ermöglicht und somit eine Funktion erfüllt. Die Pergolen erinnerten an die ursprünglichen Strukturen Tessenows, schrieb Landeskonservator Prof. Gerhard Glaser im Oktober 2001 versöhnlich, »das jetzt eingehängte Glasdach hat seinen Sinn«.

Hinsichtlich des Hotelneubaus zeigte sich die Denkmalpflege sehr entgegenkommend. Die Reste der alten Aula hätten nie für ein Hotel mit 300 Betten, die dazugehörige Gastronomie und Freizeiträume ausgereicht. Der den Maßen der Gesamtanlage und ihrem Rhythmus angepasste Neubau nach Plänen des Architekten Helmut Blöcher nimmt die Hauptachse einschließlich Terrasse und Wasserbecken auf und setzt die Symmetrie zunächst fort. An der Südseite aber stellt ein asymmetrisch angesetzter rechtwinkliger Trakt Übergang und Anschluss an die wuchtige Industriearchitektur der unmittelbar angrenzenden Chipfabrik her.

Schlüsselübergabe durch Architekt Manfred Stautmeister (Mitte) und Klaus Krawinkel (rechts) an Akademieleiter Dr. Bodo Pfeiffer am 31. Mai 2001. The handing over of the key from architect Manfred Stautmeister (centre) and Klaus Krawinkel (right) to academy head Dr. Bodo Pfeiffer, 31st of May 2001.

extensions which would otherwise have affected the functionality of the new buildings. Original outer walls were supported at substantial cost during the gutting of surviving original structures. The slender, eaves-height pergolas created along the projecting sections of the south-side buildings are reminiscent of the originals, whilst the bases of buildings which face onto the visitor car park take the form of natural, hewn Elbe sandstone walls. Terrace walls

Mit der nüchternen, fensterarmen Südwand endete sozusagen die Harmonie der Tessenowschen Anlagenkomposition. Unstrittig blieb die weitgehend originale Wiederherstellung des ehemaligen Lehrgebäudes einschließlich seiner Reliefs, das heute den Besucher von Leitung und Verwaltung empfängt. Es versteht sich auch von selbst, dass bei einer solchen Rekonstruktion nur modernste Haustechnik eingebaut wurde. Über zahlreiche Details wie beispielsweise die Gestaltung der Treppenläufe und die Einhaltung von Auflagen aber kam es immer wieder zu Differenzen mit der Denkmalpflege. Letztlich konnten solche klassischen Konflikte zwischen Nutzerinteresse und Schutzwürdigkeit aber geklärt werden. Hier vermittelte Architekt Stautmeister sehr sensibel. Im Jahre 2000 wurde relativ unkompliziert vom Regierungspräsidium Dresden die Genehmigung zum Ab-

are also of natural stone construction, and both divide and support the slope of the site and enclose appealing terraced courtyards.

The symmetry of the complex has been maintained despite the rebuilding of the three northern buildings from scratch. The two-storey, decorative pergolas and their wooden lamella were nevertheless the source of arguments until the very end of the project. Despite having once connected the boarding houses with one another, the developer felt that they were no longer viable in their original form. Though the eaves-height steel structures which have taken their place are reminiscent of the original form, the glass roof which has been added at a height of three metres now provides a protected route to the front of the hotel and therefore fulfils a function. Writing in October 2001, Saxony's then State Curator Prof. Gerhard Glaser noted in a conciliatory way that the pergolas echo the original Tessenow structures "[and] the glass roof which has been added serves its purpose".

Though officials from the Monument Preservation Authority were far more accommodating where the construction of the new hotel was concerned, the remains of the old assembly hall building would never have been sufficient for the accommodation of a 300-bed hotel and its appurtenant gastronomic and leisure facilities. Built according to designs by the architect Helmut Blöcher, the new construction has been adapted to the dimensions and rhythm of the overall complex. It adopts the main axis which extends through the terrace and fountain, and initially continues the symmetry of the ensemble before breaking from it on its south side, where an asymmetrically positioned, right-angled wing represents a point of transfer and contact between the academy site and the powerful architecture of the neighbouring chip production facility. The sober, windowless south wall effectively represents the end of the harmony of the Tessenow composition.

One issue which remained beyond dispute was the restoration of the former classroom building and its reliefs, which have now been restored to almost exactly their original forms and greet visitors to management and adminis-

Internationale Konferenz in der Aula der Akademie. International conference in the Academy's auditorium.

bruch des Pförtnerhäuschens erteilt. Es stand der Verkehrserschließung im Zusammenhang mit dem vierspurigen Ausbau der Königsbrücker Landstraße im Wege.

Schon beim Richtfest am 22. Oktober 1999 hatte Klaus Hinne, der Vorstandsvorsitzende der HVBG, von einem »architektonisch und inhaltlich anspruchsvollen Projekt« gesprochen. Die Auflagen der Denkmalpflege haben letztlich dafür gesorgt, dass die Anlage wieder den Gesamteindruck eines harmonischen Ensembles vermittelt.

trative departments. It goes without saying that a reconstruction project of this type featured the installation of only the most modern in HVAC systems. A variety of details such as stairway design and adherence to stipulations still frequently led to differences of opinion between the developer and the Monument Preservation Authority. In the end it was always possible to reach an agreement on conflicts between user requirements and the interests of monument preservation, and Stautmeister showed himself to be highly adept in the art of mediation. In the year 2000 the Dresden Regional Administrative Authority was relatively uncomplicated in its issuing of a demolition permit for the porter's lodge, which would otherwise have stood in the way of the expansion of the Königsbrücker Landstraße to a four-lane road.

Im Dienste von Arbeitssicherheit und Gesundheitsschutz

Am 15. Januar 2001 nahm die Akademie der Deutschen Gesetzlichen Unfallversicherung den Betrieb auf. Am 31. Mai des gleichen Jahres wurde die bundesweit einmalige Einrichtung mit einem Festakt offiziell eingeweiht. Acht Partner fanden schließlich unter den Dächern der ehemaligen Landesschule zusammen. Die Bildungsstätten der drei großen Berufsgenossenschaften hätten dem Bedarf entsprechend neu geschaffen werden müssen und erhielten nun in Dresden-Klotzsche ihren sinnvollen Platz. Sie haben in den nördlich der Hauptachse gelegenen drei Neubauten der Häuser sieben bis neun ihren Sitz. Die Berufsgenossenschaft für Gesundheitsdienst und Wohlfahrtspflege richtete darüber hinaus noch ein Schulungs- und Beratungszentrum ein. Der Landesverband Südost der Deutschen Gesetzlichen Unfallversicherung nutzt den südlich des Eingangs vorgelagerten Teil des ehemaligen Kramerschen Schulgebäudes. Das Netzwerk der berufsgenossenschaftlichen Prüf- und Zertifizierungsstellen »BG-PRÜFZERT« unterhält im Haus drei seine Geschäftsstelle. Die jährlich bis zu 20 000 Gäste können schließlich im Akademiehotel untergebracht werden.

Die zahlenmäßig größte Einrichtung der Akademie ist das 2001 neu geschaffene Institut Arbeit und Gesundheit der Deutschen Gesetzlichen Unfallversicherung. Sein Schwerpunkt liegt auf der Qualifizierung, wofür jährlich mehr als 300 Seminare, Workshops und Tagungen angeboten werden. Im Auftrag der gesetzlichen Unfallversicherungen berät das Institut außerdem Mitgliedsunternehmen und führt Forschungs- und Entwicklungsprojekte durch. Es beschäftigt etwa 90 Mitarbeiter auf 70 Planstellen, davon 35 eigene Dozenten. Je zehn Mitarbeiter arbeiten in den drei berufsgenossenschaftlichen Bildungsstätten und etwa 60 im Hotel. Die Akademie verfügt insgesamt über 30 Schulungsräume und 25 Musterarbeitsplätze für eine praxisnahe Ausbildung. Kongresse mit bis zu 300 Teilnehmern können ebenfalls hier abgehalten werden.

Nach fast zehn Jahren praktischer Erfahrungen mit der rekonstruierten Landesschule sind es eher Kleinigkeiten,

As early as the topping-out ceremony on the 22nd of October 1999, HVBG Chairman Klaus Hinne spoke of a project which was "ambitious in terms of both its architecture and its content". In the end, the stipulations made by the Monument Preservation Authority have ensured that the complex once again conveys the overall impression of a harmonious ensemble.

In the service of occupational safety and health

The Academy of the German Social Accident Insurance opened its doors for business as the only facility of its kind in Germany on the 15th of January 2001. An official opening ceremony was held on the 31st of May that year, with eight partners taking up residence beneath the roofs of the former Landesschule. Whereas the educational establishments previously operated by the three large Berufsgenossenschaften would have needed to be completely restructured in order to cope with developments in demand, a suitable, practical location had now been found for them in Dresden-Klotzsche. They are now housed in the newly constructed buildings 7 to 9 to the north of the main axis. The BG responsible for the health and welfare services has also set up a training and advice centre. The Regional Association (South-East) of the DGUV (the German Social Accident Insurance) uses the projecting section of the former Kramer classroom building to the south of the entrance, whilst the "BG-PRÜFZERT" network of testing and certification bodies has its offices in building 3. Up to 20,000 guests can be accommodated at the Academy Hotel on an annual basis.

In terms of numbers alone, the largest facility at the Academy is the Institute Work and Health set up by the DGUV in 2001. Its main focus is on the provision of qualification schemes, which involves the organisation of over 300 seminars, workshops and conferences each year. The BGAG also provides consultancy services to member companies on behalf of statutory accident insurance institutions and

Praxisfeld Fahrsimulation im Institut Arbeit und Gesundheit.
Practical facility: driving simulator in the Institute Work and Health.

die die Zufriedenheit mit der bewährten Konzeption von 1999 einschränken. Eine davon hat als unterirdische Ursache wiederum jene Granitplatte, die unter dem Thümmelsberg am Heiderand liegt. Trotz der Berglage staut über ihr Grundwasser. Das Problem der feuchten Keller bekamen auch Kramer und Tessenow nicht in den Griff. Möglicherweise hätte man auch die drei nördlichen Gebäude in gleicher Weise wie die südlichen mit einem unterirdischen Gang verbinden können. Und gelegentlich erscheinen die Plätze im Hotelrestaurant knapp.

Gäste der Akademie, also Führungskräfte, Personalvertreter, Sicherheitsfachkräfte, Aufsichtspersonen oder Ärzte, fühlen sich in dieser »Oase« ausgesprochen wohl. Sie bestätigen damit die Richtigkeit der Ansiedlungsentscheidung an einem Ort, dessen umgebende Natur und dessen atmosphärische Präsenz des Schulgründungsgedankens gleichermaßen stimulierend wirken.

carries out research and development projects. The Institute's 90 employees are spread across 70 posts and include 35 of its own in-house lecturers. 10 employees work at each of the three educational establishments run by the Berufsgenossenschaften, whilst the remaining 60 work in the hotel. The Academy has over 30 seminar rooms and 25 model workspaces for practical training. It can also be used to hold congresses with up to 300 participants.

With almost ten years of practical experience now having been gained at the reconstructed Landesschule, it can be said that satisfaction with the reliable concept drawn up in 1999 only tends to be tempered by minor issues. One of these issues relates to the granite slab which runs beneath the Thümmelsberg hill on the edge of Dresden Heath. Despite being on an incline, the slab accumulates ground water on its surface. This leads to damp on basement levels – a problem Kramer and Tessenow also struggled to come to terms with. One option would have been to connect the northern buildings with the same type of subterranean tunnel installed between the underground sections of the southern buildings. It also sometimes seems as if there are not enough spaces in the hotel restaurant.

Whether they are managers, staff council members, OSH professionals, labour inspectors or physicians, the guests of the Academy feel perfectly at home in this "oasis". This confirms the soundness of the decision to establish the Academy at a location with natural surroundings and an academic genius loci – each of which is as inspiring as the other.

rechts: Lobby des Akademiehotels.
right: The lobby of the Academy Hotel.

links / left
Akademiehotel von Westen.
West view of the Academy Hotel.

oben / top
Treppenturm am Akademiehotel.
Stairwell at the Academy Hotel.

ALE VERNETZUNG FORMEN EINE NEUE ARBEITSWELT
GEN UND VERSCHRÄNKEN ALLE ARBEITS
de la population mondiale ne disposent pas des
ONDIAUX CONSTITUENT UN NOUVEAU MONDE DU TRAVAIL : PERSPECTIVES D'ACTION
TOUS LES SECTEURS DE TRAVAIL ET LES DOMAINES DE LA VIE GLEICHZEITIG : RUND 80% DER WELTBEV
AINS SONT AUJOURD'HUI SOUS-EMPLOYÉS OU AU CHÔMAGE...
IßT WISSENSEXPLOSION Die Zahl der Armutsländer
LES TECHNOLOGIES DE L'INFORMATION ENVAHISSENT ET RELIENT TOUS LES SECTEURS
des connaissances
YS PAUVRES EST PASSÉ DE 25 À 48 AU COURS DES CINQ DERNIÈRES ANNÉES
1987 : 5Mrd
1980 n.Chr.
1971 : Invention de la micropuce
ns le monde . . .
BEING DIGITAL (NEGROPONTE). BEING DIGITAL
DIGITAL (NEGROPONTE). BEING DIGITAL (NEGROPONTE). BEING DIGITAL
länder, vereinigt euch (Marx). Prolétaires de tous les pays, unissez-vous (Marx).
FRANKLIN). LE TEMPS C'EST DE L'ARGENT (FRANKLIN). BEDENKE, DASS DIE ZEIT GELD IST
nfang. L'oisiveté est la mère de tous les vices. Müßiggang ist aller Laster Anfang.
Angesichts sollst du dein Brot essen (Genesis 3,19). C'est à la sueur de ton visage que tu mangeras

links / left
Verbindungsgang zwischen Haus 1
und dem Akademiehotel mit Zeitleiste zur Geschichte
der Arbeit aus dem Themenpark der EXPO 2000.
Connecting walkway between building 1 and the Academy
Hotel, featuring a timeline on the history of work originally
exhibited at EXPO 2000.

rechts / right
Treppenhaus im Akademiehotel.
Stairwell in the Academy Hotel.

Wasserflächen an der Hotelterrasse.
Water features on the hotel terrace.

oben / top
Fassadendetail am Akademiehotel.
Façade detail on the Academy Hotel.

rechts / right
Blick über die Gesamtanlage mit restaurierter Südfassade.
View across the entire complex, including the restored south façade.

Dr. phil. Ullrich Amlung
geb. 1955, Dipl.-Päd. und Volkskundler. Wissenschaftlicher Mitarbeiter am Deutschen Institut für Internationale Pädagogische Forschung, Berlin. Lehrbeauftragter an der Universität Marburg, Bildungsgeschichte und Museumspädagogik.
born 1955, graduate teacher and folklorist. Research associate at the German Institute for International Educational Research, Berlin. Part-time lecturer in educational history and museum-based educational programmes at the University of Marburg.

Dipl.-Ing. Michael Bartsch
geb. 1953, Freier Journalist und Autor. Mitteldeutschland-Korrespondent der taz in Dresden. Printmedien, Hörfunk und Moderationen mit Schwerpunkten Landespolitik, Bildung und Wissenschaft, Kulturpolitik, Theater.
born 1953, freelance journalist and author. Central German correspondent for the taz in Dresden. Active in print media, radio and chairing, specialising in the fields of state politics, education and academia, cultural politics and theatre.

Hanka Blesse M. A.
geb. 1965, Erziehungswissenschaftlerin. Berufsschullehrerin an der Berufsschule für Blinde und Sehbehinderte, Chemnitz. Magisterarbeit zum Thema »Die Nationalpolitische Erziehungsanstalt Klotzsche, Rudolf-Schröter-Schule«.
born 1965, educational scientist. Vocational teacher at the Vocational School for the Blind and Partially Sighted, Chemnitz. MA thesis written on "The National Political Educational Institution in Klotzsche, Rudolf-Schröter-Schule".

Ulrike Hübner-Grötzsch M. A.
geb. 1972, Kunsthistorikerin. Publikationen zur Architekturgeschichte der 1. Hälfte des 20. Jahrhunderts. Doktorandin zum Thema »Paul Wolf – Stadtbaurat in Dresden 1922 bis 1945«.
born 1972, art historian. Author of publications on the architectural history of the first half of the 20th century. Currently writing a doctoral thesis on "Paul Wolf – head of the Dresden Municipal Planning and Building Control Authority in Dresden from 1922 to 1945".

Ulrich Hübner M. A.
geb. 1972, Kunsthistoriker. Gebietsreferent im Landesamt für Denkmalpflege Sachsen. Publikationen zur Architekturgeschichte der 1. Hälfte des 20. Jahrhunderts, besonders Reformarchitektur. Doktorand zum Thema »Kunst und Architektur der Feuerbestattungsanlagen«.
born 1972, art historian. Regional advisor at the Saxon State Monument Protection Authority. Author of publications on the architectural history of the first half of the 20th century, especially reform architecture. Currently writing a doctoral thesis on "The Art and Architecture of Crematorial Facilities".

Götz Krüger
geb. 1957, Betriebswirtschaftler. Hobbyhistoriker, Forschungen besonders zur Geschichte der Festung Dresden, zu militärischen Ereignissen des 18. und 19. Jahrhunderts, sowjetischen Truppen in Dresden. Publikationen zur Geschichte einzelner genossenschaftlicher Wohnanlagen im Westen von Dresden.
born 1957, business administrator. Amateur historian, main focus of research on the history of Dresden Fort, military events of the 18th and 19th centuries and Soviet troops in Dresden. Author of publications on the history of individual residential cooperatives in the western area of Dresden.

Hans-Peter Lühr
geb. 1951, Lektor. Herausgeber der Dresdner Hefte, Geschäftsführer des Dresdner Geschichtsvereins. Verschiedene Publikationen zur Kultur- und Kunstgeschichte im 20. Jahrhundert.
born 1951, editor, publisher of the "Dresdner Hefte" series, head of Dresden Historical Society. Author of various publications on the cultural and artistic history of the 20th century.

Jörg-Rainer Oesen
geb. 1948, Fotograf. Studium an der Hochschule für Grafik und Buchkunst in Leipzig. Freier Fotograf, zahlreiche Preise und Auszeichnungen bei in- und ausländischen Fotowettbewerben.
born 1948, photographer. Studied at the Academy of Graphic Arts and Book Design in Leipzig. Freelance photographer, winner of numerous prizes and awards at both domestic and international photography competitions.

1.3.1731
Gründung des Königlich-Sächsischen Kadettenkorps, Standort: Altes Wackerbarthpalais, Dresden
Founding of the Royal Saxon Kadettenkorps at the Altes Wackerbarthpalais, Dresden

1876
Umzug des Kadettenkorps in die Marienallee in Dresden-Neustadt
Relocation of the Kadettenkorps to the Marienallee in the Dresden-Neustadt district

10.3.1920
Auflösung des Kadettenkorps gemäß einer Auflage des Versailler Vertrages
Closure of the Kadettenkorps in accordance with a stipulation of the Treaty of Versailles

14.4.1920
Gründung der Landesschule Dresden und Unterbringung im ehemaligen Kadettenhaus in der Marienallee
Founding of the Landesschule Dresden, accommodated in the former "Kadettenhaus" building on the Marienallee

Januar – März 1925
Beschluss zur Errichtung und Planung der Landesschule Dresden in Klotzsche auf dem Thümmelsberg durch das Sächsische Ministerium für Volksbildung. Auftragsvergabe an die Architekten Heinrich Tessenow und Oskar Kramer
Decision taken by the Saxon Ministry of Popular Education to plan and erect the Landesschule Dresden on the Thümmelsberg in Klotzsche, commissioning of architects Heinrich Tessenow and Oskar Kramer

15.10.1927
Einweihung der Landesschule Dresden in Klotzsche
Official opening of the Landesschule Dresden in Klotzsche

1.4.1934
Umwandlung der Landesschule Dresden in eine Staatliche Nationalpolitische Erziehungsanstalt (NPEA)
Transformation of the Landesschule Dresden into a state National Political Educational Institution (NPEA)

1945 – 1992
Nutzung des Geländes durch den Stab der 11. Gardepanzerdivision der sowjetischen Armee, später GUS-Armee
Site used by the Soviet Army (later the CIS Army) as the headquarters of the 11th Guards Tank Division

18./19.8.1992
Offizielle Verabschiedung der 11. Gardepanzerdivision und Verlegung nach Weißrussland
Official leaving ceremony for the departing 11th Guards Tank Division (subsequently based in Belarus)

27.5.1992
Beschluss der Unabhängigen Föderalismuskommission, eine gewerbliche Berufsgenossenschaft nach Sachsen zu verlagern
Decision taken by the Independent Federalism Commission to relocate a statutory accident insurance institution to Saxony

3.3.1993
Die Gebäude der ehemaligen Landesschule Dresden werden unter Denkmalschutz gestellt.
Listing of the buildings of the former Landesschule Dresden as a site of national heritage

26.11.1993
Beschluss der Mitgliederversammlung des Hauptverbandes der gewerblichen Berufsgenossenschaften (HVBG) zur Errichtung einer Akademie für Arbeitssicherheit und Gesundheitsschutz
Decision taken by the general assembly of the German Federation of Institutions for Statutory Accident Insurance and Prevention (HVBG) to construct an academy for occupational safety and health

9.12.1993
Zustimmender Beschluss der Unabhängigen Föderalismuskommission nach Zustimmung des Freistaates Sachsen zur Errichtung der Akademie
Concurring resolution passed by the Independent Federalism Commission further to the granting of approval for the construction of the academy by the Free State of Saxony

Oktober 1994
Übernahme der Liegenschaft der ehemaligen Landesschule Dresden durch den Bund bzw. das Land Sachsen
Takeover of the former Landesschule site by the federal government/the state of Saxony

1994
Erwerb eines Teiles des Geländes der ehemaligen Landesschule Dresden (Sportgelände) durch die Siemens AG
Section of the former Landesschule Dresden site (sports area) purchased by Siemens AG

13.6.1995
Erwerb des übrigen Geländes, einschließlich der noch erhaltenen Schul- und Internatsgebäude, durch den Hauptverband der gewerblichen Berufsgenossenschaften (HVBG), seit 2007 Deutsche Gesetzliche Unfallversicherung (DGUV)
Purchase of the remainder of the site – including surviving school buildings and boarding houses – by the German Federation of Institutions for Statutory Accident Insurance and Prevention (HVBG), renamed the German Social Accident Insurance (DGUV) in 2007

23.9.1998
Erster Spatenstich zur Errichtung der Akademie
The cutting of the first sod; construction of the academy begins

22.10.1999
Richtfest unter Beteiligung des Staatsministers für Soziales, Gesundheit und Familie, Dr. Hans Geisler, und des Dresdner Bürgermeisters für Wirtschaft und Verkehr, Rolf Wolgast
Topping-out ceremony, attended by Dr. Hans Geisler, Saxon State Minister of Social Affairs, Health and the Family, and Rolf Wolgast, Mayor for Economy and Transport in Dresden

31.5.2001
Einweihung der Akademie für Arbeitssicherheit und Gesundheitsschutz
Official opening of the academy of occupational safety and health

LAGEPLAN

Haus 1 – Institut Arbeit und Gesundheit
Ehemals Haus J (Lehrgebäude)

Haus 3 – Institut Arbeit und Gesundheit, Seminarräume und Praxisfelder
Ehemals Haus G
(Wohngebäude für Rektor sowie Rentamt)

Haus 4 – Institut Arbeit und Gesundheit, Seminarräume und Praxisfelder
Ehemals Schülerheim E

Haus 5 – Institut Arbeit und Gesundheit, Seminarräume und Praxisfelder
Ehemals Schülerheim C

Haus 6 – Institut Arbeit und Gesundheit, Seminarräume und Praxisfelder
Ehemals Schülerheim A

Haus 7 – Verwaltungs-BG
Ehemals Schülerheim B

Haus 8 – BG Gesundheitsdienst und Wohlfahrtspflege
Ehemals Schülerheim D

Haus 9 – BG Energie Textil Elektro
Ehemals Schülerheim F

Haus 10 – Akademiehotel und Restaurant
Errichtet an Stelle von Haus K
(Aula und Wirtschaftsgebäude)
sowie Haus L (Turnhalle)

Nicht erhalten bzw. nicht wiedererrichtet
Haus H (Wohngebäude für Konrektor und Beamte)
Haus M (Pförtner-Wohnhaus)
Haus N (Lehrer-Wohnhaus-Gruppe)
Kampfbahn (heute Infineon-Gelände)

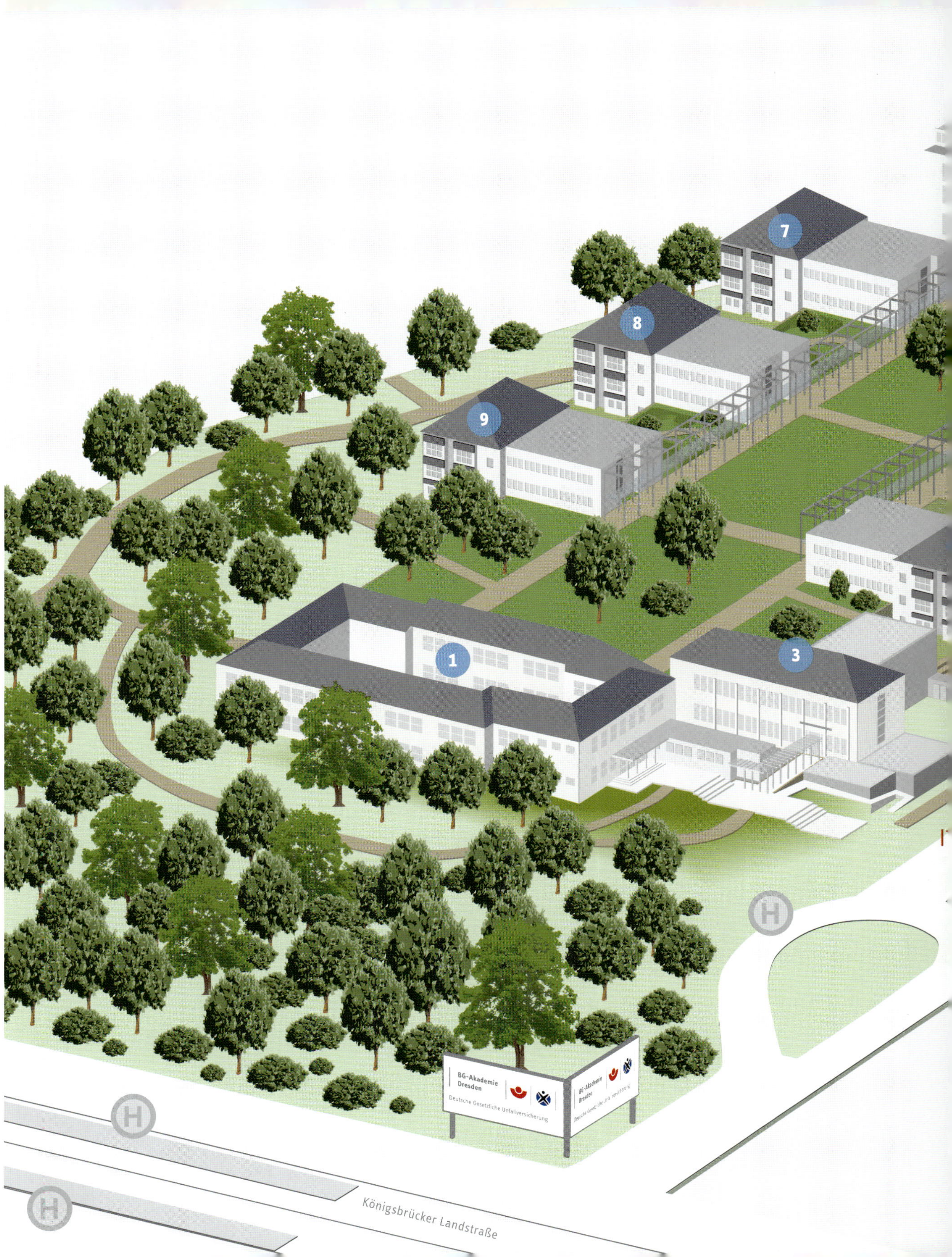

SITE PLAN

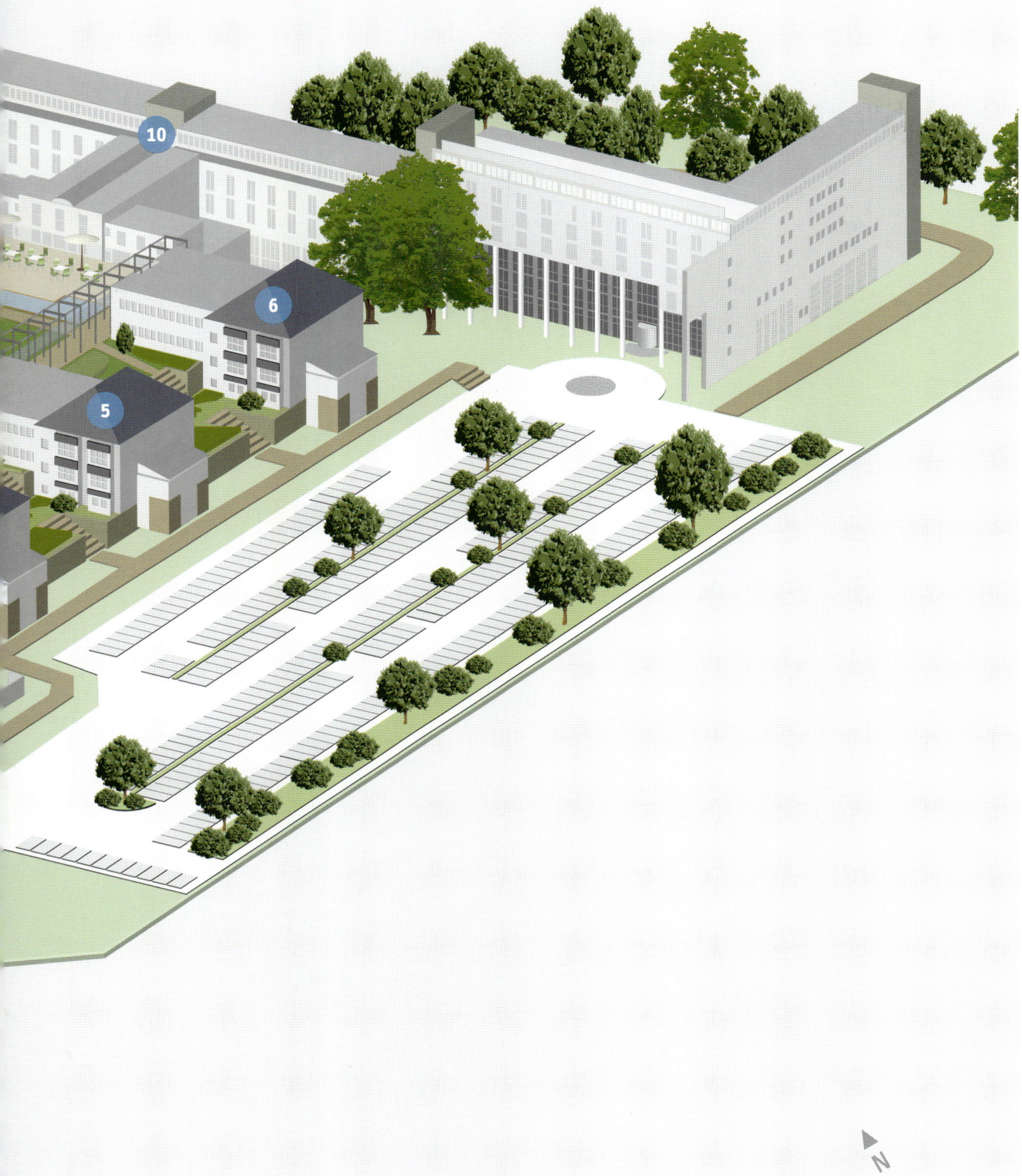

Building 1 – Institute Work and Health
Formerly building J (classroom building)

Building 3 – Institute Work and Health, seminar rooms and practical facilities
Formerly building G
(headmaster's residence and bursary)

Building 4 – Institute Work and Health, seminar rooms and practical facilities
Formerly boarding house E

Building 5 – Institute Work and Health, seminar rooms and practical facilities
Formerly boarding house C

Building 6 – Institute Work and Health, seminar rooms and practical facilities
Formerly boarding house A

Building 7 – BG responsible for the Administrative Sector
Formerly boarding house B

Building 8 – BG responsible for Health and Welfare Services
Formerly boarding house D

Building 9 – BG responsible for the Energy, Textile and Electric Sectors
Formerly boarding house F

Building 10 – Academy Hotel and Restaurant
Built in place of building K
(the assembly hall and management building)
and building L (gymnasium)

Neither retained nor reconstructed
Building H (residence for the deputy headmaster and other officials)
Building M (porter's residence)
Building N (group of teachers' residences)
Running track (on what is now the Infineon site)

Alabugin 2006-2009
Alabugin, Michail: Korrespondenz mit dem Institut Arbeit und Gesundheit der DGUV. Odessa 2006-2009

Amlung 2000
Amlung, Ullrich: Dresdner Schulwesen in der Weimarer Republik 1918-1933. In: Stadtmuseum Dresden (Hrsg.): Dresdner Geschichtsbuch 6. Altenburg 2000

Amlung 2006
Amlung, Ullrich: Dresden im Kaiserreich 1871-1918: Schulwesen In: Starke, Holger (Hrsg.): Geschichte der Stadt Dresden. Bd. 3: Von der Reichsgründung bis zur Gegenwart. Stuttgart 2006, S. 167-173

Amlung 2007
Amlung, Ullrich: Dresdner Schulwesen in der Weimarer Republik 1918-1933. In: Stadtmuseum Dresden (Hrsg.): Dresdner Geschichtsbuch. 2. Aufl. Bd. 6. 2007, S. 165-198

Amlung 2009
Amlung, Ullrich: Reformpädagogische Versuchsschulen in Dresden in der Zeit der Weimarer Republik. In: Dresdner Hefte. Beiträge zur Kulturgeschichte, Jg. 27/2009, Nr. 97. Dresden 2009, S. 16-35

Bannack 2001
Bannack, Siegfried: Chronik von Klotzsche, Dresden 2001

Behrendt 1927
Behrendt, Walter Curt: Die Landesschule Dresden, in: Zentralblatt der Bauverwaltung, Nr. 51. 1927, S. 665-671

Boesch 1997
Boesch, Martin: Dresden 1997. Zwei Bauten von Heinrich Tessenow. Ein Zwischenbericht. In: archithese 5. 1997, S. 76-79

Burkhardt 1973
Burkhardt, Karl: Die Landesschule Dresden (LSD). München 1973 (die gedruckte, unveröffentlichte Doppelseite befindet sich in Privatbesitz)

Conert 1929
Conert, Herbert: Die Neubauten der Landesschule Dresden in Klotzsche. In: Bauamt und Gemeindebau 7. 1929, S. 98-104

De Michelis 1991
De Michelis, Marco: Heinrich Tessenow 1879-1950. Das architektonische Gesamtwerk. Stuttgart 1991

Denkschrift 1926
Zur Neuordnung des höheren Schulwesens in Sachsen. Denkschrift des Ministeriums für Volksbildung. Dresden 1926

DH 140
Dresdner Heidezeitung Nr. 140 vom 23.11.1933

Dresdner Lehrerverein 1929
Dresdner Lehrerverein (Hrsg.): Führer durch Dresden zur Deutschen Lehrerversammlung vom 21. bis 24. Mai 1929. Dresden 1929

DN 332
C.G.: Die neue Landesschule - ein Kulturwerk in schwerer Zeit, in: Dresdner Nachrichten, Nr. 332. 1927, S. 7

Fischer 1927
Fischer, Curt (Hrsg.): Zur Einweihung der Landesschule Dresden in Klotzsche am 15. Oktober 1927. Dresden 1927

Fischer 1929
Fischer, Curt: Landesschule Dresden in Klotzsche. Bericht über die Zeit von Michaelis 1927 bis Ostern 1929. Dresden 1929

Grüning 1986
Grüning, Michael: Der Wachsmann-Report. Auskünfte eines Architekten. Berlin 1986

Hahn 2001
Hahn, Christa: Die Tanzstunde oder »Wie das Leben so spielt!«. In: Zur Geschichte des Standortes der Berufsgenossenschaftlichen Akademie für Arbeitssicherheit und Gesundheitsschutz - Landesschule Dresden in Klotzsche (1927-1933). Dresden 2001, S. 49-55

Häring 1928
Häring, Hugo: Neues Bauen. Moderne Bauformen 9. 1928, S. 329-376

Hofer 2005
Hofer, Sigrid: Reformarchitektur 1900-1918. Deutsche Baukünstler auf der Suche nach dem nationalen Stil. Stuttgart/London 2005

http://11td.ru
http://11td.ru: Forum ehemaliger Angehöriger der 11. Gardepanzerdivision, begründet von Igor Kormilzew (letzter Zugriff 07/2009)

Hübner/Grötzsch/Klatte 2005
Hübner, Ulrich/Grötzsch, Ulrike/Klatte, Gernot: Symbol und Wahrhaftigkeit. Reformbaukunst in Dresden. Dresden/Husum 2005

Hübner-Grötzsch/Hübner 2008
Hübner-Grötzsch, Ulrike und Ulrich Hübner: Die Architektur des Heimatstils in Sachsen. In: Sachsen - Zukunft aus Herkunft. 100 Jahre Landesverein Sächsischer Heimatschutz 1908-2008. Dresden 2008

Hübner-Grötzsch/Hübner 2009
Hübner-Grötzsch, Ulrike/Hübner, Ulrich: Dresdner Schulbauten im Geist der Reformbewegung. In: Dresdner Hefte. Beiträge zur Kulturgeschichte, Jg. 27/2009, Nr. 97. Dresden 2009, S.36-43

Jubelfest 1825
Das erste hundertjährige Jubelfest des Königlich Sächsischen Cadettenhauses, gefeiert zu Dresden den 3. October 1825. Dresden 1825

Kerner 2000
Kerner, Wolfgang: Die durch sowjetische Streitkräfte genutzten Liegenschaften Dresdens im Jahr 1990. Dresden 2000

Kleint 1943
Kleint, Walter: Die Rudolf-Schröter-Schule Sachsen. Staatliche Nationalpolitische Erziehungsanstalt - Unterbann Rudolf Schröter im Gebiet 16 HJ 1934/35. Gedenkschrift vom 25. Dezember 1943 (unveröffentlichtes Exemplar)

Kowalczuk/Wolle 2001
Kowalczuk, Ilko-Sascha/Wolle, Stefan: Roter Stern über Deutschland. Berlin 2001

Kramer 1914
Kramer, Oskar: Freistehende kleine Wohnhäuser in Stadt und Land. Dresden 1914

Kramer 1927
Kramer, Oskar: Die Neubauten der Landesschule Dresden in Klotzsche, in: Deutsche Bauzeitung 100/101. 1927, S. 817-828

Kramer 1945
Kramer, Oskar: Brief an den sowjetischen Stadtkommandanten von Dresden vom 11.6.1945. Archiv Dr. Zimmermann. Langebrück 1945

Kramer/Tessenow 1929
Oskar Kramer/Heinrich Tessenow: Die Neubauten der Landesschule Dresden in Klotzsche. In: Bauamt und Gemeindebau, Nr. 12. 1929, S. 99

Lampugnani 1991
Lampugnani, Vittorio Magnago: Heinrich Tessenow. Ausstellung im Deutschen Architektur-Museum, Frankfurt am Main 1991

Lampugnani 1998
Lampugnani, Vittorio Magnago (Hrsg.): Lexikon der Architektur des 20. Jahrhunderts. Ostfildern-Ruit 1998

Meschwitz 1907
Meschwitz, Heinrich: Geschichte des Königlich Sächsischen Kadetten- und Pagen-Korps von dessen Begründung bis zur Gegenwart. Dresden 1907

Meschwitz 1913
Meschwitz, Heinrich: Geschichte des Königlich Sächsischen Kadetten- und Pagen-Korps. Dresden 1913

Pfister 1928
Pfister, Rudolf: Tessenow. Sein Wesen und Werk. In: Baukunst 1. 1928, S. 10-24

Rother 2001
Rother, Wolfgang: Die ehemalige Landesschule Dresden in Klotzsche. Ein architekturgeschichtlicher Rückblick und Betrachtung zu den restaurierten bauplastischen Arbeiten am ehemaligen Lehrgebäude. In: Zur Geschichte des Standortes der Berufsgenossenschaftlichen Akademie für Arbeitssicherheit und Gesundheitsschutz - Landesschule Dresden in Klotzsche (1927-1933). Dresden 2001

Rundbrief 1976
E. S.: Kommentar zum Spezifischen der Anstalt Klotzsche, 25. Rundbrief. 1976

Scharfenort 1906
Scharfenort, Louis von: Militär-Erziehungs- und Bildungswesen. In: Rein, Wilhelm (Hrsg.): Encyklopädisches Handbuch der Pädagogik. Langensalza 1906, S. 849-860

Scheffler 1928
Scheffler, Karl: Heinrich Tessenow. In: Kunst und Künstler 26. 1928, S. 43-55

Schmidt 1928
Schmidt, Paul: Tessenow. Sein Leben und Schicksal. In: Baukunst 1. 1928, S. 4-9

Schmidt 1978
Schmidt, Martin: Begrüßungsansprache mit einem Rückblick auf die Landesschule Dresden. Typoskript vom 7.10.1978 (ein Exemplar befindet sich in der Sächsischen Landes- und Universitätsbibliothek Dresden)

Scholtz 1973
Scholtz, Harald: Nationalsozialistische Ausleseschulen. Internatsschulen als Herrschaftsmittel des Führerstaates. Göttingen 1973, S. 70

SHD 496
Sächsisches Hauptstaatsarchiv Dresden, Oberfinanzpräsident Dresden, Bestand 11177, Sign. 496: Bauangelegenheiten der Nationalpolitischen Erziehungsanstalt Klotzsche (1941-1942)

SHD 640
Sächsisches Hauptstaatsarchiv Dresden, Oberfinanzpräsident Dresden, Bestand 11177, Sign. 640: Bauangelegenheiten der Nationalpolitischen Erziehungsanstalt Klotzsche (1943–1945)

SHD 1306
Sächsisches Hauptstaatsarchiv Dresden, Volkskammer/Landtag, Bestand 10693, Sign. 1306: Neubau und Überlassung an Infanterieschule

SHD 11344
Sächsisches Hauptstaatsarchiv Dresden, Bestand 11344: Kadettenkorps (1694–1919)

SHD 12506
Sächsisches Hauptstaatsarchiv Dresden, Bestand 12506: Traditionsverband ehemaliger Landesschüler, Nr. 27 (Heft 12 der Landesschul-Mitteilungen vom Februar 1934)

SHD 17745
Sächsisches Hauptstaatsarchiv Dresden, Ministerium des Innern, Bestand 17745: Kadetten-Anstalten und Unteroffizier-Schulen – Landesschule Dresden (1920–1922)

SHD 21350
Sächsisches Hauptstaatsarchiv Dresden, Akten des Ministeriums für Volksbildung, Bestand 21350, S. 233

SHD 21351
Sächsisches Hauptstaatsarchiv Dresden, Akten des Ministeriums für Volksbildung, Bestand 21351, Blatt 53 ff.

SHD 21352
Sächsisches Hauptstaatsarchiv, Ministerium des Kultus und öffentlichen Unterrichts, Bestand 11125.7, Sign. 21352: Ausbau der Nationalpolitischen Erziehungs-Anstalt Klotzsche (1937–1940)

SHD 21356
Sächsisches Hauptstaatsarchiv, Akten des Ministeriums für Volksbildung, Bestand 21356, S. 122

SHD 21361
Sächsisches Hauptstaatsarchiv Dresden, Ministerium für Volksbildung, Bestand 21361: Schülerangelegenheiten an der Landesschule Dresden, ab 1.4.1934: Rudolf-Schröter-Schule in Klotzsche (1927–1938), Bll. 132 ff.

StA 2.3.1
Stadtarchiv Dresden, Hauptkanzlei, Bestand 2.3.1., Nr. II A. b. Nr. 30, den Neubau der Landesschule betreffend, Brief des Oberbürgermeisters Blüher vom 7.3.1925

StA 8.20
Stadtarchiv Dresden, Gemeindeverwaltung Klotzsche, Bestand 8.20, Nr. 531/01d, Bericht und Belege über die Verwendung der vormaligen Rudolf-Schröter-Schule 1945

Starke 2001
Starke, Holger: Bildtext »Sächsische Landesschule in Klotzsche«. In: Kregelin, Karlheinz/Starke, Holger: Dresden. Das Namenbuch der Straßen und Plätze im Norden der Stadt. Dresden 2001 (unveröffentlichtes Buchmanuskript in der Bibliothek des Stadtmuseums Dresden)

Tessenow 1986
Tessenow, Heinrich: Hausbau und dergleichen, Reprint der 4. Aufl. von 1953, Braunschweig 1986 [1. Aufl. 1916]

Verordnungsblatt 1934
Verordnungsblatt des Sächsischen Ministeriums für Volksbildung vom Jahre 1934

Wangerin/Weiss 1976
Wangerin, Gerda / Weiss, Gerhard: Heinrich Tessenow. Ein Baumeister. 1876–1950. Leben. Lehre. Werk. Essen 1976

Zentralblatt 51
W. C. B.: Die Landesschule Dresden. In: Zentralblatt der Bauverwaltung, 51. 1927, S. 665–669

Alabugin, Michail · S. 132, 133

Beda, Alexander · S. 125

Deutsche Gesetzliche Unfallversicherung
S. 9, 156, 158, 159, 160, 161, 165, 166

Dudush, Valeriy · S. 124, 127, 128

Hauptstaatsarchiv Dresden, Akten des Ministeriums für Volksbildung, Bestand 21350 · S. 95

Hauptsstaatsarchiv Dresden, Akten des Ministeriums für Volksbildung, Bestand 21355 · S. 101, 102

Hauptstaatsarchiv Dresden, Akten des Ministeriums für Volksbildung, Bestand 21369 · S. 107

Hauptstaatsarchiv Dresden, Nachlass Traditionsvereinigung Landesschule Dresden, Bestand 12506
S. 4/5, 24, 31, 32, 34, 39, 40, 41, 44, 45, 46, 60, 62, 63, 64, 65, 66, 74, 77, 79, 80, 81, 97, 98, 134, 157

Institut Arbeit und Gesundheit der Deutschen Gesetzlichen Unfallversicherung
S. 6/7, 25, 43, 78, 130, 131, 135, 137, 139, 167, 168

Kohanchik, Alexander · S. 141

Kolomeycev, Igor · S. 136, 138, 140

Landeshauptstadt Dresden, Amt für Kultur und Denkmalschutz · S. 69, 71

Landeshauptstadt Dresden, Vermessungsamt
S. 142, 145

Ralf Kruse & Thomas Seidel GbR · S. 163

Raquet, Wolfgang · S. 96, 99, 103, 105, 109

Sächsische Landesbibliothek - Staats- und Universitätsbibliothek Dresden, Abt. Deutsche Fotothek
S. 33, 35, 36, 37, 42, 61, 67, 70

Tietze, Sylvia · S. 180/181

Zimmermann, Dr. Johannes · S. 68, 71

Reproduktion aus / Copy from

Fischer, Curt (Hg.): Zur Einweihung der Landesschule Dresden in Klotzsche am 15. Oktober 1927. Dresden 1927
S. 38

Junger Wille. Kampfblatt der sächsischen Jugend 1936, S. 10 · S. 94

Meschwitz, Heinrich: Geschichte des Königlich Sächsischen Kadetten- und Pagen-Korps von dessen Begründung bis zur Gegenwart. Dresden 1907. Sächsische Landesbibliothek – Staats- und Universitätsbibliothek Dresden · S. 27, 28, 30

Meschwitz, Heinrich: Geschichte des Königlich Sächsischen Kadetten- und Pagen-Korps. Dresden 1913. Sächsische Landesbibliothek – Staats- und Universitätsbibliothek Dresden · S. 29

IMPRESSUM · IMPRINT

Herausgeber / Publisher
Deutsche Gesetzliche Unfallversicherung e.V. (DGUV)
Spitzenverband der gewerblichen Berufsgenossenschaften
und der Unfallversicherungsträger der öffentlichen Hand
www.dguv.de

Architekturfotografien / Architectural photography
Joerg-Rainer Oesen, Radebeul

Projektkoordination / Project coordination
Sabine Strickrodt, Deutsche Gesetzliche Unfallversicherung e.V.

Redaktion / Editors
Meike Griese, Michaela Klaus, Sandstein Kommunikation GmbH
Dr. Bodo Pfeiffer, Kati van der Seylberg,
Sabine Strickrodt, Deutsche Gesetzliche Unfallversicherung e.V.

Übersetzung / Translation
Peter Welchman, Schweitzer Sprachendienst Radebeul

Verlagslektorat / Publisher's proofreader
Meike Griese, Dana Hildebrand, Sandstein Kommunikation GmbH

Gestaltung / Design
Michaela Klaus, Sandstein Kommunikation GmbH
Kati van der Seylberg, Deutsche Gesetzliche Unfallversicherung e.V.

Druck und Verarbeitung / Printing and binding
Offizin Andersen Nexö Leipzig

Die Deutsche Nationalbibliothek verzeichnet diese Publikation
in der Deutschen Nationalbibliografie; detaillierte bibliografische
Daten sind im Internet über http://dnb.ddb.de abrufbar.

www.sandstein.de
ISBN 978-3-940319-77-7

Fassadendetail am Akademiehotel.
Façade detail on the Academy Hotel.